3

'4

12

This series, published for students, scholars and interested general readers, will tackle themes in gender history from the early medieval period through to the present day. Gender issues are now an integral part of all history courses and yet many traditional texts do not reflect this change. Much exciting work is now being done to redress the gender imbalances of the past, and we hope that these books will make their own substantial contribution to that process. We hope that these will both synthesise and shape future developments in gender studies.

The General Editors of the series are *Patricia Skinner* (University of Southampton) for the medieval period; *Pamela Sharpe* (University of Bristol) for the early modern period; and *Penny Summerfield* (University of Lancaster) for the modern period. *Margaret Walsh* (University of Nottingham) was the Founding Editor of the series.

Published books:

Imperial Women in Byzantium 1025–1204: Power, Patronage and Ideology
    Barbara Hill

Masculinity in Medieval Europe   *D.M. Hadley (ed.)*

Gender and Society in Renaissance Italy
    Judith C. Brown and Robert C. Davis (eds)

Widowhood in Medieval and Early Modern Europe
    Sandra Cavallo and Lyndan Warner (eds)

Gender, Church and State in Early Modern Germany:
    Essays by Merry E. Wiesner   *Merry E. Wiesner*

Manhood in Early Modern England: Honour, Sex and Marriage
    Elizabeth W. Foyster

English Masculinities, 1600–1800   *Tim Hitchcock and Michele Cohen (eds)*

Disorderly Women in Eighteenth-Century London:
    Prostitution in the Metropolis 1730–1830   *Tony Henderson*

Gender, Power and the Unitarians in England, 1760–1860   *Ruth Watts*

Practical Visionaries: Women, Education and Social Progress 1790–1930
    Mary Hilton and Pam Hirsch (eds)

Women and Work in Russia, 1880–1930: A Study in Continuity through
    Change   *Jane McDermid and Anna Hillyar*

More than Munitions: Women, Work and the Engineering Industries
    1900–1950   *Clare Wightman*

The Family Story: Blood, Contract and Intimacy, 1830–1960
    Leonore Davidoff, Megan Doolittle, Janet Fink and Katherine Holden

Women and the Second World War in France 1939–1948: Choices and
    Constraints   *Hanna Diamond*

Practical Visionaries: Women, Education and Social Progress 1790–1930

EDITED BY

MARY HILTON

AND

PAM HIRSCH

An imprint of **Pearson Education**

Harlow, England · London · New York · Reading, Massachusetts · San Francisco
Toronto · Don Mills, Ontario · Sydney · Tokyo · Singapore · Hong Kong · Seoul
Taipei · Cape Town · Madrid · Mexico City · Amsterdam · Munich · Paris · Milan

Pearson Education Limited
Edinburgh Gate
Harlow
Essex CM20 2JE
England

and Associated Companies throughout the world

Visit us on the World Wide Web at:
http://www.pearsoneduc.com

First published 2000

ISBN 0–582–40431–2 PPR

British Library Cataloguing-in-Publication Data

A catalogue record for this book is available from the British Library

Library of Congress Cataloging-in-Publication Data

Practical visionaries : women, education, and social progress, 1790–1930 / edited by
Mary Hilton and Pam Hirsch.
p. cm. — (Women and men in history)
Includes bibliographical references and index.
ISBN 0–582–40431–2 (pb)
1. Women—Education—Great Britain—History—18th century. 2.
Women—Education—Great Britain—History—19th century. 3. Women—Education—Great
Britain—History—20th century. 4. Women in education—History. 5. Women
educators—Biography. I. Series. II. Hilton, Mary, 1946– III. Hirsch, Pam.

LC2042.P72 2000
371.82′0941′0903 99–044986

Set in 10/13 pt Baskerville
Typeset by 35
Produced by Pearson Education Asia Pte Ltd
Printed in Singapore

Contents

List of Figures and Illustrations

List of Contributors

DR ANNE BLOOMFIELD is Reader in Arts Education at Nottingham Trent University where she directs an arts project for primary school children, *History in Action at Clifton Hall*, which comes out of her family history, *The Cliftons of Clifton Hall*. During 1996 she was visiting Professorial Scholar, Edith Cowan University, Perth, Western Australia. She has published on philosophical, historical and artistic aspects of movement and dance in relation to the creative self and traditional arts. She is Chairperson of the East Midlands Regions RSA (Royal Society for the Encouragement of Arts, Manufactures and Commerce), serves on the RSA Council and is a Member of the Court of the University of Derby.

DR KEVIN J. BREHONY is a Senior Lecturer in Education, Department of Education Studies and Management, the University of Reading. He has published extensively on the interface between social policy and education, both historically and also as it affects the contemporary situation. His most recent book is *Active Citizenship and the Governing of Schools* (1995) with R. Deem and S. New.

NORMA CLARKE is a Research Fellow in the Department of English at Kingston University. She has published widely on eighteenth and nineteenth century literature and has particular interests in women's writing, children's fiction (she has published a number of novels for children), Romanticism, and the social construction of the author from the late seventeenth century onwards. She is the author of *Ambitious Heights, Writing, Friendship, Love: the Jewsbury Sisters, Felicia Hemans, and Jane Welsh Carlyle* (1990). Her most recent book is *Dr Johnson's Women* (2000). She is an editor of *Gender and History*.

DR PETER CUNNINGHAM is Reader in the History of Education at Homerton College, Cambridge, with particular interest in the development of primary curriculum and in the training and professional identity of primary teachers. His study of progressivism in the post-war era was published by Falmer in 1988 and he is currently engaged in a major funded research project concerning the impact of the Second World War on teachers' attitudes and practice.

MARY JANE DRUMMOND is a Lecturer in primary education, University of Cambridge School of Education, where she researches aspects of early years care and education, and teaches on a variety of in-service courses for teachers and other educators. She has close working links with the Early Childhood Unit at the National Children's Bureau, and with them has published two in-service development packs of materials for early years educators. She has published many chapters on early education and a book, *Assessing Children's Learning* (1993).

DR ELIZABETH EDWARDS is a Senior Research Associate at Homerton College, Cambridge. Formerly she was the college's Librarian and Archivist. She has written extensively on women's experience in teacher training colleges. She has recently completed a book, to be published by UCL Press, entitled *Women in Teacher Training Colleges: A Culture of Femininity, 1900–1960.*

MARY HILTON is a Senior Lecturer in Primary Language and Literature at Homerton College, Cambridge. She has published chapters on the development of children's historical thinking and on boys' reading in the nineteenth century. She has edited *Potent Fictions: Children's Literacy and the Challenge of Popular Culture* (1996) and, together with Morag Styles and Victor Watson, *Opening the Nursery Door: Reading, Writing and Childhood 1600–1900* (1997).

DR PAM HIRSCH is a Senior Research Associate of Homerton College, Cambridge, and a member of the English Faculty and Education Faculty of the University of Cambridge. She has published on Mary Wollstonecraft, George Sand, Elizabeth Barrett Browning, Charlotte Brontë and George Eliot. Her biography *Barbara Leigh Smith Bodichon: Feminist Artist and Rebel* (1998) charts Bodichon's crucial role in the founding of the first university college for women, Girton College, Cambridge.

PROF. JANE MILLER taught in the English Department of the University of London Institute of Education until 1998. She is the author of *Many Voices: Bilingualism, Culture and Education* (1983); *Women Writing about Men* (1986); *Seductions: Studies in Reading and Culture* (1990); *More Has Meant Women: The Feminisation of Schooling* (1992) and *School for Women* (1996). She is the editor of, amongst other things, *Eccentric Propositions: Essays on Literature and the Curriculum* (1984) and the journal *Changing English.*

DR HILARY MINNS is a Lecturer in English Studies in the Institute of Education at the University of Warwick. She is author of *Read It to Me Now!* (1990, 1997), *Language, Literacy and Gender* (1991) and *Primary Language: Extending the Curriculum with Computers.* Her doctoral thesis explored the lives of migrant Irish children who came to live in Derby in the mid-nineteenth century. She is currently working on the contexts of literacy that mould the behaviour of young readers and writers who have moved beyond the stage of initial literacy learning.

DR WENDY ROBINSON is a Lecturer in Education at the Institute of Education, University of Warwick. She has published essays on the history of teacher training, the professional identity of women teachers and the education of girls. She is Secretary of the History of Education Society and joint editor of its *Bulletin*.

DR GILLIAN SUTHERLAND is Fellow, Gwatkin Lecturer and Director of Studies in History at Newnham College, Cambridge. She has published extensively on the social and political history of education, including *Policy-Making in Elementary Education 1870–1895* (Oxford, 1973), *Ability, Merit and Measurement: Mental Testing in English Education 1880–1940* (Oxford, 1984) and many essays on the higher education of women. She is currently working on a biography of Anne Jemima Clough and Blanche Athena Clough.

DR RUTH WATTS is a Senior Lecturer, University of Birmingham. She is History Tutor in the School of Education and has written much on both history in education and the history of education. Her most recent book is *Gender, Power and the Unitarians in England 1760–1860* (Harlow, 1998). She is currently researching the history of women and science and is on the executive committee of the International Standing Conference for the History of Education (ISCHE).

Acknowledgements

This book has been made possible by the constant enthusiasm and commitment of all the contributors to this intellectual project. It is the culmination of a long process of generous sharing of the fruits of individual research projects, of unexpected discoveries and of the excitement of forging connections.

Throughout the process we have benefited from the support of our home institution – Homerton College, Cambridge – including valuable insights from many of our colleagues. We would also particularly like to thank Margaret Pelling, of the University of Oxford, for her help in shaping the project.

We are grateful to our editors at Longman, to Hilary Shaw for commissioning the book in the first place and to Natasha Dupont for her indefatigable support throughout the editorial process.

We are personally indebted to both Boyd Hilton and Desmond Hirsch, the former for giving us the benefit of an historian's scrutiny of our introduction, the latter for unfailing patience as interlocutor and computer help-desk.

Most of all, in an age where the adjective 'progressive' has yet again become a pejorative term in some circles, we would like to acknowledge the many women educationists still fighting to keep alive a vision of social progress, which, at its core, implicitly recognises the right to rational autonomy of every human being, whatever their disadvantages.

Mary Hilton and Pam Hirsch
August 1999

Publisher's Acknowledgements

We are grateful to the following for permission to reproduce copyright material:

Mercy International Centre, Baggot St, Dublin for Figure 3.1; The Scottish National Portrait Gallery for Figure 4.2; Girton College Cambridge for Figures 5.1 and 5.2; Newnham College Cambridge for Figures 6.1 and 6.2; The London Borough of Barnet (Local Studies & Archive Centre) for Figure 8.1 and The Penguin Press for Figure 13.1.

Whilst every effort has been made to trace the owners of copyright material, in a few cases this has proved impossible and we take this opportunity to offer our apologies to any copyright holders whose rights we may have unwittingly infringed.

Editorial Note

The place of publication in notes and references is London unless otherwise stated.

Introduction

MARY HILTON
PAM HIRSCH

Reason has, at last, shown her captivating face, beaming with benevolence; and it will be impossible for the dark hand of despotism again to obscure its radiance, or the lurking dagger of subordinate tyrants to reach her bosom. The image of God implanted in our nature is now more rapidly expanding; and, as it opens, liberty with maternal wing seems to be soaring to regions far above vulgar annoyance, promising to shelter all mankind.

MARY WOLLSTONECRAFT, 1794[1]

Political visions, as Barbara Taylor has pointed out, are fragile: 'the history of all progressive movements is littered with half-remembered hopes, with dreams that have failed'.[2] The two centuries since Mary Wollstonecraft's vision of the power of reason and benevolence have not seen the transformation she predicted. Yet the importance of education to her theory of social progress and the centrality of its feminine component have not passed away. Through those centuries women have argued, written, taught and theorised with a passion equal to hers. Nor have they been retiring, passive or under-represented in progressive endeavour. Yet, to examine the established history of education is still to find a master narrative which consistently foregrounds the ideas and activities of men. In magisterial works like Brian Simon's *Studies in the History of Education 1780–1870* (1960) and W.A.C. Stewart and W.P. McCann's *The Educational Innovators* (1967), and in such detailed works as those of Harold Silver and Richard Selleck, women are not completely absent.[3] They appear in the texts, but always as wives, sisters, followers, assistants and believers; rarely as leaders, ideologues, founders or policy makers. The central work of philosophy, experimentation, political and institutional leadership is firmly ascribed to men.[4]

However, as our picture of nineteenth-century culture becomes richer it also becomes more dynamic. Grand narratives of the past have been disrupted by a heightened sense of differing contexts, multiple perspectives and discourses. Educational history which consistently privileged parliamentary

1

politics and doctrinal theology alongside philosophical and scientific theory foregrounded the thought of men, but recent feminist scholarship, such as the work of Leonore Davidoff and Catherine Hall, has challenged this ordering perspective and created a different lens through which to focus on the past.[5] Such scholarship, which includes the family, examines a range of reproductive practices, respects personally interpreted spiritualities and focuses clearly on the feminine, often using an eclectic range of private material once considered trivial and ephemeral, has yielded a paradigm shift in historical analysis. Now we can see that the nineteenth-century public sphere, once presented as clearly distinguishable from the private and almost exclusively masculine, was in fact more nuanced and its gender boundaries more permeable. Groundbreaking biographical scholarship on women educators, such as that by Jo Manton and Carolyn Steedman and recent gender-sensitive studies of teaching and ideology by Dina Copelman, Philip Gardner, Patricia Hollis, Jane Miller and Jane Martin, have further developed this new approach.[6] Within it is set this study of the life histories, personal ideologies, roles and relationships of a group of leading women educationists. This paradigm allows us to see that these women, having been positioned differently from men with regard to a range of social practices, brought very different *modi operandi* to the theory of education and therefore inflected it differently. Having to work in often difficult and contradictory relationships with a variety of nineteenth-century patriarchal institutions – the political press, parliamentary government, the Catholic church, elementary state schools, the pupil-teacher system, teacher training colleges and the elite universities – these outstanding women variously negotiated, expanded and subverted the roles traditionally allowed them. They then worked to reconfigure these institutions, often transforming them through their practices. It was therefore often in fiercely practical ways that our group of women leaders changed educational ideas, working at the cutting edges of theory, argument and policymaking in the period.

Each essay discusses the discrete ideas of individual women or of small groups of women and also locates those ideas historically and politically. However, the collective biographical approach of the book helps to highlight a series of vital interactions between them, which were variously familial, ideological and intellectual. Several of these women knew of each other, corresponded with, learned from, and were alert to the educational and political issues in each other's projects and legacies. In effect therefore, we outline a particular (though not exclusively) women's educational tradition, in this case a progressive one. We show specific women leaders (and we could have fielded many more) who were, like Mary Wollstonecraft, centrally concerned with questions of citizenship and social justice, and who engaged with the transformative role of education in progress towards their vision of a better social world. So, in charting these women's contributions to British education as theorists as well as practitioners, it emerges that they were also visionaries: individuals who were driven by an imaginative mission, using education as a field of endeavour to improve society in many and various ways.

Although women had a long history in the governance of religious and charitable institutions, they first emerged publicly as leading pedagogues in the late eighteenth century when the effervescent material culture of industrial capitalism created and sustained a growing middle class. Conduct books, traditionally written to raise children in the knowledge and fear of God, slowly developed into discursive manuals to help the new 'middling sort' develop the social manners and understandings necessary to prosper in a world of increased social mobility. At the same time the ideas of the Enlightenment, a new belief that reason should guide the affairs of mankind rather than superstition, faith or revelation, stimulated several progressive women to join the writers who were transforming the conduct book into a public discourse of educational principles. In this they drew on the educational works of John Locke (1632–1704) and David Hartley (1705–57). Locke's conviction that neither man nor woman was born weighed down by original sin, but instead each child's mind was a *tabula rasa* with an innate potential for reason, gave rise to a vision of the citizen as a self-determining individual whose obligation to the state came from his or her own voluntary action.[7] Subsequently Hartley developed a scientific basis for the belief that infants could be moved from early sense impressions to moral attitudes.[8] He argued that, through associating pleasant sensations with moral values in their early years, children would develop strong and good principles for life. This 'associationism', as it was called, in early education was seen as a science which offered a new authority to middle-class women educationists.

Rousseau's *Emile* (1776) dramatically entered the space created by this public discourse on education and citizenship. Pointing to the corruption of the social world, he argued that boys and girls should be removed from society and their 'natural' instincts developed in specific ways. In Rousseau's model, the male child would grow to use his reason in the service of the state, while the complementary female child would be trained to use her 'natural' instincts to become a loving wife and mother and remain within the domestic sphere. But although Rousseau was widely read, his ideas were angrily repudiated by leading women educationists of all political persuasions. Many of them had written tracts which insisted that girls should be educated in a new rational mode of womanly virtue in order to produce citizens who possessed self-command and moral autonomy.[9] Hester Chapone's *Letters on the Improvement of the Mind, addressed to a young lady* (1773) was one such text, often reprinted throughout the next half-century. Catherine Macaulay's *Letters on Education* (1790) were also widely read and greatly admired. Her younger contemporary Mary Wollstonecraft synthesised a number of radical ideas within this feminine pedagogical tradition in *Vindication of the Rights of Woman* (1792). Dismissing Rousseau's notion that a child could be educated in a desert, she spoke first of a child's education beginning in the home. Arguing that every family is a building block of the state and that 'public spirit must be nurtured by private virtue', she insisted, however, that a child's first educator, the mother, must herself 'have sense' – that is, be educated rationally.[10] As she commented, women 'may have different duties to fulfil; but they are human duties, and the principles which regulate the discharge of them, I sturdily maintain, must be the same'.[11] Her belief in educating both girls and boys to be citizens also underpinned her argument for co-educational state schools.

In this radical endeavour Mary Wollstonecraft had drawn support from a leading group of enlightenment rationalists, the Rational Dissenters, later called Unitarians.[12] The Rational Dissenters were at the forefront of educational reform at this period.[13] As Mary Hilton explains in the opening chapter, their peculiarly democratic theology not only spurned the hierarchy of the established Anglican church, but also rejected its fundamental tenet – the estrangement of God from the world and thus the notion of Christ's atonement for the sins of mankind.[14] The Rational Dissenters stressed the importance, not so much of preparing mankind for the next world as of making this world a place of justice, rationality and happiness for all. Several of the women discussed in this book found inner strength as well as familial and intellectual support in pursuing a progressive vision of the social world through their Unitarianism. Anna Barbauld, a leading Rational Dissenter, brought outstanding gifts to bear in a vision of an education which would develop reason in the growing child. She believed that the powers of reason grew through experimentation, 'argumentative discussion' and familial affection, in stark contrast to Rousseau's model of the growth of reason in his so-called 'natural' child. Her writings and her prose works for children were to nourish the next generation of middle-class women, some of whom eventually took on leadership roles themselves.[15] Her vision, like Mary Wollstonecraft's, came to be denigrated by political enemies, and obscured by the growth of evangelical Christianity in the early nineteenth century. Nevertheless, as Mary Hilton shows, she left a legacy of intense intellectualism for women, alongside her Unitarian faith in science and reason.

Anna Barbauld belonged to the same group of radical Unitarian intellectuals as the family of William Smith, the MP for Norwich, who fought to abolish slavery, advocated religious tolerance, and sought to reform Parliament by enlarging the franchise.[16] She stayed every summer with Smith, who was also a close friend of Joseph Priestley, and was a significant influence on Smith's daughter, Julia. As Pam Hirsch points out, Julia Smith in turn was significant in the upbringing and education of Barbara Leigh Smith (Bodichon). The shared familial culture and habits of these Unitarians meant that women from these families were more widely educated than most of their contemporaries.[17] As Ruth Watts shows in the next chapter, Mary Carpenter was supported by the same background of intellectual Unitarianism as Anna Barbauld and the Smiths. Although initially constrained by some of the limitations placed on women's roles in early Victorian families, she was educated by her father, the Unitarian minister Dr Lant Carpenter, and gradually emerged as a leading educationist herself. She was to be particularly concerned with children from the very poorest classes. Her conviction that all children, however seemingly vicious, could be reformed by a wise, imaginative and holistic education led to a series of writings about ragged, reformatory and industrial schools. The evidence she gave to the Royal Commission on Criminal and Destitute Children influenced the Youthful Offenders Act of 1854. Her educationally reforming establishments, such as Red Lodge in Bristol, were visited and considered by almost everyone who was interested in a progressive system for the education of the poor.

In this she stood out from the evangelical orthodoxy of the early nineteenth century. Within the Charity School Movement, such leading Evangelicals as Sarah Trimmer and Hannah More had devoted their lives to the education of children from the very poorest classes.[18] They were, however, centrally concerned with religious instruction, and in particular with the need to teach children their place in the Almighty's scheme of salvation and of the danger of eternal damnation. Many evangelical Christians believed that the poverty and distress of the hundreds of thousands who lived in the great industrial cities was chiefly attributable to the poor themselves. For them, the idleness, improvidence and licentiousness of the poor was the *sole* cause of the conditions in which they were forced to live. Thus, as John Bird Sumner, a future Archbishop of Canterbury, wrote, only gospel religion could provide an effectual remedy for the sufferings of the destitute, since it taught 'foresight, moderation, patience and contentment'.[19] 'Could we reform the improvident habits of the people', wrote the Scottish evangelical Dr Chalmers, 'it would reduce the existing poverty of the land to a very humble fraction of its present extent'.[20] In contrast, as Ruth Watts points out, Mary Carpenter believed in a kind of radical environmentalism and refused to lay the blame for their predicament on the working classes. She argued that many poor children would end up as criminals simply because of society's extreme neglect. 'If Society leaves them knowingly in the state of utter degradation in which they are then I think it more absolutely owes them reparation, far more than they could be said to owe reparation to it.'[21]

Different again from the educational work of evangelical women and the more radical initiatives of the Unitarians was the work of active orders of

Catholic nuns, who, although they did not overtly articulate their work in terms of radical social progress, were also significant providers of education. From the Reformation right up to our period the penalty for keeping a Catholic school had been lifelong imprisonment. After 1791, Catholic worship and Catholic schools were tolerated, so that convents could offer shelter to nuns fleeing from the French Revolution, some of whom set up schools in England. In the 1840s, following the Irish potato famine thousands of refugees poured into the poorest parts of England's industrial cities, swelling the number of children living in deepest poverty. At the time the education of the poor was still largely dependent on voluntary effort with little encouragement from the government. The bulk of public money (only £40,000 in 1844) went to the National Society (Anglican) and the British and Foreign School Society (Dissenters), so for the Catholic community in England getting sufficient funds for education was a significant problem. Convents sometimes established fee-paying schools for middle-class girls and used some of this income to finance poor schools. Nuns outnumbered the teaching brothers and the first Catholic inspector of schools, Thomas William Marshall, considered their schools altogether superior to those of their male counterparts. John Marmion argues that 'a significant part of the contribution made by the Religious was that they brought people of breeding and education to work in the slum schools, and without their vital contribution those schools could hardly have survived the dual problems of poverty and bigotry to become efficient places of education'.[22] For these women, joining a sisterhood offered not only an active life of service, but also membership of an intellectual community of cultured women. It was an option not available to Anglican women until 1845, when the Park Village Sisterhood, the first since the Reformation, was established in London.[23]

Hilary Minns's chapter discusses the educational work of Catherine McAuley in Ireland and England. In offering an intimate view of the teaching in Baggot Street School shortly after it had been affiliated to the National Board of Education (in order to become eligible for state aid), she demonstrates that the teaching and managerial skills of the sisters were of a high order. Indeed, being for the main part women of considerable education themselves, they can be seen as pioneers of a professional life for women. Various orders of nuns were largely responsible for the creation of a Catholic lay teaching profession; they provided colleges and staffed them and established a good supply of practice schools for their pupil teachers. Hilary Minns recounts how, aged fifty, Catherine McAuley found that the only way to give her leadership potential its full scope was to become a nun.[24] She founded the Sisters of Mercy who worked with poor girls in practical ways – training young women to be servants, teaching literacy and numeracy and encouraging able girls to become lay teachers. Catherine McAuley's Sisters of Mercy became world citizens in the course of their work in educating the children of Irish Catholic migrants in many countries.

Within Anglican society and among the more socially conservative dissenting communities, the activities of women during the first half of the nineteenth century were constrained by the new theological emphasis on the Epistles of St Paul. In the evangelical religious revivalism of the early nineteenth century women 'were granted a role in spiritual life which at one and the same time empowered and confined them'.[25] They were empowered by being considered the vital moral guardians of the family and therefore this could extend to a guardianship of their local community and even to the whole of society. Through philanthropy middle-class women found ample work and scope in the impoverished, filthy environment of early nineteenth-century cities.[26] As a result, we no longer see the nineteenth-century middle-class home as a prison for women, but, more often than not, as a centre of operations, chiefly for a variety of intellectual and philanthropic enterprises. Nevertheless, women's field of action was simultaneously confined by disabilities relating to property and by lack of parliamentary power. They were allowed a role as moral guardians, only, as it were, *in exchange* for the lack of citizens' rights. Arguably, however, the chief limiting constraint they endured was the lack of any formal education outside the home.[27]

In fact, middle-class girls could become semi-educated, thanks to the efforts of mothers, governesses, and to being allowed to listen in on the activities of tutors hired primarily for their brothers' benefit. For intellectually minded young women in households which possessed a good library, a great deal of self-education took place through reading, and reading groups were often established by women when their brothers disappeared, first to public schools and then to Oxford and Cambridge.[28] As Norma Clarke points out in her chapter, Anna Jameson is a striking example of a woman who educated herself and then established herself as the educator of 'thousands of young ladies'. Like many genteel women in precarious financial circumstances, she made her living as a governess from the age of sixteen until her marriage in 1825.[29] The career Anna Jameson established for herself was that of teacher of the liberal arts, and her books were directed not at an elite audience of university-educated men, but at a predominately feminine readership. In writing about Shakespeare's heroines, for example, she gave young women an opportunity of a focus for intellectual discussion, while their brothers learned Greek and Latin by rote at public school and university. Her books about the art treasures of Europe helped to inform and cultivate the sensibilities of young women, in substitution for the European tour which their brothers conventionally took as a rite of passage to becoming a gentleman. As an author she was very successful. Her best-known book, *Sacred and Legendary Art* (1848), ran into ten editions, but her most widely read cheaper work was a series of

essays on early Italian painters published in the *Penny Magazine* between 1843
and 1845. This was the journal of the Society for the Diffusion of Useful
Knowledge, and it was committed to 'raising among the people a sentiment
of admiration for what is beautiful'.[30] Her essays were one of the few sources
of cultural education cheaply available until the mid-1840s.[31] As Norma Clarke
shows, Anna Jameson was a significant role model in terms of female independence and influence: she even demonstrated the possibility of maintaining respectability despite being separated from her husband.[32]

The leader of the Langham Place feminists, Barbara Bodichon (née Leigh
Smith), was directly influenced by Anna Jameson when the latter came into
the orbit of William Smith's family in 1845. Coming as she did from a politically
reforming family, Barbara Bodichon inherited the expertise and the desire
to run political campaigns. Her first sortie was to publish a pamphlet outlin-
ing the inequity of the laws affecting women in England (1854), followed
by a nationwide petitioning campaign to persuade Parliament to amend the
Married Woman's Property Laws. Anna Jameson's name was one of the twenty-
four names heading the petition. Her second campaign, on the right of
middle-class women to paid employment, acknowledged the debt to Anna
Jameson's views on women and work, although emphasising that all work was
honourable, whether paid or not.[33] Then in 1866, she led the first campaign
to achieve votes for women. In her chapter on Barbara Bodichon, Pam Hirsch
shows how she drew on her Unitarian legacy of a belief in reason and enterprise to pursue her campaigns for educational reforms. Barbara Bodichon
first set up a progressive co-educational primary school in London, then
called for a higher quality of secondary education for middle-class girls, without which they could not hope to tackle university level education. Finally, in
1873, she co-founded, and put all her money into the first university college
for women, Girton College, Cambridge, testimony to her belief that the
higher education of women was the single most important way to transform
society. Pam Hirsch has paid particular attention to her abilities as a leader,
her instinctive grasp of tactics and her shrewd strategies for bringing feminist
objectives before a wider public. Barbara Bodichon persuaded Lord Brougham
to allow women to participate in the Social Science Association, probably
the most powerful liberal pressure group of the third quarter of the century.
She also set up a feminist journal, the *English Woman's Journal*, to publicise
women's causes, including education.

Gillian Sutherland's chapter next charts the founding of Newnham College,
Cambridge, at about the same time as Girton, in the early 1870s. The first
Principal, Anne Clough, came, like Barbara Bodichon, from a prominent
liberal family (indeed there was a familial connection in that Anne's brother,
the poet Arthur Hugh Clough, married Barbara Bodichon's cousin Blanche
Smith), and the two women shared a commitment to the development of
higher educational opportunities for women. Following the institution of

local examinations for boys *and* girls in 1858 by the University of Durham, the North of England Council for Promoting the Higher Education of Women was formed in 1867, of which Anne Clough was an active member.[34] This was another highly effective pressure-group, working with methodical purpose to secure academic qualifications for women. In Cambridge, Girton and Newnham began as two different institutions with different aims. At Newnham Anne Clough allowed the students to follow the studies of their choice, whether or not their work led to University examinations. This was in contrast to Emily Davies, Barbara Bodichon's co-founder and first mistress of Girton, who would allow no compromise. Driven by the need to prove women's intellectual equality, she insisted that Girton students should commit themselves to full Cambridge degree courses and sit the examinations like the men after the statutory ten terms. It seems that at first Newnham students were less affluent and socially secure than Girton students; an oral tradition has it that 'Newnham was for governesses and Girton for ladies'.[35] This difference between the two institutions soon shifted, however, so that by 1885 four-fifths of Newnham students were working for a Cambridge degree. Gillian Sutherland's essay charts not only Anne Clough's contribution to women's education but also that of her niece, Thena Clough, in the struggle to persuade the University of Cambridge to accept women as full members.

The Latin, Greek and logic required for the 'Little-Go', the Cambridge qualifying examination, was a tremendous strain on young women whose secondary education had inevitably been inadequate. The 1865 women's Memorial, of which Anne Clough was a signatory, to the Schools' Inquiry Commission persuaded Lord Taunton to investigate the state of girls' schools. The Commission subsequently castigated the inadequacy of traditional provision for girls. Its recommendation that some ancient endowments should be made over to the creation of girls' schools, was a supremely important formal acknowledgement of the predicament to which Anne Clough, Barbara Bodichon and many other women educationists had been calling attention at meetings of the Social Science Association, through the North of England Council, and in a variety of journals. The Endowed Schools Act of 1869, permitting ancient foundations to remodel endowments to meet the needs of the present day, opened up the possibility of getting funding to establish girls' schools. The Endowed Schools' Commission (1869–74) was led by Joshua Fitch, a great supporter of women's education. As he toured the country encouraging schools to remodel their endowments, he pressed them, even in the face of governors' reluctance, to use some of their endowment to create good solid secondary schools. The 1870s thus saw an expansion of schools for girls, creating new generations of young women capable of taking full advantage of the newly available university education.[36]

In Oxford the story was similar. Following a visit to Girton in 1878, Dr Edward Talbot of Keble College and his wife returned to Oxford determined to establish 'a small residential enterprise' for women.[37] They set up a group called the Association for the Education of Women (AEW), and Lady Margaret Hall and Somerville were founded almost simultaneously as residential houses from which women could attend lectures organised by the AEW. The slow struggle to persuade Oxford University to recognise women was thus similar to that in Cambridge. Many of these early Oxbridge women themselves became educationists, as teachers, heads, founders of girls' secondary schools, or as members of school boards with the power to influence policy making.[38] Overall, women's access to higher education is a story of uneven developments – too long, too complex, and too piecemeal to rehearse here. Suffice it to say that in 1878 the new charter of the University of London admitted women to its degrees, the University of Durham followed suit in 1881, while the co-educational Victoria University of Manchester (of which University College, Liverpool, and Yorkshire College, Leeds, soon became constituent colleges) opened in 1884.[39]

Jane Miller's chapter is about her great-aunt, Clara Collet (1860–1948). Clara Collet came from a slightly less affluent stratum of the middle class than Barbara Bodichon or Anne Clough, although she inherited the same radical Unitarian ideology. Ranging over several generations of Collet women, Jane Miller enables us to see her particular Unitarian legacy. Clara Collet saw very clearly that the newly opened doors of education and entry into the workplace which defined the 'new woman' did not automatically deliver them to the promised land. She attended North London Collegiate School and would have liked to have gone to Girton but it was too expensive. Instead she became an assistant mistress in a girls' high school, which was considered an attractive job for a middle-class girl at that time. However, she continued to study and to gain further academic qualifications. This enabled her to enter a career which had been opening up to women from the 1870s – the civil service. Here she increasingly turned her attention to questions of policy concerning the newly educated working woman: issues such as pay and working conditions.[40] She complained that such supposedly prestigious jobs as high school mistresses in reality entailed on women an enormous pressure of work for very poor financial reward. Clara Collet was an example of a new generation of highly educated women whose voices increasingly contributed to matters of social policy.

During the course of the nineteenth and early twentieth centuries the elementary school system slowly became less patchy as dependence on voluntary societies was reduced through a series of Acts which culminated in a compulsory school system. No doubt because there were at this time few viable employment alternatives for women, the teaching force in the elementary system became substantially feminised, increasing from 50 per cent women in the 1870s to 75 per cent by 1914.[41] Most of these elementary teachers came from the skilled working class and lower middle classes, although, as paid employment became more respectable towards the end of the nineteenth century, more daughters of the professional classes began to enter teaching.

The pupil-teacher system was inaugurated in 1846, and it was by means of this system that the majority of elementary teachers were trained until 1902.[42] Indeed, as Matthew Arnold reported to the Newcastle Commission in 1859, pupil teachers were 'the sinews of English primary instruction'.[43] The system allowed the most able pupils to be apprenticed to the headteacher of an elementary school for five years and also to obtain a secondary education through attendance at a pupil-teacher centre. Candidates who were awarded Queen's Scholarships (which meant that the government subsidised four-fifths of the cost) were further entitled to a two-year course at a teacher training college, which amounted to a tertiary education. It was a closed and arduous system. However it made it possible for some poor but highly able girls, after qualifying as elementary teachers, to be promoted to teaching a range of secondary subjects in the pupil-teacher centres. In these centres, groups of clever working-class and lower middle-class women found more prestigious work and created collegial communities.

However, from the 1850s and 1860s, thanks in part to the success of Barbara Bodichon and the Langham Place group in persuading middle-class women that paid employment was honourable, more and more of them began to enter elementary teaching. Wendy Robinson's chapter examines teacher training in this transitional stage from 1870 to 1918, and describes the conflict of class and culture that this created which accompanied the decline of the pupil-teacher centres. Following the 1902 Act, which encouraged the rise of state-aided secondary schools, the pupil-centres became a less popular option. Increasingly, a secondary pupil intending to teach could stay on at school until sixteen or seventeen, after which a year could be spent as a student teacher before going on to training college. After 1907 bursaries were offered to children staying on at school in order to become teachers later. This later start to vocational training was more acceptable to middle-class parents than apprenticeship at thirteen, and so by 1914 the pupil-teacher system had been almost totally replaced by new teacher training colleges. Through her study of Sarah Bannister, a notable woman who had herself risen through the ranks of the pupil-teacher system, Wendy Robinson shows how the poorer women of the pupil-teacher centres lost their opportunities for a shared collegial culture – devalued in the face of the 'higher' culture of the new middle-class arrangements.

In order to attract young women from lower middle-class and even professional homes, the teacher training colleges increasingly projected a genteel ethos, despite an inherent contradiction between this and the harsh realities of establishing professional status in the public world. The price these young women had to pay for properly paid employment in the elementary system was grinding hard work and rigid decorum. Elizabeth Edwards examines these strains as they were played out in a particular college, Homerton, established in Cambridge in 1895. Despite the fact that by the early twentieth century women in education had achieved a significant measure of status and authority, the search for an appropriate mode of leadership remained problematic. Elizabeth Edwards demonstrates a strategy of stylised patriarchal femininity which Homerton's Principal, Mary Miller Allan, utilised in her dealings with the world. The strains of this public stance could however be relaxed within the 'private' sphere of college, wherein single women staff found sympathy, intellectual community and the emotional possibility of homoerotic friendship.

As the elementary system brought more and more children of the industrial poor into visibility during the later nineteenth century its pedagogy, based on submissive obedience, militaristic movements such as drills and marching and the mechanical learning of literacy and number skills, came under a challenge from a new philosophy, originally imported by German émigrés into Britain. These were women from a variety of wealthy and aristocratic backgrounds who had been expelled or who had banished themselves from Germany after 1848, when the liberal climate there was dispelled by reactionary governments. They worked as teachers and proselytisers of the new system and philosophy of early childhood education – the kindergarten. This had been invented in Thuringia by Friedrich Froebel (1782–1852) but was now banned throughout Prussia because of its socialist potential.

Froebel had worked with Pestalozzi at Yverdon, whose school had been a magnet for many English educationists, including some significant women, in the early nineteenth century. Like his countryman Rousseau, Pestalozzi had developed a pedagogy that was based on the observed behaviour of the interactions between a 'good' mother and her child, which gave cultural authority to ideas already extant in women's educational work.[44] Froebel further brought two important contemporary strands of thought together into a comprehensive system. He first rejected traditionally authoritarian ideas of education – those of rote learning and rigid routine – and developed a highly complex theory of directed play based upon what he believed was the child's natural need for activity. According to the historian Ann Taylor Allen 'the aims of this system – to create a generation "free thus within itself and by its own efforts to obtain more and more independence and personality" – expressed the liberal faith in education for citizenship'.[45] Secondly he was to align himself with German feminism by locating the future creation and leadership of the institution within which this education was to take place – the kindergarten – in the hands of women. Froebel believed women to be ideally equipped for this work because they possessed an innate maternal tendency. However, as women educationists had already been advocating, he sought recognition for the *science* of proper child nurture as an occupation equal in status to the male-dominated professions which required a formal education. In wanting women to apply the insights and values gained from distinctly female experience (what we would now call subjectivity) to the wider task of the liberal reform of society, his ideas struck a chord with embedded mid-century ideology. Indeed both Mary Carpenter and Anna Jameson had articulated a social role for women in terms of 'mothering' their community.[46] The reforming power of 'social motherhood' was already an important rhetorical strategy sanctioning women's authority in the public domain. As Ann Taylor Allen has pointed out, 'far from the reactionary affirmation of traditional subservience which some feminist historians have denounced, the nineteenth-century glorification of mother-hood was initially a progressive trend whose origins, like those of liberal thought in general, may be traced primarily to the Enlightenment'.[47]

What came to be recognised world-wide as the Froebel movement argu-ably would not have taken hold had it not been for some deeply committed German women, perhaps the most important being Baroness Bertha von Marenholz-Bulow. She blamed the death of her only child on the severity of his early formal education, and committed the rest of her life to what she termed 'the Cause' – that all children should be protected from what her own child had had to suffer. In this way she translated a private experience into a public commitment to improving the lot of all children, travelling throughout Europe, holding meetings, visiting infant schools and speaking publicly about Froebel's philosophy and methods.[48] As early as 1854 a private kindergarten was started in London by a leading Froebelian, and over the following twenty years more were started there and in some provincial cities. In Britain many women educationists, frequently from Unitarian or Jewish backgrounds, worked in or established kindergartens. Several of these women became leaders engaging in a wide range of educational movements, for example, the sisters Emily and Maria Shirreff. Emily Shirreff served as Mistress at the College for Women in Hitchin for two terms in 1870 and the two sisters together established the Girls' Public Day School Company (GPDSC) in 1872.[49] In 1874 a Froebel Society was founded by Maria Shirreff Grey, who was instrumental in attaching a kindergarten to most of the GPDSC schools. Since these schools primarily served the young children of middle- and upper middle-class parents, the benefit of progressive ideas was initially limited to what Gareth Stedman Jones has called the urban gentry.[50]

Nevertheless, by the 1880s, when the worst features of the 'payment by results' system were diminishing in infant schools, there developed within the state system a unique generation of women elementary teachers.[51] These dedicated and inspiring exponents of progressive ideas skilfully managed the tensions which their new approach was bound to provoke when applied within the physical limitations and conservative ethos of the Board schools. Anne Bloomfield's chapter illustrates how strong individuals could overcome conventional beliefs and practices through the work of Jane Roadknight, whose interventions led to changes in the system. Notwithstanding the poor physical condition of the children, and the inflexible architecture of the Board schools – in particular desks fixed to the floor and infant galleries which embodied an authoritarian and mechanical view of learning – she established a network system that disseminated, endorsed and implemented the new pedagogy for infant education. Never afraid to venture into the worst slum areas, her lived ideology, interpreted within the urban environment of Nottingham, was taken up by many members of the infant school teaching force, transforming Froebelian-based ideas into practical realities. Jane Roadknight's inspirational powers of leadership and organisation, revealed through her Inspector's annual reports, monitor the evolution of change, the rise in educational standards, improvements in health and a new-found freedom in many infant schools.

Inevitably, the original Froebelian philosophy was challenged and modified by the many women within the movement as the problems and practicalities of applying its methods to the poorest children in society created a variety of contested priorities. By the early twentieth century the movement had become a powerful locus of liberal and socialist thought, as the visible signs of under-nourishment inscribed on the bodies of poor children – high infant mortality, stunted growth, rickets, death from tuberculosis – mocked British notions of Imperial superiority. Kevin Brehony's chapter explores the way in which the new generation of professional women who came to prominence in the Froebel movement at the turn of the century challenged Froebelian orthodoxy. Maria Findlay and other Froebelian women attacked the way in which the older school of Froebelians clung to an idealist and mystical legitimation of the pedagogy – particularly the mother songs, gifts and occupations. They sought instead to replace it with a new active pedagogy, one which could be adapted to children of the urban poor. His essay goes on to consider how these professional women's primary concern for the children of the slums became articulated as a state-centred, collectivist educational project which was markedly at odds with their mainly Gladstonian Liberal upbringing.

Froebelian rhetoric, developed by women educationists, therefore underpinned progressive ideology within the state system, arguably until the 1960s and the Plowden Report. Partly as a result, the ideas of Maria Montessori, although influential, never became fully mainstream. Dr Montessori was an academically able woman, a doctor, and a professor of anthropology at the University of Rome. From 1907 she was the Directress of the Casa de Bambini in Rome, designed to serve slum children whose mothers worked outside their own homes. Her books, beginning with *A Method of Scientific Pedagogy* (1909), encouraged teachers to experiment and to record their observations of the mental, spiritual and physical attributes of the children in their care. Peter Cunningham's essay explores the impact of her ideas, the way they touched on the new concerns of middle-class mothers, and the role of male promoters and publishers within the educational establishment. He investigates the cultural authority deriving from her scientific background at a time when psychology and 'child study' were contributing to a redefinition of childhood. He goes on to consider the world-wide interest in her methods, exploring the role of travel, photography and film in assisting the dissemination of her ideas in the internationalist context of educational progressivism. He also points out that the Froebelian revisionists in Britain, led by the powerfully influential Margaret McMillan, were highly critical, finding Montessori's sense training – first developed for brain-damaged children – inappropriate for normal children.[52]

Finally, Mary Jane Drummond explores Susan Isaacs's establishment of the Maltings House School in Cambridge, 1924–7, which enabled Isaacs to undertake an active project, the main point of which was to study the ways in which individual children thought in order to help them learn. Although this progressive school served only a select group of children, often from academic homes, her theories embodied in her books *Intellectual Growth of Young Children* (1930), *The Children We Teach* (1932) and *Social Development in Young Children* (1933), remained key texts in the study of child development. Mary Jane Drummond shows the significance of Susan Isaacs's unique combination of qualifications, and her own early experience, which led her to study children's lives with sympathetic attentiveness and scientific rigour. What she learned about children's learning, both at the Maltings House and from her practice as a psychoanalyst, became the basis for studies in child development which were enormously influential in the training of new generations of nursery and primary teachers.

In this book, we trace the lives and work of a group of women leaders who, taken together, embody a particular yet multi-faceted tradition. It will be seen that this is not an essentialising project that sets women educationists apart as contributors to a Whiggish story of social reform. Rather, the details of each woman's strategies in making interventions in the social and political world in order to effect change reveal a constant series of dialectical tensions in play over the whole period, between such polarities as authority and freedom, public and private, patriarchy and matriarchy, middle class and working class. We are not therefore describing a feminist totality, but a relational articulation with all its attendant historical specifics. In each case the work of individual women had concrete effects on *different* disadvantaged groups. However, in doing this, we show that they drew on each other's intellectual and political legacies, support and solutions.

Lilian Shiman has pointed out, 'we know that some Victorian men quite consciously sought to suppress accounts of female activism as a bad example for their wives and daughters. Considerable effort is needed therefore to learn about women who sought meaningful public lives despite societal pressure against them.'[53] Yet all these women displayed unabashed agency, albeit within their own historical situations, often setting the terms for political debates, and entering public, ideological arguments over the nature of society, in print and on platform. Taken together, these women's habits of travel (three went to India, one travelled to America and Algiers, Montessori travelled world-wide), their public appearances, their political activism and their acknowledged intellectual and practical authority represent a major challenge to separate spheres historiography. Nearly all these women were household names in their local communities, while several were national and international figures.

Mary Wollstonecraft was one of the first and most influential women educationists to point out that 'a false system of education' for girls was injurious to the progress of society.[54] The infantilisation of falsely educated women meant that wives and daughters behaved like slaves, and this made their male relations, in effect, the slaves of slaves.[55] Worse still, she believed the irrational woman was totally unsuited to raising rational citizens. It will be obvious that in this sense the two central themes of this book are inevitably interlocked. The consistent concerns of women represented here – the liberalisation of education for young children, particularly those of the poorest classes, and the concomitant establishment of better and higher education for girls and women – remain intertwined in progressive ideology. In addition, Mary Wollstonecraft's sense that education was never marginal to, but was inevitably locked into, the political domain, underpins the ideas of nearly all our women. Like them, she regarded the middle class as the class most likely to be able to institute personal development, political change and social progress. These women leaders were all middle-class and likewise they were all legatees of a shared liberal inheritance.[56] As Marxist historians have suggested, however, their sense of political possibilities for change was perhaps limited by the 'naturalising' features of their bourgeois project. Eventually Margaret McMillan was to push at its boundaries by attempting to politicise the body of the working-class child. As Carolyn Steedman has shown in her biography of McMillan, 'the cause of childhood, conceived of as a social mission that transcended mere political divisions, could be viewed as the final resting place of a socialism that did not base itself in an economic understanding of a society's divisions, but saw rather the uplifting of broad masses of abandoned humanity as one of its central projects'.[57] Even the socialist Margaret McMillan, then, shared what could be seen as the liberal blindspot, an inability to conceive of progress in society in more structural economic terms.

Whatever the limitations of the projects of these 'welfare liberals', nevertheless, each chapter, in examining discretely the work of leading women educationists, shows them practising the art of the possible in particular, frequently difficult circumstances.[58] Despite the complexities and constraints they faced, they negotiated the dominant discourses and systems of their times in practical ways to realise their visions.

NOTES

1. Mary Wollstonecraft, *An Historical and Moral View of the Origin and Progress of the French Revolution and the Effect it has Produced in Europe* (1794), p. 19.
2. Barbara Taylor, *Eve and the New Jerusalem: Socialism and Feminism in the Nineteenth Century* (1983), p. ix.
3. R.J.W. Selleck, *The New Education 1870–1914* (1972); B. Simon, *The Two Nations and the Educational Structure 1780–1850* (1974); W.A.C. Stewart and W.P. McCann, *The Educational Innovators* (1967); H. Silver, *English Education and the Radicals 1780–1850* (1975).
4. This point is made generally by Sheila Rowbotham, *Hidden From History* (1973) and more specifically by June Purvis, *A History of Women's Education* (Buckinghamshire, 1991).
5. Leonore Davidoff, *The Best Circles* (1973); Leonore Davidoff and Catherine Hall, *Family Fortunes: Men and Women of the English Middle Class 1780–1850* (1987).
6. Jo Manton, *Mary Carpenter and the Children of the Streets* (1976); Carolyn Steedman, *Childhood, Culture and Class in Britain: Margaret McMillan 1860–1931* (1990); Dina Copelman, *London's Women Teachers: Gender, Class and Feminism 1870–1930* (1996); Philip Gardner, *The Lost Elementary Schools of Victorian England* (1984); Jane Martin, *Women and the Politics of Schooling in Victorian and Edwardian England* (1999); Jane Miller, *School for Women* (1996); Alison Oram, *Women Teachers and Feminist Politics 1900–39* (Manchester, 1996).
7. John Locke, *Essay Concerning Human Understanding* (1690); *Some Thoughts Concerning Education* (1693).
8. *Observations of Man* (1743).
9. Mitzi Myers, 'Impeccable Governesses, Rational Dames, and Moral Mothers: Mary Wollstonecraft and the Female Tradition in Georgian Children's Books', *Children's Literature* 14 (1986), pp. 31–59.
10. *Vindication of the Rights of Women* (Harmondsworth, 1986), p. 251.
11. *Ibid.*, p. 139.
12. See Pam Hirsch, 'Mary Wollstonecraft: A Problematic Legacy', in *Wollstonecraft's Daughters: Womanhood in England and France 1780–1920*, ed. Clarissa Campbell Orr (Manchester, 1996), pp. 43–60.
13. Raymond V. Holt, *The Unitarian Contribution to Social Progress* (1952).
14. Boyd Hilton, *The Age of Atonement: The Influence of Evangelicalism on Social and Economic Thought 1785–1865* (Oxford, 1997).
15. *Life of Frances Power Cobbe by Herself*, 2 vols (Cambridge, 1894), 1, 32.
16. Chapter 1, 'The Smiths' in Pam Hirsch, *Barbara Leigh Smith Bodichon: Feminist, Artist and Rebel* (1998).
17. F.K. Prochaska, *Women and Philanthropy in Nineteenth Century England* (Oxford, 1980).
18. M.G. Jones, *The Charity School Movement,* (Cambridge, 1938), pp. 155–60.
19. Quoted by Norris Pope, *Dickens and Charity* (Basingstoke, 1978), p. 6.
20. Rev W. Hanna, *Memoirs of the Life and Writings of Thomas Chalmers* (Edinburgh, 1949–52), 1, 384–5.
21. Jo Manton, *Mary Carpenter and the Children of the Streets* (1976), p. 14.
22. John P. Marmion, *Recusant History* 17, 1 (1984) pp. 67–83; p. 77.
23. This seems particularly timely, as the 1851 census showed that there were over half a million 'surplus' single women in the population, so that the importance for women of communities outside their own families was pressing.
24. Hazel Mills, writing of the work of French nuns for the education of the poor, comments that it allowed many women to pursue the extensive plans of usefulness and independence which Mary Wollstonecraft had advocated. See ' "Saintes soeurs" and "femme fortes": alternative accounts of the route to womanly civic virtue, and the history of French feminism' in *Wollstonecraft's Daughters*, op. cit. (see n. 12).
25. Philippa Levine, *Victorian Feminism 1850–1900* (London, 1987), p. 12.
26. F.K. Prochaska, *Women and Philanthropy in Nineteenth Century England* (Oxford, 1980).
27. Jeanne Peterson, 'No Angels in the House: the Victorian Myth and the Paget Women', *American Historical Review* 89 (1984), pp. 677–708.

28. Elizabeth Barrett Browning is one example of a sister suffering from the loss of a brother's tutor in Greek. See Pam Hirsch, 'Gender Negotiations in Nineteenth-Century Women's Autobiographical Writing' in *The Uses of Autobiography*, ed. Julia Swindells (1995).

29. Her first published book was *A First or Mother's Dictionary for Children* (1825).

30. *The Penny Magazine*, 17 November 1832, p. 326.

31. Adele M. Holcomb, 'Anna Jameson (1794–1860): Sacred Art and Social Vision', *Women as Interpreters of the Visual Arts, 1820–1979*, ed. Claire Richter Sherman with Adele M. Holcombe (Westport, Conn., 1981), p. 105. Jameson's essays were reprinted as *Memoirs of the Early Italian Painters* (1845).

32. See Carol Gilligan's work on the importance of female role models for teenage girls in, e.g., *Making Connections: the Relational Worlds of Adolescent Girls at Emma Willard School*, eds. Carol Gilligan, Nona P. Lyons and Trudy J. Hanmer (Cambridge, Mass., 1990).

33. Barbara Leigh Smith, *Women and Work* (1857).

34. Blanche Athena Clough, *A Memoir of Anne Jemima Clough* (1897), pp. 118–19.

35. Gillian Sutherland, 'Emily Davies, the Sidgwicks and the Education of Women in Cambridge' in *Cambridge Minds*, ed. Richard Mason (Cambridge, 1995), pp. 34–47; p. 38.

36. Gillian Avery, *The Best Type of Girl: A History of Girls' Independent Schools* (1991).

37. Vera Brittain, *The Women at Oxford* (1960), p. 50.

38. See Patricia Hollis, *Ladies Elect: Women in English Local Government 1865–1914* (Oxford, 1987); Polly Hill, *The Early Cambridge Women Students: The Sociological, Demographic and Sexual Contexts and the Women's Subsequent Careers* (Cambridge, 1995).

39. H. Hale Bellot, *The University of London: A History* (privately printed, 1969); W.H.G. Armytage, 'Portents and Polytechnics: the Efflorescence of Civic University Colleges in England 1867–1898', *The Universities Review* (October, 1952), pp. 5–19; C.E. Whiting, *The University of Durham 1832–1932* (London, 1932).

40. Clara Collet, *Educated Working Women* (1902).

41. Frances Widdowson, *Going Up into the Next Class: Women and Elementary Teacher Training 1840–1914* (1980).

42. R. Johnson, 'Educational Policy and Social Control in Early Victorian England', *Past and Present* 49 (1970), pp. 96–119; p. 119.

43. *Report* of Newcastle Commission, p. 106, quoted by H.C. Barnard, *A History of English Education* (1961), p. 185.

44. See J.H. Pestalozzi, *How Gertrude Teaches her Children*, translated by Lucy E. Holland and F.C. Turner (1900).

45. Ann Taylor Allen, 'Spiritual Motherhood: German Feminists and the Kindergarten Movement 1848–1911', *History of Education Quarterly* (Fall 1982), pp. 319–39; p. 322.

46. Eileen Janes Yeo, 'Social Motherhood and the Sexual Communion of Labour in British Social Science, 1850–1950', *Women's History Review* 1, 1 (1992), pp. 63–87.

47. Ann Taylor Allen, 'Spiritual Motherhood', p. 320.

48. *Friedrich Froebel and English Education*, ed. Evelyn Lawrence (1969).

49. Josephine Kamm, *Indicative Past: A Hundred Years of the Girls' Public Day School Trust* (1971). It changed from a limited company to a charitable trust in the 1920s (GPDST).

50. Gareth Stedman Jones, *Outcast London: A Study in the Relationship between Classes in Victorian Society* (1984).

51. The Revised Code of 1862 was the result of the Report of the Newcastle Commission which incorporated the principle of payments by results into the distribution of maintenance grants for elementary schools. The Revised Code was modified in 1867 and successive Codes over the next thirty years removed the worst features of payment by results till the principle itself was dropped. See J. Stuart Maclure, *Educational Documents: England and Wales 1816–1963* (1965), pp. 79–82.

52. Elsie Murray, *A Story of Infant Schools and Kindergartens* (1912), ch. 12.

53. Lilian Lewis Shiman, *Women and Leadership in Nineteenth Century England* (Basingstoke, 1992), p. xi.

54. Mary Wollstonecraft, *Vindication of the Rights of Woman* (Harmondsworth, 1986), p. 79.

55. *Ibid.*, p. 145.

56. Melissa A. Butler, 'Early Liberal Roots of Feminism: John Locke and the Attack on Patriarchy', *American Political Science* 72, 1 (1978); Stefan Collini, *Public Moralists: Political Thought and Intellectual Life in Britain 1850–1930* (Oxford, 1991), ch. 4 'The Culture of Altruism'.

57. Carolyn Steedman, *Childhood, Culture and Class: Margaret McMillan 1860–1931* (1990), p. 60.

58. See chapter 1 of Rosemarie Putnam Tong, *Feminist Thought* (Oxford, 1998).

PART ONE

The Emergence of Progressive Women Educators

CHAPTER ONE

'Child of Reason': Anna Barbauld and the Origins of Progressive Pedagogy

MARY HILTON

Progressive education, now somewhat in retreat in Britain, has constantly been assumed to postulate a Romantic and innocent child, a view first articulated by Rousseau. His idealised growing child, whose special nature and developing reason require a necessary freedom from all the corrupting restraints of society, has prevailed in the history of education.[1] A dialectical polarity has thus been erected between this representation and that of the puritan child, full of original sin, which view supported the evangelical fervour of much early nineteenth-century education. By examining the work of a distinguished pre-Romantic woman writer and educationist I wish to continue the recent challenge to this particular history of progressive ideology, returning to the rise of education during the Enlightenment as a central concern of liberal protestants, and the rather different ways the idea of reason was there configured and developed.[2]

Anna Barbauld was one of the most notable eighteenth-century women educationists who wrote directly for children. Her first poetry was published in 1773, and she was considered a talented literary woman even before she wrote her popular *Early Lessons* (1778) and *Hymns in Prose* (1781). She went on to write further poetry, tracts, sermons, hymns, essays and criticism. Here was a leading woman writer whose educational work was contiguous with her role as a civic personage, who crossed easily and gracefully from the discourse of political polemic to that of poetry, from educative stories for children to literary parody and learned criticism. As a result, however, her reputation was ambiguous.

On the one hand, she was remembered as a leading representative of liberal dissent and an almost perfect exemplar of eighteenth-century civility. According to her niece, 'she was possessed of great beauty, distinct traces of which remained to the latest period of her life. Her person was slender, her complexion exquisitely fair, with the bloom of perfect health.'[3] She was an outstanding conversationalist, witty and subtle in thought, brave and elevated in writing, liberal in her opinions, just and reasonable in her attitudes to children, friends and (most notably) other writers. 'I always wish to find great virtues where there are great talents, and to love what I admire', wrote the bluestocking Mrs Montagu, queen of London's literary society, in 1774, 'so, to tell you the truth, I made many enquiries into your character as soon as I was acquainted with your works, and it gave me intimate pleasure to find the moral character returned the lustre it received from the mental accomplishments'.[4]

On the other hand, following the French Revolution of 1789 she became, like other dissenters and radicals, alienated from the growing conservative hegemony and was publicly denigrated. By the early nineteenth century, the urbane civic world of her upbringing – the world in which she had been so admired – had hardened into a public arena of unrest and hostility, marked by war, scarcity, rampant industrialisation, evangelical religiosity and romantic nationalism. The swingeing attacks made on her last poem in 1812 have acquired lasting notoriety,[5] as has Lamb's famous diatribe against 'the cursed Barbauld crew, the blasts and blights of all that is human in man and child',[6] while Coleridge's coarse name-calling still induces a feeling of distaste.[7] Yet it is important for historians of education to recognise the political and gendered nature of these attacks, if they are to appreciate the radical nature of her thought, and the ways in which her educational views sprang from what Marlon Ross has called her position of 'double dissent' – as both a woman and a dissenter.[8]

Anna Barbauld (1743–1825) was born Anna Laetitia Aikin, daughter of Dr John Aikin and his wife, Jane Jennings. Both her parents were well educated and came from rational dissenting families. Until she was fifteen and her brother eleven her father ran a boys' school for the sons of dissenters at Kibworth. When a new dissenting academy was formed at Warrington, John Aikin was appointed Tutor in Languages and Belles Lettres. Three years later he became Tutor in Divinity in succession to Dr John Taylor of Norwich, while Joseph Priestley was chosen to fill his former post. Priestley was already known for his knowledge of natural philosophy, though he had not begun his experiments with electricity nor yet made his discovery of oxygen. Other residents included men and women who shone in literature, science and theology, and whose liberal humanism and wide learning were outstanding. Anna Barbauld's niece Lucy Aikin wrote later,

> Neither Oxford nor Cambridge could boast of brighter names in literature or science than several of these dissenting tutors – humbly content in an obscure town, and on a scanty pittance . . . They and theirs lived together like one large family, and in the facility of their intercourse they found large compensation for its deficiency in luxury and splendour.[9]

The history of liberal social progress from the late eighteenth to the middle of the nineteenth century is, in a large part, the history of Rational Dissent, later known as Unitarianism. The causes of women's emancipation[10] and education[11], science and technology, the alleviation of urban poverty, political reform and the abolition of slavery[12] were all promoted by a handful of enlightened Unitarian families connected by this particular form of dissenting Christianity. All Dissenters denounced the privileges of the established church and objected to its episcopalian traditions and rituals. However, unlike Methodists and the ranks of so-called 'New Dissent', Rational Dissenters embraced a radical theology, denying the doctrines of the Trinity and original sin, and therefore of Christ's separate act of redemption for the sins of humankind. The worship of Christ as part of God seemed unnecessary as well as blasphemous to them because they did not believe that humankind was estranged from God. Their democratic and liberal approach to the scriptures – based on the view that all people could read and interpret them, and that all had access to salvation – thus denied the hierarchical ecclesiology of the Book of Common Prayer.

The very conditions of their existence as religious communities made Rational Dissenters alert to the threat which the state, including the Church of England, always posed to their autonomy.[13] Their belief that the independent action of rational individuals should be left to regulate matters in everyday life, and that individuals should be free to read and write, to worship at any religious gathering, and to educate their children however they wished, showed their deep tolerance for difference and diversity. Central to this belief in diversity and freedom was education. Priestley wrote on the essential breadth of liberal education:

> By *natural philosophy* we mean the knowledge of the external world, but by *moral philosophy* we mean the knowledge of the structure of our own minds, and its various affections and operations, of which it must be acknowledged that very little is yet known, but into which we begin to get some light, especially from the observations of Mr Hobbes, Mr Locke, and, above all, Dr Hartley. This knowledge of human nature is the proper groundwork of every thing that is called *political knowledge*, or a knowledge of the interests and conduct of men as connected in society . . . .[14]

Anna Barbauld's association with Joseph Priestley and his wife was early, adoring, and for her critically influential. He had arrived at Warrington Academy when she was eighteen, encouraged her to write and publish her first poetry, and contributed to the open, rational and affectionate intellectual exchange that she had already experienced with her father, a colleague and friend of Priestley. Priestley was always a contentious figure. His *History of the Corruptions of Christianity* (1782) and *History of Early Opinions Concerning*

Jesus Christ (1786) became notorious as assaults upon received religion. He was a prominent intellectual of Rational Dissent, experimenting and teaching across a broad front in the confident belief that the natural sciences provided evidence of the unfolding of divine purpose. Anna Aikin (as she was then) was deeply aware of his radical sympathies and devotion to natural philosophy, both of which are ironically juxtaposed in her early poem, *The Mouse's Petition to Doctor Priestley having been Found in the Trap where he had been Confined all Night by Dr Priestley, For the Sake of Making Experiments with Different Kinds of Air* (1773):

> If e'er thy breast with freedom glowed,
> And spurned a tyrant's chain
> Let not thy strong oppressive force
> A free-born mouse detain . . .
>
> The well-taught philosophic mind
> To all compassion gives;
> Casts round the world an equal eye,
> And feels for all that lives.[15]

Her witty poem about his study – 'Papers and books, a strange mixed olio,/ From shilling touch to pompous folio' – was tragically prophetic in that, twenty years later, his study was to be ransacked by a hostile 'King and Country' mob, his books and instruments destroyed.

Like all Rational Dissenting academies, Warrington was deeply committed to the works of Locke. Locke's writings had covered a wide range of subjects, but it was the overall intellectual scheme explicated in his *Two Treatises of Government* that gave Rational Dissent its moral and political justification and placed his philosophy firmly on the dissenting academy curriculum. It was written towards the end of the seventeenth century in opposition to Sir Robert Filmer's *Patriarcha*. Filmer, a hierarchical Anglican, had argued that humans were by biological and theological necessity born into a state of helpless physical and legal impotence, that they live their lives as the property of a sovereign power whose authority had been conferred on Adam, the first father, directly by God, and that all subsequent fathers had enjoyed a similar authority over their children, as kings had over their subjects. To Locke the idea of such absolute power over other humans, particularly such total despotism over children, was blasphemous. Locke held that the legitimacy of the legal order which existed among mankind was derived solely from their acceptance of it. For Locke (as for Rational Dissenters), authority works *upwards* as humans confront each other in a social world created by the intricate patterns of their own compulsions. Thoughtless servility carries a moral burden, so that, when civil or religious liberty is threatened, there is an individual responsibility to make explicit dignified but total dissent. As John Dunn writes regarding Locke's ideas,

> Even the stupid have souls and hence cannot escape from their responsibility for the cognition of their elementary duties, both religious and political . . . In the relationship with God in which, through the mediation of grace, they come to know the truths of religion, all men are equal.[16]

That Anna Barbauld absorbed these philosophical lessons is clear from several of the treatises she wrote. *Civic Sermons to the People* (1792) and *Address to the Opposers of the Repeal of the Test and Corporation Acts* (1791) are model statements of Lockean principle on the proper basis of civic consent and the imperative of dignified dissent, while in her sermon *Reasons for National Penitence* (1793) she wrote,

> The energy of laws is instrumental, and secondary only; and they derive their sanction and authority from the will of the people. I have reverted to the origin of civil government, that it might clearly appear to you, that every one of you is involved in the guilt of public and national offences.[17]

Indeed, like other Rational Dissenters, she was politically active in several Opposition campaigns of the 1770s and 1780s. She condemned the British war against the American colonies and spoke out against the slave trade. Her famous poem *Epistle to William Wilberforce* (1791) on the rejection of his bill for the abolition of the slave trade showed again her commitment to civil rights and the freedom of the individual. It has a modern radical resonance:

> . . . Where seasoned tools of Avarice prevail,
> A Nation's eloquence, combined, must fail . . .

Rational Dissenters argued for liberty, not just for themselves but for all who suffered from state interference, and during and after the American War of Independence they provided the leading voices in effective political polemic. In 1790, when Fox brought forward his motion for the repeal of the Test and Corporation Acts (the acts which debarred dissenters from Oxford and Cambridge and most of the professions), Priestley wrote his *Letters to Burke* which achieved instant notoriety. Anna Barbauld also entered the lists against Burke with her incisive pamphlet *Address to the Opposers of the Repeal of the Corporation and Test Acts* (1791):

> The old cry of 'The Church is in danger' has again been made to vibrate in our ears . . . What! fenced and guarded as she is with her exclusive privileges and rich emoluments, stately with her learned halls and endowed colleges, with all the attraction of her wealth, and the thunder of her censures; all that the orator calls 'the majesty of the church' about her, – and does she, resting in security under the broad buckler of the state, does she tremble at the naked and unarmed sectary?[18]

Again she promotes a Lockean view of civic responsibility:

> You have set a mark of separation upon us, and it is not in our power to take it
> off; but it is in our power to determine whether it shall be a disgraceful stigma
> or an honourable distinction. If, by the continued peaceableness of our de-
> meanour, and the serious sobriety of our conversation, – a sobriety for which
> we have not yet quite ceased to be distinguished; if, by our ardent love of liberty
> which you are pretty ready to allow us, we deserve esteem, we shall enjoy it.

Locke's writings had also encompassed the central importance of education
and the growth of reason in the individual child. In his *Essay Concerning
Human Understanding* (1690) and *Some Thoughts Concerning Education* (1693)
Locke had provided the eighteenth century with what seemed to be a defini-
tive and rational basis for the study of human development and an explanation of the crucial formative importance of early experiences. According to
Locke, the child was not a diminutive adult but a tender infant without
innate ideas or principles, certainly without sin. This tiny infant, through
observing external sensible objects, has conveyed into its mind distinct per-
ceptions of things, according to the various ways those objects affect him or
her. In time its mind reflects on its own operations about these ideas and
thereby stores itself with a new set of ideas. This principle that the infant
child is furnished with ideas through the early association of sensations with
feelings, then reflects upon these ideas, unites them, compares them, and by
breaking them apart develops the ability to abstract, still underlies much
liberal educational thought. In the eighteenth century it was developed by
David Hartley in his influential *Observations of Man* (1749). Locke and, later,
Hartley were widely read and enlightened educational theory rested heavily
on their work.[19] Associationism, as it became called, gave a central role to
mothers and became a popular science for women. They, being the earliest
carers of the instinctual infant, were the adults most likely to set up the
proper (or improper) associations between sensations and feelings.

If Locke provided eighteenth-century Rational Dissenters such as Anna
Barbauld with a political world-view and an educational rationale, then the
works of Paley encapsulated her comfortable sense of a benign Providence.
Paley did not publish his *Principles of Moral and Political Philosophy* until 1785,
or his *Natural Theology* until 1802, but his theological schema can be identified
with that mood of holistic optimism which characterised the decade leading
up to 1776, and which has been called 'the high summer of the English
Enlightenment, a time in which all men of taste and letters, however dis-
parate in faith or morals, could meet in urbane society'.[20] *Natural Theology*
demonstrates the existence of God from the 'book of nature'. The justification of pain, disease and death and all other physical evil is shown as consistent with the design and contrivance of a beneficent creator. Indeed,

a world furnished with advantages on one side, and beset with difficulties, wants and inconveniences on the other, is the proper abode of free, rational and active natures, being the fittest to stimulate and exercise their faculties.[21]

Paley argued that happiness is not to be found in the pleasures of the senses or in elevated rank or luxury, but rather in the exercise of the social affections, good habits, and the good health of body and spirit. In his eighteenth-century apologetic he linked the laws of nature to social equilibrium: 'all which we enjoy, and a great part of what we suffer, is put in our own power'.[22] For Paley life itself was a time of moral and rational education, God having provided a range of good and evil possibilities which free and rational beings could exploit in order to develop their virtue. For a liberal educationist such as Anna Barbauld, this was the paradigm that framed the nature of childhood. Her plea for Coleridge – 'Heaven conduct thee with a parent's love'[23] – implied a belief in a firm but ultimately benevolent authority which allowed the growing reason considerable latitude.

Anna Barbauld was a keen and spirited reader of Paley who, although he was a member of the Anglican church, held latitudinarian views akin to those of the Rational Dissenters. This popular tradition believed that religious awe derived from observations of nature. In 1774 Anna had married Rochemont Barbauld, a clergyman of French descent, and together they ran a boys' school in Palgrave in Suffolk. They did not have children of their own but adopted a nephew, Charles Aikin, at the age of two. During her time at Palgrave she published *Early Lessons for Children* (1778), written for little Charles, and *Hymns in Prose* (1781). The *Early Lessons* demonstrate her Paleyan sense of a benign creator and of the value of contentment:

> But the poor lad looked up in his face with a smile of great contentment, and told him that as he was very happy in the sunshine so he was not afraid of the storm . . . Truly, thought the gentleman, it is a noble thing not to be disturbed by trifles, and to be happy though we may not have fine clothes, which are of no good in a storm, nor a grand house, which is not half so constant or so good a shelter as a good heart and a cheerful mind.[24]

Similarly *Hymns in Prose* united her associationist belief in the importance of indelible impressions in early childhood with her Paleyan sense of awe in the contemplation of God's hand in the works of nature:

> Come, let us walk abroad; let us talk of the works of God . . . Every plant hath a separate inhabitant . . . Who causeth them to grow every where . . . and giveth them colours and smells, and spreadeth out their thin transparent leaves? . . . Lo, these are part of his works; and a little portion of his wonders. There is little need that I should tell you of God, for everything speaks of Him.[25]

The Barbaulds closed their school in 1785, and after travelling on the Continent for a year they settled in Hampstead, where her husband officiated

Fig 1.1   *'But the poor lad looked up in his face with a smile of great contentment, and told him that as he was very happy in the sunshine so he was not afraid of the storm.' Anna Barbauld's* Lessons for Children *(1778) demonstrate her Enlightenment view of a benign Providence.*

at the small dissenting chapel and she pursued her literary work. Over the forty years that Anna Barbauld wrote and published she developed and maintained a consistent ideology. In common with the Bluestockings, the renowned circle of leading literary women, she held that reason in men and women should guide their conduct towards a better knowledge of God, and towards an increase of virtuous conduct in the social world. Reason, however, is not a static sense that is given to some rather than others. Rather, as Locke had argued, all people have a 'candle' within them that makes them responsible for their freedom and capable of improvement in virtue.

Also in the increasing and effervescent material commerce of the eighteenth century, where patrimony was shifting from more static forms of inherited land to transmission of entrepreneurial capital associated with business, Lockean 'virtue' now seemed vital within the new *visible* culture. Spiritual righteousness, even learned skills, were no longer central to education. It was now manners and attitudes, an ease with both superiors and inferiors, a genuine dislike of vice and bad company, good habits for life and above all an affectionate and loving relationship with elderly parents which would ensure the transmission of more volatile forms of patrimony. Locke's concerns were not confined to an apprenticeship in skills or knowledge or even classical learning, but were focused on a broader conception of 'mentality'. Education is no longer simply instruction but a much grander project, enveloping the infant child in its whole familial culture, intricately involving the growth of reason through affectionate example and discussion.

Anna Barbauld's essay *On Education* reveals her development of these principles. Her advice to a wealthy man on how to rear his son is both a reiteration of the effect of early impressions and associations ('The moment he was able to form an idea his education was already begun') and also a treatise on attitudes and mentality. She brushes aside 'instruction' in order to focus, like Locke, on the early attitudes he will develop relevant to virtue and conduct. These are almost entirely transferred *by example*:

> Education, in its largest sense, is a thing of great scope and extent. It includes the whole process by which a human being is formed to be what he is, in habits, principles and cultivation of every kind. But of this, a very small part is in the power even of the parent himself; a smaller still can be directed by purchased tuition of any kind . . . Do you ask then, what will educate your son? Your example will educate him; your conversation with your friends; the business he sees you transact; the likings and dislikings you express; these will educate him.[26]

So much for boys. However, her attitude towards the education of girls was even more domestic and far more authoritarian. In repudiating, as early as 1774, an offer by the bluestocking Mrs Montagu of the headship of an academy for female education, she wrote a much-quoted letter in which is inscribed a complete absence of today's feminism:

> The best way for women to acquire knowledge is from conversation with a
> father, a brother or friend, in the way of family intercourse and easy conversa-
> tion, and by such a course of reading as they may recommend.[27]

Yet her narrower views on the upbringing of girls came not only, as she
claimed, from her lack of familiarity with that process, but also sprang from
her theological beliefs. Rational Dissenting intellectuals, of whom she was
an outstanding example, saw God in everything: man, woman, animal and
matter. There was no estrangement between God and mankind as in most
parts of the Anglican tradition, no essential mediation between God the
Father and mankind through his son Jesus Christ. So for her the social roles
allowed to men and women were but one facet of a beneficent Providence,
which inhabited everything. This powerful theological monism enabled her
to maintain an ironic distance from both genders, a satirical gaze which has
puzzled and intrigued seekers after Enlightenment feminism. She could be
as witty and ironical about masculine stupidity as she was about feminine
tyranny.[28] Her utter conviction of the intellectual equality between the sexes
enabled her to encourage the most intense study for girls alongside their
roles as sisters, wives and mothers, to sustain intellectual and political discourse with her women friends, and to establish herself as a leading *woman*
writer and essayist, whilst conforming to a rigid pattern of female decorum.
The later Unitarian tradition of intellectual womanhood, exemplified by such
women writers as Harriet Martineau and Sarah Austin, looked to Anna
Barbauld as an outstanding leader in conduct and intelligence.[29]

One of the greatest concerns for Rational Dissenters in the grand project
of education was to achieve a coherence between the growth of reason in the
individual and his or her necessary early submission to God's authority. At
the heart of the Warrington curriculum was a vital commitment to liberal
education, a sense that all ideas, from whatever authority, are there to be
interrogated. Priestley and Anna Barbauld's father, Dr Aikin, were both famous
for their easy familiarity with students and ideas. Priestley wrote:

> If the subject be a controversial one, let him [the student] refer to books
> written on both sides of the question . . . Let the lecturer give his pupils all
> encouragement to enter occasionally in the conversation, by proposing queries,
> or making any objections or remarks that may occur to them . . . For my own
> part I would not forgo the pleasure and advantage which accrue, both to my
> pupils and myself, from . . . this familiar way of discoursing upon a subject.[30]

However, these Dissenters, being strong associationists, believed firmly in the
authoritative planting of religious and moral ideas in early childhood. Priestley
was against Rousseau's idea 'that nothing should be inculcated upon children which they cannot perfectly understand and see the reason of'. On the
contrary, he wrote,

a general notion [should] be gradually impressed upon their minds, that some reverence is due to a power which they do not see, and that there exists an authority to which all mankind, the rich and great, as well as the poor and mean, must equally bow.[31]

In her *Hymns in Prose*, Anna Barbauld commences an instructive catechism by asking the 'child of reason' where he had been and what he had seen. He replies that he had been in the meadow looking at the cattle and wheat. But, she asks,

Didst thou observe nothing besides? Return again, child of reason, for there are greater things than these. God was among the fields; and dids't thou not perceive him? His beauty was upon the meadows; his smile enlivened the sun-shine.

Thus for Anna Barbauld reason was not, as it has since come to be character-ised, a cold and utilitarian faculty of the mind, an objective thinking without passion, prejudice or superstition, but rather an intellectual quickness and balanced appreciation of God's wonders and polarities. There is an affinity here with Addison's famous ode, which became a popular eighteenth-century Protestant hymn:

> What though in solemn Silence, all
> Move round the dark terrestrial Ball?
> What tho' nor real Voice nor Sound
> Amid their radiant orbs be found?
> In *Reason's* Ear they all rejoice'
> And utter forth a glorious voice
> For ever singing as they shine,
> 'The Hand that made us is Divine'.

As George Dekker has observed with regard to this ode, 'the Reason that can hear the *musica mundana* is not the Reason of the soundless, voiceless Newtonian universe. It must be an inspired, creative faculty in man himself.'[32] To Anna Barbauld also, as to Addison, reason is an affective faculty which connects mankind to the system of the universe. She places understanding within a paradigm created by reason, and like Hartley she claims that reason is *developed* from early associations and ideas. In this eighteenth-century meta-physical ordering of consciousness, understanding is a process whereby the mind brings what is given in sensation under the control of a framework of necessary concepts or categories. But the central ideas of reason, in which are embedded a moral and ontological order, guide the understanding. Thus one cannot simply understand how nature as such is an ordered whole or a design, and the overarching ideas of inspired reason must play their part in guiding experience or in leading the understanding to look for connections and relationships between things.[33]

Anna Barbauld dealt directly with the question of reason and authority in a short essay *On Prejudice*, in which she examined Rousseau's idea of the suspension of belief:

> Give your child, it is said, no *prejudices*: let reason be the only foundation of his opinions; where he cannot reason, let him suspend his belief. Let your great care be, that as he grows up he has nothing to unlearn; and never make use of authority in matters of opinion, for authority is no test of truth.

But, she asks,

> Is it desirable that a child should grow up without opinions to regulate his conduct, till he is able to form them fairly by the exercise of his own abilities? Such an exercise requires at least the sober period of matured reason; reason not only sharpened by argumentative discussion, but informed by experience.

She then takes Rousseau's idea apart:

> Besides, taking it for granted (which however is utterly impossible) that a youth could be brought up to the age of fifteen or sixteen without prejudice in favour of any opinions whatever, and that he is then set to examine for himself some important proposition, – how is he to set about it? Who is to recommend books to him? Who is to give him the previous information necessary to comprehend the question? Who is to tell him whether or no it is important? Whoever does these will infallibly lay a bias upon his mind.

She finishes with a resounding liberal argument:

> Let his conviction of all the truths you deem important be mixed up with every warm affection of his nature, and identified with his most cherished recollections – the time will come soon enough when his confidence in you will have received a check . . . Do not expect the mind of your son to resemble yours . . . He was formed, like you, to use his own judgement, and he claims the high privilege of his nature.[34]

It is not surprising, therefore, that Barbauld refuted Rousseau in her beliefs and practices. Her sense of the vitality of textual knowledge and the importance of learning to read was, in itself, a refutation of Rousseau's untainted 'natural' child (he considered the only text suitable for children to be Defoe's *Robinson Crusoe*). Despite her early success in the literary world, she believed that writing for children was extremely important ('The task is humble, but not mean, for to lay the first stone of a noble building and to plant the first idea in a human mind can be no dishonour to any hand').[35] The school she and her husband ran at Palgrave was well known for its enlightened yet textually rich curriculum. Several distinguished scholars long after remembered her writing lessons. Her energies in putting on dramatic performances, and her gifted ways of making texts come alive through performance, showed in these years. Many remembered her gentle yet perceptive critical sense that she expended all her life on the written works of others.[36]

In Anna Barbauld's work it is possible to trace an argument that an affectionate and strong familial cultural matrix is not necessarily at odds with a growing child's development as a fully rational, and therefore potentially dissenting, being. In opposition to Rousseau's romantic radicalism of the 'natural' child, her own conformable social behaviour, combined with considered public opposition to major issues of her day, shows the ways that liberal thought, honed by affective yet rational 'argumentative discussion', developed within Rational Dissenting families in the eighteenth century. Her familial yet respectful view of the autonomous growing child – as someone whom adults have an intense didactic responsibility to encourage to experiment, to think for themselves, to read and discuss and to argue rationally – was to be submerged in the early nineteenth century by two powerful intellectual movements: evangelicalism and Romanticism.

Until the French Revolution in 1789 the Rational Dissenters, led by Richard Price and Joseph Priestley, continued to harry for constitutional reform. By 1792, however, the turmoil of violence in France led conservative society to jettison Enlightenment values altogether, fearing that they would produce anarchy and disaffection. The 'Jacobin' threat allegedly posed by radicals and Dissenters gave this conservative ideology considerable appeal and resilience. Not only did the French Revolution and war create national anxiety at home, but the population had exploded from under eight million in 1750 to nearly 11 million in 1801. Economic changes were destroying traditional patterns of life, while rural poverty increased dramatically, creating heavy pressure on Poor Law provision. In the 1790s dearth seriously affected the lives of numbers of people and food riots took place. In 1798 the young Robert Malthus, who had been educated at Warrington and was a friend of the Aikin family, published his influential *Essay* on the new science of political economy. In it he argued that famine and poverty were inevitable since, in the imperfect social system created by mankind, population would always outstrip the supply of food. Suddenly it seemed that God's benevolence was more remote from the day-to-day workings of human beings than most liberal Anglicans and Dissenters had believed. Anna Barbauld was to share the wide pessimism about the decay of Britain that Malthus's work engendered.

Like the other Rational Dissenters, Anna Barbauld, for all her graciousness and Enlightenment civility, was now, after the early 1790s, to share the decades of unrest and denigration for dissenters and radicals. In her *Address to the Opposers of the Repeal of the Test and Corporation Acts* (1792) she had written about France:

> You see a mighty empire breaking from bondage, and exerting the energies of
> recovered freedom, and . . . England, who has long reproached her with being
> a slave, now censures her for daring to be free.

Her brother John Aikin's medical practice in Great Yarmouth collapsed and
he moved with his family to Stoke Newington. Mr Barbauld's mental health
began to decline and he had to give up his pastorship of the Unitarian
chapel in Hampstead. The Barbaulds moved to be near the Aikins in Stoke
Newington. After Priestley's house and laboratory were destroyed by a Church
and King mob, forcing him to emigrate to America, she wrote indignantly:

> . . . the slander of a passing age
> Imports not . . .
> . . . Calm thou can'st consign it
> To the slow payment of that distant day, –
> If distant, – when thy name, to Freedom's joined,
> Shall meet the thanks of a regenerate land.[37]

She continued to live in Stoke Newington with her husband whose mental
illness, by the new century, made him dangerous. After making several attempts
on her life he was kept in a separate establishment and committed suicide in
1808. She kept up her literary work which culminated when, in 1812, then
aged 68, she published a long poem simply entitled *Eighteen Hundred and
Eleven*.

She first prophesies Britain's complete commercial collapse:

> Thy baseless wealth dissolves in air away,
> Like mists that melt before the morning ray

– to be followed by total ruination:

> Night, Gothic Night, again may shade the plains
> Where Power is seated, and where Science reigns;
> England, the seat of arts, be only known
> By the grey ruin and the mouldering stone;
> That Time may tear the garland from her brow,
> And Europe sit in dust, as Asia now.

In a private sense Anna Barbauld had much to mourn, but in her writings
she had always looked outwards to the public realm rather than inwards, and
here she well expresses a rational depression and a sense of national *civic*
loss. What is fascinating, historically, is that she inscribes a roll of honour, or
rather a hall of fame, of great thinkers of the previous century, which poetic
conceit she uses to express a sense of the architectonic and public scale of
past greatness. In a poem of monumental pathos she recreates for the reader

her lost Augustan civic world, with its philosophers, scientists, statesmen, poets and reformers now troped as inspirers of the new world of the Americas. 'Thy Lockes, Thy Paleys shall instruct their youth', she defiantly intones, and further on: 'Join with their Franklin, Priestley's injured name, / Whom, then, each continent shall proudly claim.'

In its anxiety and gloom about 'baseless wealth' the poem addressed a general feeling of potential commercial ruin that had reached its acme by 1811. The *New Annual Register* of 1810 drew attention to the wartime in-security of wealth which depended on bills that might not be creditworthy: 'there is much reason to dread that the commerce of Britain has seen its best days'.[38] According to Geoffrey Carnall several writers at this time envisaged the ruin of London, in whose very greatness lay the seeds of premature and rapid decay.[39] Gibbon's *The History of the Decline and Fall of the Roman Empire* (1776–88) had also pointed to an inevitable decay of great empires, advanced and corrupted societies which contrast with the heroic simplicity, freedom and individualism of primitive precursors such as the Roman republic. The war was not going well and the intellectual and political climate was full of contestation and unease. In this year Jane Austen started to write *Mansfield Park*, her most morally anxious novel. Anna Barbauld's friend Crabbe Robinson felt distaste for her poem and its unfortunate reminder of her radical views:

At this time dear Mrs Barbauld incurred great reproach by writing 1811 . . . There was a disheartening and even dastardly tone in it which even I with all my love for her could not excuse. . . . I find in my journal occasional expres-sions of displeasure at the unqualified Jacobinism of her politics, and lately, on looking over her otherwise admirable *Sins of the Government, Sins of the Nation*, I was surprised that I had not before noticed what was then become offensive, the unqualified assertion that the numerical majority of every country ought to be the legislators![40]

Soon after it was published in June 1812 Anna Barbauld's poem was viciously criticised in the *Quarterly Review* and, as a result, she never wrote again for publication. J.W. Croker was an MP, a 'Tory' hack, a man of limited imagina-tion but acidulous prose.[41] Both the economy and the prospects for the outcome of the war had improved by 1812 which enabled him, after a bitterly contemptuous introduction, to write:

We do not know where Mrs Anna Letitia now resides, though we can venture to assert that it is not on Parnassus: it must, however, be in some equally unfrequented, though less classical region: [her depiction of Britain] is no more like a scene that is really before our eyes, than Mrs Barbauld's satire is like her 'Lessons for Children', or her 'Hymns in Prose.'[42]

But the real reason for Croker's acid was Anna Barbauld's political sympathies. She was a woman intellectual, a Rational Dissenter and a political liberal and he was writing in the Tory *Quarterly Review*. His last sentence reveals much of his true position:

> We also assure her, that we should not by any means impute it to a want of taste or patriotism on her part, if, for her country, her fears were less confident, and for America her hopes less ardent; and if she would leave both the victims and the heroes of her political prejudices to the respective judgement which the impartiality of posterity will not fail to pronounce.[43]

Thus Anna Barbauld left posterity a map of her ideological reference points in a work which etched the changes from Enlightenment culture to nineteenth-century pessimism. Her last poem epitomised the rupture in eighteenth-century faith in reason and civility. In the turbulent decades that followed, the middle and upper classes became obsessed by catastrophes: by wars, famines, pestilences, revolutions, volcanoes and especially the great commercial upheavals which periodically threatened to topple the capitalist system. An evangelical ethos – according to which such sufferings could be seen to be part of God's plan, and children once again as vessels of original sin – dominated throughout. The leading Evangelical Wilberforce wrote in 1803, 'it ought to be the grand object of every moral writer . . . to produce in us that true and just sense of the intensity of malignity of sin . . . and of the real magnitude of our danger'.[44] There was a widespread return to the revealed word of God in the scriptures, particularly to the patriarchal epistles of St Paul. In such a climate Anna Barbauld's rational ideology based on natural theology and freedom for the individual was found dangerously wanting. Nor did it appeal to those poets who, in the early nineteenth century, began taking an inward or subjective direction, searching for self in the sublimity of nature.[45] Here Rousseau's natural and innocent child supported a new intellectual cult of childhood which, for the male Romantic poets, provided the soil for the exploration of the poetic psyche and the development of the masculine ego.[46] Caught in the new political and gender realignments of these movements, the literary achievements and the progressive educational philosophy of this outstanding woman were denigrated, belittled and rendered almost invisible to history.

NOTES

1. John Darling, *Child-Centred Education and its Critics* (London, 1994), pp. 6–31; W.A.C. Stewart and W.P. McCann, *The Educational Innovators, Vol. 1 1750–1880* (London, 1967), vol. 1 pp. 23–35.

2. Ruth Watts, *Gender, Power and the Unitarians in England 1760–1860* (London, 1998), pp. 25–52.

3. Lucy Aikin, 'Memoir', in L. Aikin, ed., *The Works of Anna Laetitia Barbauld* 2 vols (1825), vol. 1 p. x.

4. Letter to Anna Aikin (1774) from Elizabeth Montagu, quoted in Mrs Henry Martin, *Memories of Seventy Years* (1884), p. 115.

5. Josephine McDonagh, 'Barbauld's domestic economy', in Anne Janowitz, ed., *Romanticism and Gender* (Cambridge, 1998), pp. 62–77.

6. Norma Clarke, ' "The Cursed Barbauld Crew": women writers and writing for children in the late eighteenth century', in M. Hilton, M. Styles, and V. Watson, eds., *Opening the Nursery Door: Reading, Writing and Childhood, 1600–1900* (1996), pp. 91–103.

7. He called her 'Mrs Bare and bold', despite his earlier respect for her and her affection for him as a younger Unitarian intellectual.

8. Marlon Ross, 'Configurations of feminine reform: the woman writer and the tradition of dissent', in Carol Shiner Wilson and Joel Haefner, eds., *Revisioning Romanticism* (Pennsylvania, 1994), p. 93.

9. Lucy Aikin to Henry Bright, quoted in Betsy Rodgers, *Georgian Chronicle: Mrs Barbauld and her Family* (1958), p. 48.

10. Kathryn Gleadle, *The Early Feminists: Radical Unitarians and the Emergence of the Women's Rights Movement, 1831–51* (1995).

11. Ruth Watts, 'Knowledge is Power: Unitarians, gender and education in the eighteenth and early nineteenth centuries', *Gender and Education* 1 (1989), pp. 35–50.

12. Raymond V. Holt, *The Unitarian Contribution to Social Progress in England* (1938).

13. John Seed, 'Rational Dissent and political opposition 1770–1790', in Knud Haakonssen, ed., *Enlightenment and Religion: Rational Dissent in Eighteenth Century Britain* (Cambridge, 1996), p. 158.

14. Joseph Priestley, *Miscellaneous Observations Relating to Education* (1780), p. 27.

15. A.L. Aikin, *Poems* (1773).

16. John Dunn, 'The politics of Locke in England and America', in John W. Yolton, ed., *John Locke: Problems and Perspectives: a Collection of New Essays* (Cambridge, 1969), pp. 55–6.

17. A.L. Barbauld, *Sins of the Government, Sins of the Nation* (1793).

18. Barbauld, *Works*, vol II p. 357.

19. Samuel F. Pickering, Jr, *John Locke and Children's Books in Eighteenth-Century England* (Tennessee, 1981), p. 7.

20. A.M.C. Waterman, *Revolution, Economics and Religion: Christian Political Economy, 1798–1833* (Cambridge, 1991), p. 115.

21. *Ibid.*, p. 128.

22. *Ibid.*, p. 132.

23. 'To Mr S.T. Coleridge', Barbauld, *Works*, vol. I, p. 209.

24. A.L. Barbauld, *Lessons for Children* (1788). Victorian reprint of *Early Lessons*.

25. A.L. Barbauld, *Hymns in Prose for Children* (1788), p. 10.

26. Barbauld, *Works*, vol. II, p. 306.

27. L. Aikin, 'Memoir', in Barbauld, *Works*, vol. I, pp. xviii, xxii.

28. Marlon B. Ross, *The Contours of Masculine Desire: Romanticism and the Rise of Women's Poetry* (Oxford, 1989), pp. 215–21.

29. Harriet Martineau, *Autobiography, vol. 1* (1877), Vol. I p. 101; Janet Ross, *Three Generations of English Women: Memoirs and Correspondence of Susannah Taylor, Sarah Austin, and Lady Duff Gordon* (1893), pp. 30–7.

30. Joseph Priestley, *Miscellaneous Observations relating to Education* (1780), p. 219.

31. *Ibid.*, p. 86.

32. George Dekker, *Coleridge and the Literature of Sensibility* (1978), pp. 156–61.

33. T.J. Diffey, 'The roots of imagination: the philosophical context', in S. Prickett, ed., *The Context of English Literature: the Romantics* (1981), p. 188.

34. Barbauld, *Works*, vol. II, pp. 322–37.

35. A.L. Le Breton, *Memoir of Mrs Barbauld* (1874), p. 50.

36. Rodgers, *Georgian Chronicle*, pp. 76–9 (see n. 9).

37. *To Doctor Priestley* (1792), Barbauld, *Works*, vol. I, pp. 183–4.

38. *New Annual Register* (1810), p. 265.

39. Geoffrey Carnall, *Robert Southey and his Age: The Development of a Conservative Mind* (Oxford, 1960), p. 11.

40. Edith J., Morley, ed., *Henry Crabbe Robinson on Books and their Writers*, vol. 1 (1938), p. 64.

41. The term 'Tory' was just coming into use to describe the government and its conservative supporters.

42. W. Croker, *Quarterly Review* (March/June 1812), p. 313.

43. *Ibid.*

44. Boyd Hilton, *The Age of Atonement: The Influence of Evangelicalism on Social and Economic Thought 1785–1865* (Oxford, 1988), p. 4.

45. Anne K. Mellor, *Romanticism and Gender* (1993), pp. 17–29; A.D. Harvey, *English Poetry in a Changing Society 1780–1825* (1980).

46. Norma Clarke, ' "The Cursed Barbauld Crew" ' (see n. 6 above).

CHAPTER TWO

Mary Carpenter: Educator of the Children of the 'Perishing and Dangerous Classes'

RUTH WATTS

Mary Carpenter is honoured as a national educational reformer in Bristol Cathedral.[1] Her significance both as an educational reformer and as a role model for women in the nineteenth century has recently become more widely broadcast in women's history although her place as a leading pedagogue in educational history still needs to be asserted. This chapter will firstly look briefly at Mary Carpenter's actual achievements and then explore the religious, educational and social influences that affected her, the networks in which she worked and her emergence as an active agent of educational and social change. It will be argued that Mary Carpenter forged her own vision of social progress, using her considerable powers of organisation, analysis and persuasion to carry her ideals even to parliamentary level. Her ideals epitomised the type of caring power particularly claimed by women. At the same time, her gradual emergence as a confident public figure demonstrated women's capabilities and, thereby, helped change attitudes towards women.

Mary Carpenter (1807–1877) was the daughter of Anna Penn and the Unitarian minister and progressive teacher Dr Lant Carpenter. Given an excellent rational education, Mary, with her mother and two sisters, took over her father's school in Bristol and turned it into a reputable school for girls. Undoubtedly, the Unitarianism in which Mary Carpenter was brought up was one of the most powerful influences on her life. The Unitarians' denial of original sin and their optimistic belief in the goodness and potential possibilities of humanity were allied to an eager anticipation of the unravelling of the laws of nature by reason, experience and experiment. Moral perfection rather than ardent spirituality was the Unitarian ideal. Its realisation was to be found through a careful intellectual, physical and moral education from birth based largely on Joseph Priestley's psychological theory, which in turn was derived from David Hartley's work concerning the association of ideas. A modern and scientific approach in both method and subject made Unitarians pioneers in education as in theology. Such an emphasis, although

39

extolling rationality and sounding dry and cold, led many of its adherents to an enthusiastic and active espousal of new ideas in all aspects of life.[2] From the 1830s Unitarianism itself was gentled by the influence of thinkers such as the American Unitarian William Ellery Channing and the English James Martineau whose ideas, nevertheless, reinforced the Unitarian commitment to moral evolution within an open-ended religion. Mary Carpenter keenly participated in the debate around such ideas, publishing a small, anonymous book on universal religious truths in 1845. Close to her charismatic father, she imbibed from him an almost evangelical fervour usually anathema to Unitarians. Those Unitarians whom, like her, Douglas Stange has termed 'evangelical Unitarians' did share with orthodox evangelicals an adoration of Jesus Christ, intense feelings and a warm concern for all manner of human beings. What they did not share was the evangelicals' emphasis on the total depravity of humankind, their anti-intellectualism, conservatism and their desire to convert all to one unchanging way of religion. Nor did they stress humility and obedience as so-called 'feminine virtues'. Rather they wished all to think for themselves and women to be educated to make their own judgements.[3]

The Unitarian focus on a careful, rational education had particular significance for Unitarian girls. Accepting that it was education that made people what they were, Unitarians did not believe that women were inferior intellectually, as was so often assumed, including by many clergymen, doctors and conservative women.[4] Indeed, they argued, women needed mental development as much as men since, without it, they could neither achieve true morality and virtue themselves nor educate children properly. Unitarian women, therefore, were notable for being educated far above the norm. Mary Carpenter had the added advantage of being educated in her father's boys' school, one of the best in Unitarian education. Thus, unlike most females, she was able to study classics, and unlike many middle-class boys, she learnt mathematics, science and English literature. Loving art and later poetry too, she also delighted in the mental philosophy of David Hartley, the cornerstone of Priestley's associationist psychology. There was no higher education for women available despite her own father's earlier efforts, although even he put some limits on women's capacity for the highest creative thought. Generally, however, Unitarians agreed with George Armstrong, Carpenter's co-pastor from 1837, that there should be no monopoly of study or subject by either sex and that good wives and mothers could equally be 'learned' and 'enlightened' with 'vigorous ideas'.[5]

Nevertheless, Mary Carpenter was unable to become a minister as two of her brothers did or a scientist as another, William, did to great repute. The teaching labours of herself and her sisters helped provide the means for their brothers' excellent higher education but the same opportunities were not open to them. Born into the middle class, but not rich enough to be unemployed, teaching was the only obvious 'respectable' road open to women. At least, among Unitarians, this was given status and both Mary Carpenter's mother and aunt had been teachers.[6] Furthermore, despite the bitter hostility to their religious views, Unitarian cultural leadership enabled female Unitarians to be part of an enterprising, energetic community, at its best brimming with intellectual vitality. Some Unitarian homes, including that of the Carpenters, were educative centres in themselves. Women fared less well in scientific and learned societies, even the multitude established and supported by Unitarians. It was difficult to fight such attitudes as Unitarians sought to compensate for their extremely unpopular religious and often political views by aspiring to be 'respectable', but this in turn limited their women's lives by the prevailing notions of propriety. Mary Carpenter too, like many other spinsters, was first restrained by deference to the wishes of her mother.[7]

A more 'public' role for women was acceptable in unpaid charity work and Sunday school teaching. Mary Carpenter early taught in her chapel's Sunday schools, becoming the chief manager of the girls' school. She was deeply influenced in turn by her father who welcomed and drew the poor in large numbers to the opulent and hitherto exclusive chapel at Lewin's Mead; and by Joseph Tuckerman, the American Unitarian from Boston whose life she published in 1849. Tuckerman's insistence on respect for the unique capacities, needs and value of every individual, including the poorest, the most deprived and most depraved, became the central focus of Mary Carpenter's religion and work. She was inspired by his cogent denial that there could be a human being with 'no element of goodness; . . . no inextinguishable spark . . . which . . . may not be blown into a flame'. She agreed that the 'propertied classes' would benefit morally and spiritually by having more contact with the poor and was excited by Tuckerman's vision of non-proselytising domestic missions to help the neediest in society with sympathetic moral guidance and some practical assistance.[8]

In this Mary Carpenter was not alone. Tuckerman inspired the humane enthusiasm of other English Unitarians so that in the 1830s, domestic missions were established in many of the large urban centres where they had chapels. Other denominations, mainly evangelical Anglicans inspired by Thomas Chalmers in Scotland, also had city and town missions. Those of the Unitarians, however, were characterised by their openness to all, educational zeal, and urging of self-help and moral reformation within a general religious framework rather than any particular creed. Undoubtedly some supporters, particularly the wealthier, were motivated by fears of social unrest and willingly emphasised the moral causes of poverty rather than economic and structural ones. Around their dedicated missions, however, spawned an abundance of educational, social and recreational facilities that optimistically would help the depressed masses realise their own 'capabilities and dignity as rational, intellectual and spiritual beings'.[9]

Unitarians, therefore, were exercised by the 'problem' of the urban poor. They were amongst the first to respond 'scientifically', collecting statistics to demonstrate the relationship between poverty, lack of education and crime, for example.[10] Mary Carpenter eagerly adopted such an approach. She became the indefatigable secretary and chief organiser of the Women's Working and Visiting Society established at Lewin's Mead in 1835. The poor areas of Bristol were divided into five districts where female visitors called upon families of children at any of the chapel's Sunday schools. Mary Carpenter deliberately took the worst areas and a large proportion of the initial visits. The careful organisation, detailed reports and willingness to adapt from experience were all to be hallmarks of her reform work. So were the principles enunciated, not least the respect for other people's religious views which attracted many of the poor to use the excellent, non-denominational Unitarian Sunday schools. The visitors counselled 'forethought and economy', helped those who were sick, advised others, tried to procure work for the unemployed and, in carefully considered desperate cases, gave money. Respect for all, therefore, was set firmly within the confines of discriminate charity and a counsel of self-help.[11]

Through Mary Carpenter's reports, however, emerges a deeply felt realisation of the 'many wants of the poor', the difficulties of advising those 'whose regular earnings are barely sufficient to support a rising family', and the near impossibility of such people avoiding debt if the family experienced sickness or unforeseen misfortune. Her reports were vigorously and cogently written and her visiting obviously strengthened her conviction of the benefits of such personal contacts between the classes and, overwhelmingly, of how education was 'almost uniformly, highly prized among the poor'.[12]

Mary Carpenter was thus located in a Unitarian network of crucial importance to her as she developed her ideas and activities. Significantly it included women as well as men. Lady Byron, for example, who moved to Bristol in 1844, gave her moral and all-important financial support. Her deep involvement in educational schemes for the working classes extended to supporting ventures of Matthew Davenport Hill, another firm supporter of Mary Carpenter and one who likewise came from a family keenly interested in the holistic, humane and individualistic educational methods of Pestalozzi and, indeed, in educational innovation generally. He was also involved in the struggle for women's rights, as was Mary Carpenter's exhausted but admiring co-worker from 1858 to 1859, Frances Power Cobbe. This network grew in Bristol with Matthew Hill's daughters later joined by the Winkworth sisters – all women pioneering new roles. Another supporter, Russell Scott Junior, was linked through his father to the humble cobbler and inspiration for ragged schools, John Pounds.[13]

Mary Carpenter drew on this Unitarian network of both women and men for material, intellectual and moral support. She also had other helpers especially once the reformatory movement got under way.[14] She used her Unitarian world-view, however, to create her own space, transforming her cultural, theological and political inheritance into an original contribution to educational pedagogy, particularly with respect to the children of the urban poor. Through her own actions and writings she forged her own philosophy, so to these we must now turn.

It is important to understand Mary Carpenter's personal interpretation of the most progressive and scientific educational theory of the day, particularly as it concerned the education of the urban poor. Her educational philosophy was demonstrated clearly in both her actual work in ragged, industrial and reformatory schools and in her pedagogical writings, especially *Ragged Schools* (1849), *Reformatory Schools* (1851) and *Juvenile Delinquents, their Condition and Treatment* (1853). She was absolutely convinced that virtue, fulfilment and happiness were based on a good education and that, conversely, vice and crime coexisted largely with educational deficiency. Thus there needed to be schools for all, but separate ones for the poorest in society who were not wanted in the ordinary fee-paying day elementary schools because they were ill-clad, outcast and possibly 'vicious'. Drawing from developments already in existence especially in Aberdeen, Hamburg and Mettray, Mary Carpenter believed three particular types of school to be urgently necessary, two of them new. For those very poor without proper clothing she wanted good free day schools, an improved version of those already popularly known as ragged schools. Secondly, for the neglected children of the very poor found wandering in the streets, involved in petty misdemeanours or known to the police as constantly on the edge of crime, she desired industrial schools. Compulsory for those sent to them, these should offer a free meal and industrial training alongside an elementary education. Thirdly, for offenders actually convicted in court, reformatory schools should be established emphasising reform not punishment.[15]

Mary Carpenter's individual contribution was not only her constant lobbying for and organisation of reform but also her insistence on basic principles, without which, for her, the whole initiative would be meaningless. If, as in workhouses, children were 'enslaved', 'crushed' in will and affection, neglected physically and overfed with the wrong type of intellectual and religious training, she argued, they were almost bound to a life of degradation and 'fearful consequences' might ensue. Success was only possible where all, no matter how deprived or depraved, were wisely given respect, love and care in line with the associationist psychology in which she had been educated herself. A teacher should not regard pupils as 'a collection of little machines' to 'set in motion and keep going until a certain amount of [mechanical] work is done', but should recognise in each child their distinct personality and be able to draw out their various powers by sympathy and a fully harmonious education, helping each to be engaged in their 'own intellectual and moral improvement'. Only in a family-like atmosphere could the individual become strong and healthy in both mind and body and, thus, if the state had to assume the care of a child it must provide the best equivalent of a good home possible for them. This was true for all children although especially so for girls. Mary Carpenter allowed of no stunted, impoverished or ugly conditions for the education of even the poorest in society, for since children became like their surroundings, beauty was not 'an unnecessary luxury in a schoolroom'. Her ragged school in St James's Back, for example, was enlivened by every kind of visual aid inside and, when in 1850 she was able to buy the filthy, dangerous court in which it was situated, she immediately improved the dwellings by adding baths, washhouses, waterworks and a playground. To these practical measures she added the trusting and imaginative touch of planting creepers against the walls. Her reformatory school for girls, Red Lodge, was a lovely building.[16]

To these principles, so unlike the rigidity of the Revised Code for elementary schools of 1862, was added that of preparing pupils to take care of themselves in the outside world and having ready advice and sympathy for those discharged from industrial and reformatory schools. Having studied examples in France and America, Mary Carpenter argued cogently over many years for a Central Committee of Management in London with a regional network. She ensured that boys and girls released from her own industrial school and Red Lodge at least received such care.[17] Similarly, she revealed her passionate hatred of the retributive theology of many Christians. The evangelical certainty that all humankind was 'utterly sinful' led its adherents, women and men, to make heroic efforts to convert others, from kings to the poorest outcasts of society. It also led to demands for punishment for those who infringed the moral code and laws of a 'Christian' society. The contrasting Unitarian denial of original sin and optimistic hope for the perfectibility of humanity on earth allowed for a stress on changing the environment which caused transgression rather than severe punishment which might harden the offender. Thus Mary Carpenter argued it was not that children owed retribution to society, but 'Society owed retribution to them'. Therefore she fought bitterly and forcefully against juvenile imprisonment and the clause in the Youthful Offenders Act of 1854 which committed convicted delinquents to prison for fourteen days before entering a reformatory. Privately pouring out her love for the young offenders in her charge, she publicly reiterated the virtue of industrial schools in having no such stigma attached.[18]

Mary Carpenter's firm belief in rational moral principle infusing the whole of education rather than mere inculcation of religious doctrine mirrors those of other Unitarians in this period. So did her increasing conviction that, although the voluntary principle could not meet the various demands for elementary education, government control would mean regimental conformity which would not answer sensitively the needs of deprived or depraved children. Her solution was to have government aid backing voluntary initiative to an even greater degree than in ordinary elementary education. She disagreed with the London Ragged School Union that government inspection would interfere with teaching or religion, finding it 'amazing' that the Council on Education did not give aid to enable volunteers to reach '*a class untouched by any other existing agency*'. But as she was certain that ragged schools could not meet the requirements of the 1862 Revised Code, she wished them to be allowed to develop as those who ran them thought best. She believed the best answer for juvenile offenders was reformatory schools, 'based on voluntary action' but with government grants and sufficient inspection to ensure that the proper conditions were reached. Unlike workhouses, they would supply 'voluntary benevolence, or rather Christian love' which a child's nature craved and that 'certain freedom which cannot be conceded by purely official control'.[19] In the light of experience she realised by the 1870s that the ragged schools could not cope with the numbers of destitute and neglected children and so urged the establishment of day industrial feeding schools, aided by school boards. She countered arguments that this meant the state paid for parental irresponsibility by forcibly stating that a proper educational system with a hierarchy of different types of schools to mop up the various layers of destitution and need would end the cost of pauperism and crime.[20]

Mary Carpenter's philosophy was a curious mixture of compassion, radical awareness of society's responsibilities and yet a more common 'paternalism' which asserted that she and other reformers knew better than the families of destitute children what was good for them. Children could be removed from home to be 'reformed' or educated although compulsory schooling was not yet the law. Rather than profligate parents receive an allowance for them, it was better for children to be paid for in proper institutions either by the state or, in the case of industrial schools, by the parents themselves. This was hardly thinking that the 'sacred' principle of parental freedom did not matter for such children since Mary Carpenter was prepared to compel *all* children to go to school before this became a general political principle. In the case of industrial schooling, she would make children not actually convicted of crime go as a preventative measure against worse consequences. She did want decent, not any menial, employment for such youngsters, as her own provisions, for example at Red Lodge, proved. Furthermore, she also recognised that the 'crimes' of the poor were termed misdemeanours when committed by upper-class children. She even quoted the case of Lord Eldon who once robbed an orchard but was sent home by the magistrates to his parents for correction.[21]

Mary Carpenter did, in fact, realise the structural causes of poverty but wanted to empower the poor through giving them education rather than by changing the economic situation. The contradictions in her arguments have been very ably analysed by Richard Selleck. Like others of her day, even reformers and even Matthew Hill, she employed attitudes and terminology redolent of hard, patronising political economy. Yet her principles were deeply enmeshed in a humanitarian and environmentalist educational philosophy that was concerned with empowering people, not judging them for circumstances they could not help nor avoid. Such confusion bedevilled the efforts of many Unitarians, some of whom could be overbearingly paternalistic. Mary Carpenter herself believed that whether people approached the matter from Christian benevolence or political economy made little difference.[22]

Similarly, on gender issues, Mary Carpenter's deeply held views, modified by experience, led her to enunciate principles of equality but difference. Like her fellow Unitarian Anna Barbauld, she was strongly influenced by Hartleyan and Priestleyan psychology. Her chief educator, her father, had been one of the leading developers of this educational philosophy in the early nineteenth century and had recommended as a useful example of it, *Evenings at Home,* the popular book for children Anna Barbauld had written with her brother John Aikin.[23] Mary Carpenter too, therefore, believed that circumstance or education in its widest sense largely formed all children, male or female, who were thus much more equally capable of intellectual, physical and moral development than traditional educational norms realised. She accepted that the two sexes had been created 'for totally different spheres'. Thus one had 'greater power and energy' while the other had 'greater susceptibility and delicacy of organisation'. Each, however, she urged, 'should respect the different gifts of the other' and have a 'free and equal opportunity' to develop their powers. In the rare circumstances where this happened, she knew from direct experience that girls of fifteen to sixteen could surpass boys even in classics and maths, subjects usually denied them. With good teaching, girls could equal boys in the elementary schools even though they spent two hours a day on needlework. Such equality of intellect was not evident in ragged and reformatory schools, however, because girls were dulled by the bad influences of home where they were little better than drudges, while boys' powers were 'quickened' by the excitement of outdoor life. Similarly, she realised that there could be no equality of intellect between middle-class adults as only males were developed by 'the work of life'. Although recent examinations showed girls were capable of more than previously thought, very few had chance to prove it, so she was ever grateful that her father had given her an equal education, long believing that in both sexes the mind should be trained to observe, reason and think critically. This she saw as the basis of all her achievements.[24]

Nevertheless Mary Carpenter believed that boys and girls should have a different 'general training' to match their future social positions and physical natures. She could agree with Anna Barbauld and her brother both that '. . . all things are not equally necessary to everyone . . . it is the purpose of all education to fit persons for the station in life in which they are hereafter to live' and in their more positive depiction of the mother and daughter who followed a walk to the market-place by a visit to the booksellers. She gave many examples herself to prove that proficiency in the domestic arts and intellectual achievement could run together, and she wanted physical exercise for girls.[25] Even so, she always saw women first as domestic creatures and this affected her ideas on how girls of the destitute and 'perishing' classes should be treated.

Initially, at her first reformatory school at Kingswood in Bristol, Mary Carpenter put boys and girls together. She was soon convinced that the girls needed a different experience, not least because they tended to be much more hardened cases. This, she explained, was because, unlike boys, girls were only sent when all else had failed, for any dealings with the magistrates lost them their character. Only by putting girls of such great 'moral depravity' in a sympathetic, homely environment could they learn self-discipline, internalise a desire for reform and receive the education that would allow 'Christian women' to 'fearlessly seek' them as servants. Such an education should be wholesome intellectual nourishment to prevent their minds preying on 'garbage'. Such an institution should be in a healthy spot, secure but comfortable, neat and convenient, with opportunities for natural activity and play, so that its inmates would be proud to call it 'our home'. In addition, it should be managed and visited by ladies. Mary Carpenter stuck essentially to these principles despite some bitter experiences at Red Lodge where some of the bolder, precocious intake were neither immediately 'sensible to kindness' nor very obviously developing a rekindled 'divine nature'. Convinced by experience that the most lawless needed separate institutions, for them as for pauper children she still wished the same interesting intellectual education, worthwhile industrial training and innocent amusement. Interestingly, perhaps her most successful personal educational venture on these lines was her industrial school for *boys* in Bristol.[26]

The educational reforms and principles she so ardently upheld had to be fought for by Mary Carpenter over many years, against strong opposition including that of many male reformers. She achieved much through the modern political tactics of the organisation of conferences, lobbying of officialdom and politicians and constant publicising of her views. Through having to mobilise all her own talents she became increasingly convinced that women had a special role to play in public life. Sure that 'professional' involvement by 'ladies' in social and educational concerns would benefit all classes, she wanted women on committees of every institution which included girls. She believed, for example, that this would alleviate the dulling, degrading influences of workhouse barracks on girls. This both fitted her notions of the benefits of the 'voluntary principle' and fed her growing acceptance that she and other women could and should take an active 'citizenship' role. Her own burning necessity to be heard and win passionately desired reforms forced her increasing appearance in public life through writings and conferences. Despite early family difficulties over this, she became a well-known public figure. At first she very 'properly' remained silent at the very conferences she herself had worked hard to arrange and in 1852 almost stayed away from the parliamentary committee enquiring into destitute and criminal children which had (most unusually) asked her to report to them. Yet it was her certainty that her 'woman's nature' quite unfitted her for public action that led her to act on her own. She also concluded that her womanly nature was what best fitted God's purpose.[27]

From 1857, Mary Carpenter found an effective forum in which to air her projected reforms in the newly formed National Association for the Promotion of the Social Sciences (NAPSS). Here she literally found her voice, putting aside her silent role to argue analytically and rationally but also passionately and graphically for educational and social reform in both Britain and India. By 1867, she even gave papers extempore. Other women reformers gave papers in this organisation which, linking leading social reformers, was unusual in including women from its beginning. None of them spoke so regularly, however, or on so many different topics in the first twenty years as Mary Carpenter. She lectured more often at many conferences than most men. She also spoke often, forcibly and at length in the discussions following the papers, basing her arguments on detailed analysis, experience and plentiful illustration and taking account of common fears and misconceptions. After her death in 1877 the President, George Hastings, made a moving tribute in recognition of her services to the NAPSS.[28]

Her emergence as a public voice, constantly reiterating her principles against what she perceived as the misunderstandings of magistrates and others, helped develop Mary Carpenter's own ideas on women's rights. She publicly supported the Women's Movement's drive to obtain better education and thereby employment for middle-class girls, arguing herself for the establishment of normal training schools so teachers could be properly trained for the new schools. During her visit to the USA in 1873 she was first astonished and then impressed at finding women successfully holding positions of trust in the treasury at Washington, at all levels of education, in printing offices and hospitals. Their success, based on 'a thoroughly good education, equal to that received by boys', should, she urged, be emulated in England. Likewise, she argued for Indian women to have government normal schools where they could learn the science and art of teaching and thence upgrade female education there.[29]

On other rights of women, Mary Carpenter had to be persuaded by experience and by the arguments of those within the network of Unitarians and their friends in which she moved. As late as 1873 she refused to chair the executive committee of the International Arbitration Association because this was outside her 'womanly sphere' yet in the same year, in New York, she began to speak from pulpits. Her very gendered opinion of women helped develop her appreciation of their 'rights'. Thus she opposed bitterly the double standards over desperate women guilty of the infanticide of illegitimate children, arguing that it was unfair that 'the real offender', the man who caused the woman's plight, escaped the censure of society. She became vice-president of the mixed National Association against the Contagious Diseases Acts and supported the struggle to obtain the admission of women to medical degrees at the University of London. Unfavourable to the idea of women's suffrage at first, the influence of John Stuart Mill helped change her mind until, in 1877, she was on the same platform as her friend Frances Power Cobbe where they took turns to propose or second the resolutions on women's suffrage.[30]

It is clear that Mary Carpenter became an increasingly influential figure. She helped make reformatory education a central issue for many years at the NAPSS, for example. She had a pivotal role in a network of social and educational reformers and, indeed, became an international figure, welcomed in European countries, the USA and India. She proved that women could make sustained arguments from evidence carefully collected and selected. In 1860, her address to the statistical section of the British Association for the Advancement of Science, from which she had been debarred as a woman in 1836, marked a milestone in the acceptance of women as figures of authority.[31] Admired by other women pioneers such as Dorothea Dix and Frances Power Cobbe, she spurred on others by her example. She was upheld as a role model by the *Englishwomen's Review* especially because of her work in India and her particular 'imperial role' for women.[32]

Mary Carpenter was, indeed, helping to forge both a science of education and a caring role for women which gave them a particular type of power. Not alone in either endeavour, as she herself willingly acknowledged, she nevertheless carved a prominent educational and reforming niche for herself in contemporary politics. Sensitive always to the gendered roles assigned to women and men in Victorian society, she became increasingly aware not only of how women could use that role to forge their own distinctive contribution to social justice, but also of how they themselves could and should have greater opportunities and rights. Not without faults and suffering occasional severe depressions, she nevertheless believed that she knew what was right for the less fortunate in both England and abroad. Yet she wanted to empower more than control, even if her methods were often high-handed, for she did not consider others inferior, only deprived of the lucky upbringing, education and moral influences she had had.[33]

Mary Carpenter's former neglect in history was partly due to her being a Unitarian. In the rounder picture of educational developments now being drawn and the greater recognition of female endeavour in the construction of history, she has a better chance of achieving her rightful due.

NOTES

1. Bristol Cathedral inscription.

2. *Dictionary of National Biography* (*DNB*) IX (1887), pp. 159–61; Ruth Watts, *Gender, Power and the Unitarians in England 1760–1860* (1998), pp. 3, 35–40, *passim.*

3. Watts, *Gender,* pp. 29–31, 82, 100–1, 103, 112; J.E. Carpenter, *The Life and Work of Mary Carpenter* (1881), pp. 17–18, 66–7; William B. Carpenter, *Sketch of the Life and Work of Mary Carpenter of Bristol* (Bristol, 1877), pp. 3–4; Douglas Charles Stange, *British Unitarians against American Slavery, 1833–65* (1984), pp. 222–3; Jane Rendall, *The Origins of Modern Feminism: Women in Britain, France and the United States, 1780–1860* (1985), pp. 73–7, 87–96, 106; Ian Bradley, *The Call to Seriousness: The Evangelical Impact on the Victorians* (New York, 1976), pp. 20–56.

4. See e.g. Janet Horowitz Murray, *Strong-Minded Women* (Harmondsworth, 1984), pp. 195–255 *passim.*

5. R.L. Carpenter, *Memoir of the Revd. Lant Carpenter LL.D* (1842), pp. 99, 342–52, 497; J.E. Carpenter, *Mary Carpenter,* pp. 5–25, 47–51, 62–4; Lant Carpenter, *Sermons on Practical Subjects* (Bristol, 1840), p. 263; Bristol Reference Library, B19568, *Selections from the Writings of Rev. George Armstrong* (private circulation, 1892), p. 48.

6. *DNB* IX, pp. 162–3, 166–8; R.L. Carpenter, *In Memory of Mary Carpenter* (1878).

7. Watts, *Gender,* pp. 63–6, 89, 108, 117, 129–30, 148–53, 200.

8. R.L. Carpenter, *Lant Carpenter,* pp. 242–3, 474–5; Mary Carpenter, *Joseph Tuckerman* (1849), pp. 30–2, 45, 64–5, *passim.*

9. Watts, *Gender,* pp. 178–86; David Steers, 'The origin and development of the domestic mission movement especially in Liverpool and Manchester', *Transactions of the Unitarian Historical Society* (*TUHS*) XXI, 2 (1996), pp. 79–103.

10. See e.g. R.J.W. Selleck, *James Kay Shuttleworth: Journey of an Outsider* (Ilford, 1994), pp. 82–7.

11. Bristol Central Library BL 2D B7054, *First Report of the Lewin's Mead Chapel Working and Visiting Society* (1836); *Second Report* (1836), p. 3; *Fifth Report* (1841), p. 2.

12. *Ibid., Second Report,* pp. 2–6; *Third Report* (1837), p. 2.

13. R. & F.D. Hill, *The Recorder of Birmingham. A Memoir of Matthew Davenport Hill* (1878), *passim;* H. McLachlan, 'The Taylors and Scotts of the Manchester Guardian', *TUHS* (1927), p. 33; Watts, *Gender,* pp. 112–14, 130–2, 176, 206; Bristol Central Library B115 68 L98.2 Car. F.P. Cobbe, *Personal Recollections of Mary Carpenter* (no date or provenance given), pp. 279–300; Philippa Levine, *Feminist Lives in Victorian England* (Oxford, 1990), pp. 26–8.

14. J.E. Carpenter, *Mary Carpenter,* pp. 125ff., 138, *passim.*

15. Mary Carpenter, *Reformatory Schools for the Children of the Perishing and Dangerous Classes and for Juvenile Offenders* (New York, 1969; 1st edn 1851), pp. 19–39; J.E. Carpenter, *Mary Carpenter,* pp. 118–19, 144.

16. Mary Carpenter, 'On the principles of education', *NAPSS 1860* (1861), pp. 391–7; 'The application of the principles of education to schools for the lower classes of society', *NAPSS 1861* (1862), pp. 344–9; J.E. Carpenter, *Mary Carpenter,* pp. 88–92, 113.

17. J.E. Carpenter, *Mary Carpenter,* p. 236; Mary Carpenter, 'On the supplementary measures needed for reformatories for the diminution of juvenile crime', *NAPSS 1860* (1861), pp. 491–2; 'Reformatories for convicted girls', *NAPSS 1857* (1858), p. 346; 'On the essential principles of the reformatory movement', *NAPSS 1862* (1863), pp. 449–50.

18. J.E. Carpenter, *Mary Carpenter*, pp. 131–3, 161; Mary Carpenter, 'On the non-imprisonment of children', *NAPSS 1864* (1865), pp. 247–55; Bradley, *Seriousness*, pp. 20, 34–53.

19. Mary Carpenter, 'On the connexion of voluntary effort with government aid', *NAPSS 1861* (1862), pp. 441–6; 'On the relation of ragged schools to the educational movement', *NAPSS 1857* (1858), pp. 226–7; 'The duty of government to aid in the education of children of the perishing and neglected classes', *NAPSS 1864* (1865), pp. 436–43; 'Essential principles', p. 444.

20. Mary Carpenter, 'Day industrial feeding schools', *NAPSS 1876* (1877), p. 380; 'How may the education of neglected children be best provided for?', *NAPSS 1871* (1872), pp. 335–41.

21. Mary Carpenter, *Reformatory Schools*, pp. 40–57; '. . . supplementary measures', pp. 493–7; '. . . convicted girls', p. 346. See, in contrast, Barbara Weinburger, 'The children of the perishing and dangerous classes: industrial and reformatory schools and the elementary education system', in *Childhood, Youth and Education in the Late Nineteenth Century* (History of Education Society, 1980), p. 68.

22. R.J.W. Selleck, 'Mary Carpenter: A confident and contradictory reformer', *History of Education* 14 (June 1985), No. 2, pp. 111–15; Watts, *Gender*, pp. 177–8, 181–6; Mary Carpenter, 'neglected children', pp. 335–41.

23. Lant Carpenter, *Principles of Education* (1820), pp. 120, *passim*; John Aikin & Anna Laetitia Barbauld, *Evenings at Home* (1st edn 1793).

24. Mary Carpenter, 'On female education', *NAPSS 1869* (1870), pp. 351–2.

25. *Ibid.*, p. 353; Aikin & Barbauld, *Evenings* (1868 edn), pp. 37–42.

26. Mary Carpenter, '. . . convicted girls', pp. 339–45; 'On the education of pauper girls', *NAPSS 1862* (1863), pp. 286–92; Ruby Saywell, *Mary Carpenter of Bristol* (Bristol, 1964), pp. 9–16; Jo Manton, *Mary Carpenter and the Children of the Streets* (1976), pp. 154–5.

27. Mary Carpenter, 'Pauper girls', pp. 291–2; 'On the treatment of female convicts', *NAPSS 1863* (1864), pp. 415–21; J.E. Carpenter, *Mary Carpenter*, pp. 129–31, 135, 152.

28. See NAPSS transactions 1857–77 and above notes and especially G.W. Hastings, 'Introduction', *NAPSS 1857* (1858), p. xxvi; tribute to Mary Carpenter, *NAPSS 1877* (1878), pp. 148–50; J.E. Carpenter, *Mary Carpenter*, pp. 222, 276–7.

29. Mary Carpenter, 'Female education', pp. 353–5; Discussion on female education, *NAPSS 1873* (1874), pp. 363–6; Discussion on secondary education for girls, *NAPSS 1872* (1873), pp. 272–3; 'On female education in India', *NAPSS 1867* (1868), pp. 408–13 and *NAPSS 1876* (1877), pp. 471–4.

30. J.E. Carpenter, *Mary Carpenter*, pp. 312–38, 381; Mary Carpenter, Discussion on infanticide, *NAPSS 1869* (1870), p. 215; Cobbe, *Personal Recollections*, pp. 299–300.

31. Mary Carpenter, 'Female education in India', pp. 405–18; J.E. Carpenter, *Mary Carpenter*, pp. 212–13, 312–13, 321ff.

32. Francis Tiffany, *Life of Dorothea Dix* (Boston, 1891), p. 317; Cobbe, *Personal Recollections*, pp. 279–300; Barbara Caine, *English Feminism* (Oxford, 1997), pp. 88, 127–8.

33. See e.g. Mary Carpenter , 'Voluntary effort', pp. 441, 444; F.K. Prochaska, *Women and Philanthropy in 19th Century England* (Oxford, 1980), pp. 146–8, 174–5.

CHAPTER THREE

Catherine McAuley and the Education of Irish Roman Catholic Children in the Mid-Nineteenth Century

HILARY MINNS

The education of poor Catholic girls in the first half of the nineteenth century, both in Ireland and Britain, is an under-researched area, perhaps because it sits uneasily between broad historical studies of educational provision for the children of the poor, and general biographies of the religious women who became major providers of formal Catholic education for poor girls.[1] This essay explores the educational work of one of these women – Catherine McAuley. She was the founder of the Sisters of Mercy, one of a small number of institutions to pioneer the education of poor Catholic girls in the nineteenth century. Her work had a stabilising influence on the lives of numerous Catholic girls and young women from poor families, because it gave them access to a basic secular education, not only in a community of other girls, but in the company of committed, intelligent women. When Catherine McAuley died in 1841 she had already established twelve convents, ten of them in Ireland and two in England. This essay explores the foundations of her work in Dublin and then, in order to show how this work flourished after her death, it focuses on the educational provision at a Mercy Convent set up in Derby, in the English Midlands, eight years after Catherine McAuley died.

Catherine McAuley was one of a small number of quite exceptional middle-class Irish women who worked with the sick poor in eighteenth- and nineteenth-century Ireland and set up educational institutions for poor Catholic girls to help them make something of their lives and to nurture their spiritual development. Susan O'Brien argues that it was the 'willingness of thousands of women to make vows', coupled with the 'growing demand from the church for the education, nursing and welfare services which women could supply', that brought about the phenomenal growth in female religious institutions in the nineteenth century.[2] Catherine McAuley was part of what Mary Peckham Magray terms the 'female culture of charitable and evangelical organisation'.[3] She followed in the footsteps of other Irish Catholic women, most notably Nano Nagle, Teresa Mulally and Mary Aikenhead, all of whom established religious foundations with the aim of helping the poor. Nagle (1718–1784) developed and supported poor schools in Cork and founded a convent to teach the children of the poor.[4] Teresa Mulally (1728–1803) drew on Nagle's inspiration and founded the Presentation Sisters, the first religious institute in Ireland to devote itself to educational work among the female poor. She also set up an orphanage and a poor school where basic secular education and industrial training were combined with religious instruction.[5] Mary Aikenhead (1787–1858) continued Mulally's work, and founded the Sisters of Charity in 1815.[6]

The humanitarian and educational work of these women coincided with a period in which restrictions against Catholics were gradually eased.[7] At the beginning of the nineteenth century there was considerable interest in educating the children of the poor in Ireland. A government commission set up in 1809 reported on the 'improvident neglect of the education of the poor' and recommended the creation of a national system of education in Ireland, open to children of all denominations, under the supervision of a state board of control.[8] The Society for Promoting the Education of the Poor in Ireland (also known as the Kildare Place Society) was set up in 1811 to promote the education of poor children in non-denominational institutions. The society initially had the support of both Protestants and Catholics, and Daniel O'Connell, who had led the movement to repeal the 1801 Act of Union between Britain and Ireland, served on its managerial board. Despite genuine attempts by the Kildare Place Society to support non-denominational teaching, Catholics became increasingly uneasy about the Protestant tendencies of the society and its teachers, and they began withdrawing their children from its schools. A royal commission of 1825 was set up to investigate the situation, and this led to the establishment of the Irish Board of Education in 1831 – a national system that was in place some 40 years before similar state systems were set up in England and Scotland.[9] Both Protestants and Catholics were represented on the Board of Commissioners.

Catherine McAuley's own objectives were clear: she wished to visit and take care of the sick in hospital and in their homes, to educate poor Catholic girls, and to provide accommodation and domestic training for vulnerable young women 'out of situation' before finding them positions with suitable families. All this she achieved; in addition, she organised pension schools for middle-class girls in some of her foundations and trained young women for work as governesses. Her aims might not therefore appear radical today – there was no suggestion, for example, that the daughters of the poor should ever be taught to rise above their allotted station in life – but, nevertheless,

Catherine McAuley takes her place alongside other practical visionaries because her work enabled thousands of poor Catholic girls from the third decade of the nineteenth century onwards to receive a sound basic education, not only in Ireland and Britain, but further afield in North and South America, Newfoundland, the West Indies, Africa, Australia and New Zealand.[10]

Catherine McAuley was born in 1778 into a comfortable middle-class Catholic home outside Dublin. Her father had been a country gentleman who dealt in land and property. He died when she was two years old, and her mother moved her young family back to Dublin. Catherine McAuley was educated in the manner of refined young women of her day, taking lessons in French and learning to play the piano. She enjoyed writing and once wrote that 'rhyming was her pastime, her folly, her play, from which she never could stop'.[11] When Catherine McAuley was seventeen years old her mother died, and she went to live with her uncle for a time before accepting a position as companion-housekeeper to William Callaghan and his wife, a couple who had recently returned from India. Having no children of their own, they enjoyed the friendship of this lively, serious and companionable young woman, and for the next two decades she lived with them at Coolock House, their country estate just outside Dublin, and learnt valuable lessons in household management that were to serve her well later. She learnt spiritual lessons too as she accompanied the Quaker Mrs Callaghan on her frequent visits to poor families in the district – an experience that deepened her acute sense of moral responsibility. Catherine McAuley's passionate urge to alleviate the sufferings of the poor was the spiritual force that drove her deepest impulses. Her religion always remained the most profound and regulating influence on her life – as it was of course for many nineteenth-century lay women.[12]

In 1822, at the age of 44, Catherine McAuley's life was set to take a new direction. Mrs Callaghan had died in 1819 and her husband died three years later, leaving his estate to Catherine McAuley. Peckham Magray itemises her fortune as £30,000 in the Bank of Ireland, £600 per year, Coolock House, some jewellery and several life insurance policies.[13] She thus found herself in a position of enormous power – an unmarried woman, with the vitality and confidence of early middle age, in possession of a great deal of money. She continued her work with the poor, and adopted four children of a cousin who had died, as well as two orphaned children from the village. At this time she became a frequent visitor to the Presentation Sisters' Middle Abbey Poor School in Dublin, where she taught the children home crafts and, already showing an entrepreneurial spirit, rented premises near the school to use as a repository for displaying and selling the children's work to her rich friends.[14]

Catherine McAuley admired the work of the Sisters of Charity and learned much from her visits to their convent school in George's Hill about the practical organisation of education and charitable relief for the sick poor. Even so, she was not drawn to the conformity of conventual life. Instead, a clear and rather audacious vision began to shape itself in this restless woman's mind. She would use her legacy to build a school, an orphanage and a house of industry for poor women in the heart of Dublin. She held discussions with priests and architects, chose a suitable site, sold her home, and set to work nourishing her vision by commissioning a building which would stand as an enduring monument to her Christian ideals of mercy and kindness.

The House of Mercy was opened in 1827, when Catherine McAuley was 49 years old. It is a heavy substantial building, standing solidly on the corner of Lower Baggot Street in Dublin, and was designed with classrooms, a chapel, dormitories, and some smaller rooms for herself and her companions. The House of Mercy must have been a source of great pride to her, and there is no doubt that her enthusiasm inspired around twelve young middle-class lay women to work alongside her in her mission; some of them also gave financial support.[15] The house provided these women with what Peckham Magray terms a network of 'continuity and comradeship'. This was particularly the case since many of them were related – several, for example, were nieces of Daniel O'Connell. Indeed, Peckham Magray notes that 16 per cent of the 129 women who entered the Convent of Mercy in Lower Baggot Street, Dublin, between 1847 and 1877 were siblings.[16]

Savage points out that this kind of 'organised lay-effort among women was almost unknown' in the nineteenth century.[17] It needed a leader who combined genuine modesty and compassion with an enormous capacity for life-enhancement to give followers the courage to adopt this rather unorthodox lifestyle. The work of the house presented these women with an intellectual challenge at a time when there were few openings of this kind available to women and it became for them, according to Peckham Magray, a 'culturally validated mission of philanthropic work among the Catholic poor'.[18] It is important to remember that the premises at Lower Baggot Street did not at first form part of a religious house, nor were the Catholic women who worked alongside Catherine McAuley part of a religious order. They took no vows and were free to visit friends and family if they chose to do so. This informal community of lay women, living in an atmosphere of mutual trust and support, probably experienced freedoms they would not have known either as daughters or wives; outwardly conformist, they were nevertheless in revolt against domestic boredom and lives of dependency, and by opting for a disciplined life of austerity, they carved out a challenging career for themselves at a time when middle-class women were expected to retreat into the home.

Catherine McAuley designed a simple costume for herself and the other women that reflected a community whose lives were spent in austerity, simplicity and obedience.[19] The daily routine in the House of Mercy was fashioned around a life of prayer and religious observance. The lifestyle was hard and demanding, the women ate little, and they were expected to visit the sick poor in unwholesome environments that often drained their health.

During the Dublin cholera epidemic of 1832, for example, the Sisters spent many hours with the sick and some of them succumbed to illness themselves. Nevertheless, Catherine McAuley and her group of Sisters were free to think, to speak and to engage with ideas in an atmosphere of trust and mutual support. Indeed, their leader encouraged debate. 'Never suppose you can make me feel displeasure by giving any opinion that occurs to you', she once wrote to a Sister.[20] Paradoxically, by later taking the veil, she put herself in a position where she was able to wield enormous influence and to make contact with people not only in Ireland and Britain but beyond, in the wider world.

In spite of outward conformity, there was growing pressure within sections of the Catholic church for Catherine McAuley to found a religious order. In Degnan's view it appeared 'highly unorthodox' for a group of Catholic lay women to be living together in a lay community.[21] Catherine McAuley ran the house with an enormous degree of independent authority. She was, after all, a woman of considerable wealth, accustomed to living with servants, with a carriage at her disposal, and used to having the company of intelligent, lively women. On one significant occasion Canon Matthius Kelly suggested to Catherine McAuley that she and her lay followers should regularize the matter by transferring the house to the Sisters of Charity – though Archbishop Murray called personally the following day to refute this.[22] But Catherine McAuley gradually came to understand that her work could have more influence beyond Dublin – and beyond her own lifetime – if she took conventual status.[23] Her own religious congregation would then stand as a visible expression of her spiritual power and tenacity of purpose. In important ways she had already demonstrated to the church that her attention to cholera victims, orphans and poor girls was an indispensable part of Catholic welfare provision, and providing she could establish her own active – rather than contemplative – order, she knew she could continue her mission. 'We who began were prepared to do whatever was recommended', she wrote later.[24] And so, at the age of 50, Catherine McAuley made the decision to undergo a formal fifteen-month novitiate training with the Presentation Sisters in order to learn the rudiments of religious life.[25]

The physical and emotional cost of this novitiate to Catherine McAuley must have been colossal, but it was clear that she was determined on a course that would enable her to continue to work with the poor. She reasoned that she would 'rather be cold and hungry than deprive the poor of any consolation she could give to them'.[26] It is small wonder, then, that the novitiate became part of her purpose, and it was entirely within her character to accept any hardship and pain necessary for the implementation of her ideals of duty towards the sick poor. In 1831, at the age of 53, she completed her novitiate, and became the superior of her own – and the first – Convent of Mercy. Several of the lay women who had joined her in Lower Baggot Street undertook their own novitiates so that they could continue their work with her in the wider community. Catherine McAuley drew up her Rule, written in her own hand. She based it on the Presentation Rule, following a convention in which foundresses 'borrowed' from one another's formal constitutions. Indeed, the passages dealing with education were lifted freely from those of the Presentation Rule.[27]

Catherine McAuley now had a little more freedom to turn her attention to educational matters and for the next four years she taught in her own poor schools, modelling her educational work on the practice she had observed at the George's Hill and the Middle Abbey poor schools in Dublin. She had earlier visited the Kildare Place Society schools to study their teaching methods, curriculum and organisation, as well as journeying to France with her friend Fanny Tighe to investigate methods of education there for the children of the poor.[28] She developed strong views on teaching and learning and set great store by the relationships fostered between teacher and taught. 'Children', she wrote, 'must be made to feel their teachers are their best friends – if we draw the strings too tight, they will snap.'[29] In 1831 formal control of the education system passed to a new Board of Commissioners of National Education, which was established as a non-denominational system under the control of the government. In 1834 Catherine McAuley applied to the National Board for her school to be affiliated, since she felt that the children would benefit from regular examination. Equally important, her school would become eligible for state aid. In 1839 the Lower Baggot Street school was affiliated to the Board. In order to receive the annual grant her schools, in common with all affiliated schools, had to agree to use government-sponsored non-sectarian textbooks.[30]

A classroom scene in the Lower Baggot Street school was sketched by Sister Mary Clare Agnew in 1840, one year before Catherine McAuley's death. We see through the artist's eyes what learning looked like for 200 or more little girls gathered together in one huge schoolroom, around the sweeping curves of their semi-circular draft stations. The drawing is one of a remarkable series showing the Sisters at work, and gives insights into the schooling and social condition of the poor in the mid-nineteenth century, as well as being an indication of the philosophy that underpinned the lessons these Catholic girls received. The overall plan of the schoolroom shows that a form of the Lancasterian system was operating, with monitorial teaching duties delegated to younger Sisters. This method of teaching was originally promoted

Fig 3.1   *Girls from Dublin's poorest families gather round their teachers in the schoolroom at Lower Baggot Street for their morning lesson. This orderly scene was sketched by Sister Clare Agnew in 1840.*

by Joseph Lancaster and Andrew Bell as a method of instructing large numbers of children economically, since the teacher taught the oldest pupils, who themselves taught groups of younger children, and in this way several hundred children could be taught in a large room at any one time.[31]

The Lower Baggot Street school day began with a thirty-minute religious lesson based on the Catechism, followed by conventional school work. Each lesson began and ended with a prayer. The teaching of the Catechism was not, of course, unusual and each girl may have owned her own copy, with its 370 or so questions and answers, which they were expected to learn by heart. 'Train the children for this world, but so that they will not forget the other world', Catherine McAuley explained, and to this end the concept of faith was implanted in the minds of the children.[32]

In Figure 3.1, one girl has been sent to kneel in the corner of the room with her book, perhaps as a punishment for not learning her lesson. It is likely that she would not have been punished physically, since Catherine McAuley encouraged the Sisters to be 'gentle, humble, patient, hard-working, obedient, charitable, but above all simple and joyous'.[33] She said that wherever possible the administration of reproof was to be verbal and controlled. Harold Silver reminds us that historians 'have assumed that physical punishment was the rule in the Victorian elementary school – because it was the rule in the grammar and public school'.[34] There is an indication here that these girls were not physically punished. Catherine McAuley's guidance reflected her belief in the positive relationship between teacher and taught, based on mutual respect and an acceptable version of nineteenth-century classroom democracy.

The presiding Sister is sitting on a raised platform, giving her a view of the entire room, again reflecting Lancasterian organisational planning. Each Sister, in the role of monitress or pupil-teacher, is in charge of her own group of about twenty girls of differing ages gathered round her for their lesson. Most are barefooted, and the older girls wear shawls, perhaps signifying a step towards the adoption of full adult dress as they move towards womanhood.[35] Their hair is short, probably to manage the problem of infestation, and their hands are folded as if in prayer. They are all looking at their teachers, except for two girls in the centre of the frame, who appear to be talking to each other and are being admonished. Other groups are out of sight to the left of the picture.

A reading lesson appears to be in progress. One small girl in the foreground holds up a letter 'A', so perhaps her group is learning the alphabet. Each Sister is holding a book in her hand – the Bible perhaps, or a reading primer. The children do not have books of their own and are therefore not able to see what their teacher is reading, though they can watch the way she holds the book and turns the pages, and in this way they see the act of reading modelled for them, something they might never have witnessed at home. As they listen to the teacher read to them they are also learning about the rhythms and cadences of written English, and perhaps also memorising the text. There is a clock on the wall, so the girls are probably required to learn to tell the time, and two charts, one on each side of the clock, with the Roman numerals I–VI on the left and I–X on the right. The text is difficult to decipher but it is possible that it represents the Ten Commandments and the Beatitudes – with their emphasis on kindness and mercy reflecting the work of the Sisters of Mercy.[36] The Sisters themselves needed considerable skill to teach in this large room, learning strategies for projecting their voices, for providing encouragement, for holding the attention of little girls standing on a hard floor, and for always being aware of the timing of each lesson. Catherine McAuley knew about the physical and emotional toll of teaching and in her Rule she asked her Sisters to 'cheerfully accept all of the labour and fatigue of it'.[37]

These girls were poor, perhaps the daughters of labourers or weavers, and some were orphans who lived permanently in the convent. While most of the girls probably had no education at all before they came to Lower Baggot Street, others might have attended a Kildare Place Society school or been drawn to Lower Baggot Street because of its Catholic teaching. They were all part of a social and economic system that had low expectations for its poor children. Many would eventually go into service and it was in their interests to learn domestic skills and sewing at school. Their principal role was to care for their husbands and children, to cook and clean; not, of course, to engage in intellectual matters.[38] Yet here they were being taught basic literacy and numeracy, and might have been the first members of their families to read about geography, history and the phenomena of the natural world in their reading books.[39]

One of Catherine McAuley's central purposes in building the House of Mercy was to develop a house of industry for young women who were 'out of situation'. Her early work with Mrs Callaghan had convinced her that some kind of training in a practical occupation was the sole means by which many poor young women could gain a livelihood and learn to stand on their own feet. This appeal to rational good sense was overwhelming and reflected her response to the economy of the nineteenth-century market place and the social organisation of the lives of the poor. When these young women had completed their course the Sisters provided them with a 'testimonial of good conduct' to help them obtain a situation. 'Slovenliness', 'faulty manners' and 'crude speech' were corrected so that they could be recommended to prospective employers.[40] Though this policy may appear harsh and punitive, Catherine McAuley was no sentimentalist: she understood how difficult it was for Irish women from the lower classes to find work as servants, particularly if they emigrated to Britain, and she was determined to prepare them for their future role. In his report of 1851, ten years after Catherine McAuley's death, HMI W. MacDermott inspected 'thirty-two young women whom [the Sisters] instruct in the laundry department in the very best mode of washing and making up linen' and he noted that the 'establishment [was] one of inestimable worth'.[41]

Catherine McAuley died in Dublin in 1841, and it must have given her profound satisfaction to know that her work was not going to die with her. Sr M. Frances Gibson was one of many sisters who expressed her sense of loss keenly: 'Mother, don't leave us! What will the congregation do if you die?' To which Catherine McAuley is said to have replied, with characteristic charity: 'If the Order be my work, the sooner it falls to the ground the better. If it is God's work, it needs no one.'[42]

Her work was indeed still desperately needed, and not only in Ireland but in Britain too, where the arrival of thousands of Irish Catholic immigrants from the 1840s onwards posed an enormous problem for both church and secular authorities. The Irish poor, victims of the famine and its dire social consequences, soon became 'a problem for bishop and priest', according to Jennifer Supple.[43] The lack of Roman Catholic schools presented the Catholic authorities with a crisis in educational provision. John Marmion believes they had 'a major problem on their hands'.[44] During the 1840s and 1850s it is estimated that over 2,000,000 people left Ireland in response to repeated famines and their social aftermath.[45] Some emigrated to America, but many remained on the British mainland, and settled in the towns and cities that offered them work. The cultural and language differences of the Irish immigrants, their Celtic superstitions and overwhelming poverty, surprised and bewildered many traditional English Catholics, some of whom were particularly antagonistic towards the new waves of Irish immigrants.

It became essential to organise schooling for the children of the Irish immigrants. The Catholic Poor School Committee (hereafter CPSC) was a potent force behind the Catholic education system in Britain. It was established in 1847 at the instigation of its first president, Charles Langdale, to negotiate with the Committee of Council of Education over grants to its schools. The First Report of the CPSC (1848) states that 'the number of Catholic children now destitute of means of education is no less than 40,000, and this number is daily augmented by conversions to the faith, by immigration from Ireland, and by the ordinary increase in the population'.[46] The government agreed that grants should be given to Catholic schools on condition that they were open to inspection, though the CPSC was allowed to appoint inspectors of its own faith.[47] Thomas William Marshall was appointed HMI for Catholic schools in England, Wales and Scotland, and he held the post until 1860. Marmion believes that 'his reports reveal a man who had a deep concern for the plight of poor children'.[48]

A further problem for the Catholic authorities was the staffing of their schools, and there is no doubt that the Catholic authorities recognised the value of the Sisters who worked with the Irish poor during this period and educated their children. Money was a constant problem, and they were relieved not to have to recruit and pay lay schoolmistresses 'in consequence of the large and happily growing number of religious ladies who devote themselves to the education of the poor'.[49]

Between 1840 and 1860 over one thousand Irish-born people came to live in Derby, and a great many more passed through the town on their way to America, or to other towns and cities in Britain.[50] It must have been a great relief to the priests in Derby to have the support of the Sisters of Mercy, who arrived in the town in 1849 with an established reputation among the members of the CPSC as 'most efficient teachers'.[51] Francis Bridgeman, the Mother Superior of the Kinsale convent, arrived in Derby with a small group of Sisters, and the convent annalist recorded with satisfaction: 'Day and Night Schools were opened immediately and great numbers of young women attended the latter, as they were employed in working in the factories during the day time and were eager to receive instructions from the Sisters.'[52] Their work continued to expand, and the Second Annual Report of the CPSC noted that 70 girls were receiving education in Derby's Catholic poor schools.[53] By 1851 eight Sisters, fourteen lay servants and nineteen scholars were living in the Derby convent, and by the following year the Sisters were running three schools in the town. Marshall complimented the work of these schools, with their intake of 190 girls, and there is no doubt that Catherine McAuley would have been justifiably proud of the Sisters in Derby. In his report of 1852 Marshall stated:

> Desks and furniture – good and abundant. Books and apparatus – good and abundant. Organisation – thoroughly complete and effective. Instruction and discipline – excellent.
>
> Methods – system of the Sisters of Mercy applied in every subject with consummate skill. Teachers – singularly able and skilful and possessing in the largest measure the art of influencing and instructing children. Special – this remarkable and very interesting school continues to be conducted with rare skill and judgement, and I have only to repeat the admiration which I have expressed on former occasions when speaking of the results obtained in it. The instruction is of the highest order, all the methods singularly effective. I can see that it is not possible to carry an elementary school to a higher degree of perfection.[54]

It is likely that a modified Lancasterian system was still in use at these schools right through the 1850s, since Marshall indicates in his report four years later that the girls' schools were staffed by a mistress, twelve assistants and three apprentices.[55] Poor Catholic boys in Derby were also able to receive an education, but not of course from the Sisters of Mercy. The Catholic authorities in Derby employed a master, James Murphy, from the Model School in Dublin to teach at the newly built boys' school in 1852, but Marshall's report for that year rather tactfully states that 'discipline' was 'not yet fully established' because the school had only been open for four months, though he added that 'the instruction was patient and intelligent, and the teacher seem[ed] . . . to have laid the foundation for future success and [was] certainly capable of creating an efficient school'.[56]

Opportunities for professional work of any kind were slight for the children of the poor, but one route that was open to a few, both boys and girls, was through the apprentice-teacher system. It would have given Catherine McAuley a great deal of satisfaction to know that the girls' schools in Derby proved to be a fruitful training ground for young women who showed ability to become lay teachers in elementary Catholic schools. Trainees across the country swelled the numbers of Catholic teachers and at the same time they brought much-needed finance to the schools in the form of annual grants.[57] It has been possible to trace two girls in Derby who trained as lay teachers at the convent. Bessie Keily (sometimes spelled Keeley) appears in the census for Derby in 1851 as a sixteen-year-old 'scholar' who lived at the convent. She was also named in the CPSC's reports as an assistant teacher, and must therefore have been working in a monitorial capacity in the girls' schools. The account states that 'upon a further report from Mr Marshall' she was 'entitled to a payment of 3s'.[58] The following year the Inspector nominated her for a gratuity of £3 in recognition of her work.[59] The second apprentice-teacher was Susan Riley. She was born in Yorkshire and first appears in the census for Derby in 1851, aged thirteen, also living at the convent. In 1856, at the age of seventeen, and after working for five years as a pupil-teacher in the girls' schools, she won a First Class Queen's Scholarship worth £17 and a personal allowance of £3.[60] She went to St Leonard's-on-Sea training college as a first year student.[61] By Christmas 1858 she had become a certificated teacher and was sent to St Wilfred's School in Preston where she taught poor children in the town.[62] The success of these two young women possibly repres-ents Catherine McAuley's greatest achievement – the stabilising influence on the lives of girls and young women from poor families whose futures she helped to shape and, she would argue, on *their* families. Her respect for women's abilities was a reflection of her own belief in herself. What marks Catherine McAuley out as a practical visionary was her ability to translate religious and compassionate fervour into action, and to give other people a belief in their own abilities.

When Catherine McAuley died in 1841 there were almost 100 Sisters of Mercy to continue her work; fifteen years later this number had risen to almost 3,000.[63] Fifteen sisters died in their first years of service at Lower Baggot Street, while another 54 became either Mother Superiors of their own convents, or left the Lower Baggot Street community to become Sisters in other convents.[64] O'Brien believes that 'the experience of the women religious was in advance of the general development of a professional life for women'.[65] It seems that the women themselves recognised this. Their com-pensation for a life of austerity was civilised companionship, stimulation and enormous fulfilment. Today there are over 20,000 Sisters of Mercy working across the world, in Ireland, Britain, Iceland, North America, Newfoundland, Canada, British Columbia, Central and South America and the West Indies; Africa, India, Guam, New Guinea, the Philippines, the Friendly Isles and the Lebanon; Australia, Tasmania and New Zealand.

What has been most striking in researching and writing this essay has been the sense of Catherine McAuley's enduring presence among Sisters working today in Ireland and Britain. They speak of her with love and reverence, and there is no doubt that in some sense she is still there working with them, alongside them, giving each individual community and each individual sister in that community a sense of completeness and mutual recognition and understanding, as no doubt she would have wished.

ACKNOWLEDGEMENTS

I am grateful to the Mercy International Centre, Dublin, for permission to reproduce the illustration of the schoolroom in Lower Baggot Street by Sister Mary Clare Agnew. My thanks to Mike Torbe for reading and commenting on drafts of this article and to Sister Eleanor Little, Sister Magdalena Frisby, Sister Imelda Hogan, Sister Agnes Gleeson and Marianne Cosgrave for their continuing support.

NOTES

1. Mary Hickman points out that the Commission for Racial Equality's report *Schools of Faith. Religious Schools in a Multicultural Society* (1990) 'ignores the history of the Roman Catholic state schools which originated to educate Irish working-class Catholics'. 'Integration or Segregation? The education of the Irish in Britain in Roman Catholic voluntary-aided schools', *British Journal of Sociology of Education* 14/3 (1993), p. 285.

2. S. O'Brien, '*Terra Incognita:* The nun in nineteenth-century England', *Past and Present* 121 (1988), p. 114.

3. M. Peckham Magray, *The Transforming Power of Nuns: Women, Religion and Cultural Change in Ireland, 1750–1900* (Oxford, 1998), p. viii.

4. T.J. Walsh, *Nano Nagle and the Presentation Sisters* (Monastereven, Co. Kildare, 1980) [first published 1959].

5. R.B. Savage, *A Valiant Dublin Woman: The Story of George's Hill (1766–1940)* (Dublin, 1940).

6. Sarah Atkinson, *The Life of Mother Mary Aikenhead* (Dublin, 1879).

7. For a discussion of the Penal Code and its effects on the education of Catholic children see P.J. Dowling, *A History of Irish Education: A Study in Conflicting Loyalties* (Cork, 1971), pp. 7, 73–82.

8. T. Bernard, ed., *Of the Education of the Poor: Being the First part of A Digest of the Reports of the Society for Bettering the Condition of the Poor* (1970) [first published 1809], report No. LXIV, p. 66.

9. For further discussion see John Coolahan, *Irish Education: Its History and Structure* (Dublin, 1981), pp. 2–20.

10. R.B. Savage, *Catherine McAuley: the First Sister of Mercy* (Dublin, 1949), p. 393.

11. *Ibid.*, p. 20.

12. M. Luddy, *Women in Ireland, 1800–1918* (Cork, 1995), p. 72.

13. Peckham Magray, *Transforming Power*, pp. 143–4.

14. Savage, *Catherine McAuley*, pp. 44–5.

15. M. Degnan, *Mercy Unto Thousands* (Dublin, 1958), p. 77.

16. Peckham Magray, *Transforming Power*, p. 52.

17. Savage, *Catherine McAuley*, p. 59.

18. Peckham Magray, *Transforming Power*, p. 34.

19. Savage, *Catherine McAuley*, p. 83.

20. M.I. Neumann, ed., *Letters of Catherine McAuley* (Baltimore, 1969), p. 165.

21. Degnan, *Mercy Unto Thousands*, pp. 98–9.

22. Savage, *Catherine McAuley*, p. 105.

23. *Ibid.*, p. 106.

24. Neumann, *Letters*, pp. 154–5.

25. For an interesting discussion of this issue see Peckham Magray, *Transforming Power*, pp. 21–3.

26. Neumann, *Letters*, p. 142.

27. Savage, *George's Hill*, p. 248.

28. Savage, *Catherine McAuley*, pp. 53–67.

29. A. Bolster, *Catherine McAuley, and the Story of a Woman of Prayer and Compassion* (Strasbourg, 1982), p. 23.

30. Peckham Magray, *Transforming Power*, p. 81.

31. For a useful discussion of the monitorial system see T. May, *The Victorian Schoolroom* (Princes Risborough, 1995).

32. M. Nathy, *Catherine McAuley, Mercy Foundress* (Dublin, 1979), p. 21.

33. *Ibid.*

34. Harold Silver, *Education as History: Interpreting Nineteenth- and Twentieth-Century Education* (1983), p. 26.

35. K. Calvert, *Children in the House: the Material Culture of Early Childhood, 1600–1900* (Boston, Mass., 1992), p. 83.

36. I am grateful to Mary Jane Drummond for her helpful comments on these charts.

37. *Rules and Constitutions of the Institute of the Religious Called the Sisters of Mercy* (Pittsburgh, 1852).

38. Luddy, *Women in Ireland*, p. 90.

39. For a discussion of the Irish Lesson Books which might have been used in these schools see H. Minns, ' "I knew a duck": reading and learning in Derby's poor schools', in M. Hilton, M. Styles, V. Watson, eds., *Opening the Nursery Door: Reading, Writing and Childhood, 1600–1900* (1997).

40. Degnan, *Mercy Unto Thousands*, p. 79.

41. Report of Wm MacDermott, Esq., District Inspector on the Baggot Street Industrial School. Appendix to the 18th Report of the Commissioners of National Education in Ireland (1851), pp. 102–5, No. 29.

42. H.M. Burns, S. Carney, *Praying With Catherine McAuley* (Winona, Minnesota, 1996), p. 46.

43. J. Supple, 'The Catholic clergy of Yorkshire, 1850–1900', in *Northern History (Great Britain)* 21 (1985), p. 222.

44. J. Marmion, 'The beginnings of the Catholic poor schools in England', *Recusant History* 17/1 (1984), p. 69.

45. D. Fitzpatrick, *Irish Emigration, 1801–1921* (Dublin, 1984), p. 7.

46. 1st Annual Report, Catholic Poor School Committee (1848), p. 53.

47. T. Fitzpatrick, 'Catholic education in Glasgow, Lanarkshire and South-west Scotland before 1872', *Innes Review* 36/2 (1985), p. 94.

48. Marmion, 'Beginnings', p. 70.

49. 4th Annual Report, Catholic Poor School Committee (1851), p. 9.

50. For further discussion of Irish immigration in Derby see H. Minns, ' "Rough-headed urchins and bonnetless girls": A study of Irish childhood in Derby in the mid-nineteenth century' (1996), Ph.D. University of Warwick.

51. *The Catholic School*, Feb. 1850, p. 234.

52. Annals, Convent of Mercy, Derby (1849).

53. 2nd Annual Report, Catholic Poor School Committee (1849), p. 54.

54. *The Catholic School* 2/12 (1853), p. 41.

55. *The Catholic School* 3/5 (1 Sept 1856), p. 250.

56. *The Catholic School* 2 (Aug 1850–Feb 1853), p. 51.

57. For a discussion of grants to pupil-teachers see N. Smelser, *Social Paralysis and Social Change: British Working-Class Education in the Nineteenth Century* (Berkeley, California, 1991), p. 275.

58. 3rd Annual Report, Catholic Poor School Committee (1850), p. 9.

59. 4th Annual Report, Catholic Poor School Committee (1851), p. 7.

60. 9th Annual Report, Catholic Poor School Committee (1856), p. 70.

61. 10th Annual Report, Catholic Poor School Committee (1857), App. G, lxiii.

62. 11th Annual Report, Catholic Poor School Committee (1858), App. F.

63. Savage, *Catherine McAuley*, p. 393.

64. Peckham Magray, *Transforming Power*, pp. 61–2.

65. O'Brien, '*Terra Incognita*', p. 115.

PART TWO

The Struggle for Better Education for Middle-Class Women

CHAPTER FOUR

Anna Jameson: 'The Idol of Thousands of Young Ladies'

NORMA CLARKE

'everywhere the mind is, or should be, its own world, its own country, its own home'.

ANNA JAMESON, *WINTER STUDIES AND SUMMER RAMBLES*[1]

In histories of early feminism, Anna Jameson (1794–1860) plays a small but significant part: she is the mentor figure for those mid-nineteenth-century activists who, in the words of Martha Vicinus, 'laid the foundation for a generation who built institutions that then grew in directions well beyond their original conception'. Vicinus calls Anna Jameson one of the 'heroic pioneers', a leader in the ideological battle for women's rights.[2] Ray Strachey, in her classic account of the nineteenth-century struggle for women's emancipation, *The Cause*, tells us she was 'the idol of thousands of young ladies'.[3] More recently, both Judith Johnston and Barbara Caine confirm her importance as an inspirational figure.[4] Like Caroline Norton, Anna Jameson was personally representative of the inequalities and unhappinesses produced by the laws and customs relating to marriage in England in the first half of the nineteenth century: she was the unhappy wife of an unsatisfactory husband. Though she and Robert Jameson separated after four years, the rest of Anna Jameson's adult life was dominated by the struggle to obtain agreed and reliable financial support from him. These experiences informed her political understanding of the situation of women in the 1830s and 1840s. Caroline Norton's personal quest for justice led to changes in the laws concerning property, marriage and child custody, but she did not identify herself with newly emergent feminist activism.[5] Anna Jameson, by contrast, was swept up by the enthusiasm of the younger generation. She joined the committee for reform of the married women's property laws, was a signatory to its petition and a great encourager of others. An established professional writer with an international reputation, a woman of wisdom and wit, independent, much-travelled, hard-working, gritty and experienced, she was exactly the

heavyweight quasi-maternal figure to inspire and reassure the younger generation of feminists who gathered around Barbara Bodichon at Langham
Place in the 1850s.

If Ray Strachey is correct in her representation of Anna Jameson as 'the
idol of thousands of young ladies' (and there is no reason to suppose she
isn't), it is worth asking ourselves what kind of example Anna Jameson was
to young women in the mid- and later nineteenth century. What did she
embody and espouse? In what sense was she understood as being worthy
of emulation? In particular, since the education of girls was a subject of
practical and theoretical importance to her, what was Anna Jameson's vision
as an educationist? What aspirations did she have and pass on to those who
came under her influence? Ray Strachey describes two lectures, 'Sisters of
Charity' and 'Community of Labour', given by Anna Jameson in 1855 and
1856 which, she says, 'created a real sensation in literary and philanthropic
London'. These lectures, delivered towards the end of her life, were a passionate plea to a society infatuated with an ideology of womanhood which
narrowed and trivialised women's scope. The plea was that society's understanding of women's lives should embrace work and meaning, for women
had more to offer society than their decorative accomplishments. The lectures
(which were published and widely read) described the useful work done by
women in organised groups, such as the sisterhoods and nursing establishments on the Continent, and argued for cooperation between men and
women in all areas of social work. For women to be equipped to work
alongside men, they had to be properly trained. Anna Jameson, Strachey tells
us, 'was profoundly moved by the stir of social conscience which was going
on around her and saw, with an almost desperate passion, the waste which
was involved in the untrained lives of women'.[6]

Anna Jameson, then, seen from the perspective of feminist history, was an
inspirational figure because she urged – 'with an almost desperate passion' –
the importance of training and education for young women. Like most inspirational figures, the passion she communicated to others was fed by her own
experiences in a number of ways. She lived out her belief in training and
education by systematically making herself proficient in a number of specialised scholarly arenas. In all of these – literary criticism, biography, art history,
and cataloguing of works of art – she became a much-respected authority.
Additionally, she developed her skills as an artist and etcher so that she was
able to engrave her own plates for her books. But that was not all. Throughout her life, Anna Jameson travelled a good deal and wherever she went she
wrote about the social and literary milieu. She was an acute and dedicated
social observer whose impulse was to get out and see, and record what she
saw and thought, especially where it concerned the treatment of women. She
had a great deal of energy and many talents. Having begun as a governess,

Fig 4.1 *Anna Jameson's drawing of Domenichino's St Catherine, the patron saint of female intellect and eloquence, in her book* Sacred and Legendary Art.

she transformed herself into a teacher of that ever-expanding community school, the Victorian reading public. This was a public with a voracious appetite for knowledge and an almost religious belief in the ethos of self-advancement that knowledge was seen to serve. Anna Jameson emblematised this ethos: she was the self-made, self-helped individual that Victorian culture mythologised and that she, in her turn, sought to encourage. Starting from very little, by putting her God-given gifts to good use, working extremely hard, she received her due rewards. One of those rewards was a cultural position which gave her the authority to speak out and be listened to – as in her 1855 and 1856 lectures – on large social issues. Very few women managed to achieve such a position.[7]

More prosaically, Anna Jameson's energetic pursuit of knowledge and her fluency in purveying what she had learnt to an eager reading public was driven by financial considerations. Like many other women in the early nineteenth century, she had to earn a living. From a young age, she had taken on the responsibility of supporting her parents and two unmarried sisters. Later, in 1839, when her married sister's financial affairs collapsed, she added her niece Gerardine to the list of dependents. There was never enough money; there was always a great deal of work in often very straitened circumstances. Her situation required her to be inventive, energetic, independent, and shrewd. She had to generate money-spinning ideas, persuade publishers and readers of their worth, and carry them out. Her writings on art history are an interesting example of her ability to identify newly emerging subjects for popular education of the sort her writings offered. We might think of art history as a rather esoteric subject, but this was not the context in which Anna Jameson began writing about art in the 1820s and 1830s. Her context was the expansion of tourism, and art tourism, following on the opening up of the Continent after the battle of Waterloo and end of the Napoleonic wars in 1815. Her first book, *Diary of an Ennuyée* (1826), a fictionalised combining of travel writings with diary jottings with accounts of Italian paintings seen in the Vatican Museum and elsewhere, drew on her experiences as a governess touring with her aristocratic employers.[8] Meanwhile, back home, the collections that had been amassed by wealthy aristocratic travellers over the previous centuries had begun to be catalogued and to be seen as – to some limited extent – held in trust for the nation. Certainly, art was marked out as of educational importance, and the opening of public galleries of art in this country came with a specific educational agenda. The National Gallery, which opened in 1834, existed 'not to delight the connoisseur, but to improve the public taste'.[9] Throughout the 1830s, Anna Jameson made it her business to visit and catalogue all the public galleries in and near London (as well as many private collections) so that in 1842 she was able to publish a substantial volume, *A Handbook to the Public Galleries of Art in and near London*. This is exactly what it says: a guidebook and a register, with full indexes and critical, historical and biographical notices of the artists included. It is compendious, thorough, and fully researched; a tool for looking and learning.[10] The book was widely reviewed in favourable terms, being received as a contribution to public education. As the *British and Foreign Review* put it, art had a civilising and domesticating effect, it opened the minds of the masses:

> The Government has learnt to recognise the importance of these aids to the people's education; and we already see the fruits of their liberal measures, in the important fact, that a power of seeing, has . . . led to a power . . . of appreciating. Here lie the proofs, in the appearance of such books as Mrs Jameson's . . . works full of knowledge and right criticism, which are in the hands of thousands, instructing the studious, making studious the idle-minded; making Art . . . work in the hearts and minds of those who never before looked beyond the canvass of the picture. [11]

To have as an objective the task of 'making studious the idle-minded' takes on a particular spin when we consider the ideology of proper womanhood that dominated the early decades of the nineteenth century. Anna Jameson's assertion in her earlier work, *Winter Studies and Summer Rambles* – 'everywhere the mind is, or should be, its own world, its own country, its own home' – is an extraordinary assertion of ungendered self-sufficiency. To speak of work as an absolute good was a Victorian piety; but that hard intellectual work might lead women from comfortable studiousness to an awkward and emphatic independence, at home in rooms, countries and worlds of their own, was not part of the deal. Thomas Carlyle, the leading exponent of what he called the Gospel of Work, had a grudging respect for Anna Jameson as a literary professional like himself, but he found her assertiveness unattractive. To him she was a 'little, hard, proud, redhaired, freckled, fierce-eyed, square-mouthed woman; shrewd, harsh, cockneyish-irrational'.[12] He attempted to dismiss her as 'one of the swarm that came out with the Annuals' – that is, one of the many women producing what we might call coffee-table books of verse and prose. Harriet Martineau categorised her as a writer of 'light' literature.[13] The term was not meant as a compliment, but I think it warrants some attention.

By 'light' Martineau effectively means 'popular'. It may also be the case that in her early works, Anna Jameson's targeting of a specifically female audience for her books, and her concentration on female subjects, rendered her productions 'light' by definition according to the gender codings of the time. In the 1820s, when Anna Jameson began thinking about publishing, to be young and female was a highly marketable proposition. The poet Felicia Hemans had published three books of verse before she married, not yet twenty, in 1812. L.E.L. (the poet Laetitia Landon) was not much older when

Fig 4.2   *By 1845, when this occupational photograph was taken, Anna Jameson was
an established author with specialised expertise. The portrait represents a woman briefly
interrupted in her labours. One arm rests on a substantial book, probably one of her own
authorship. She appears to have just removed a pair of spectacles and, hanging from a ribbon
round her neck, the most significant professional accoutrement is shown, a magnifying glass
for scrutinising engravings.*

she became all the rage in the mid-1820s. Anna Jameson followed her highly successful *Diary of an Ennuyee* (1826) with *Loves of the Poets* (1829) (in the third edition the title was altered to the more elaborated *Memoirs of Women Loved & Celebrated by the Poets*); *Memoirs of Celebrated Female Sovereigns* (1831) and *Characteristics of Women, Moral, Poetical and Historical* (1832). As these titles reveal, Anna Jameson grasped early on the commercial possibilities of the subject Woman which by the 1840s and 1850s was to grip the Victorian imagination and lead to the situation which Virginia Woolf dryly noted in *A Room of One's Own*, which is that Woman was 'the most discussed animal in the universe'.[14] In books of history, biography and literary criticism, Anna Jameson used the figure of the female in an ambitious new way, taking woman as her subject (that was hardly new) but at the same time deploying the figure of the female writer with great dexterity, making it visible in her text. Many were to commodify Woman, packaging the current ideologies of womanhood to reach out for the social role of published author; what makes Anna Jameson distinct is her projection, within this popular 'light' writing, of an image of herself as a serious thinker, and one whose thoughts arise as much from observed experience as from books. This may not seem particularly radical, but I would like to suggest that it is.

The rhetorical space Anna Jameson created for herself was one in which she could speak about Woman from the point of view and experience of a woman, in a female voice which somehow belonged to a being unfettered by gendered prescription. Her lived experience embodied a practical vision of a freely enacted life quite at odds with the dependency and subordination increasingly being insisted upon: married, but single; not a mother, but in quasi-maternal role vis-à-vis her sisters, parents and niece; working extremely hard in a sphere which took her out into different venues – art collections, libraries, social and literary gatherings of every kind – as well as to many different countries. All this powerfully foregrounded the element of independent choice, and of movement guided by individual judgement. To be a traveller, especially a traveller alone, which she often was, is to be licensed to look, make observations and comparisons, ask questions, draw conclusions. It's a learning posture. It also leads directly to the role of teacher: she brings back the results of her inquiries and teaches them to those who stayed behind. This traveller is a self-appointed conduit for curious knowledge who has acquired the authority of a personal experience that others do not share and cannot challenge. The creation of such a *persona* probably explains why Anna Jameson always seems to be travelling alone whether she actually is or not: the *idea* of the solitary voyager is the leading idea she sought to convey in her books. This is true not only of the books which were obviously about her travels; it is also true of her literary criticism and other works. Anna Jameson's travels are the free travellings of the mind as well as the body. Intellectually, she casts herself as an explorer, seeking to understand her primary subject: Woman. What she brings back from her travels is not just knowledge but something more nebulous which she seeks, like all good teachers, to impart. This more nebulous understanding has to do with the inter-relationship of teaching, learning, writing and reading with lived experience.

Anna Jameson had a dynamic view of the interlocking of study and development, of objects of knowledge and the emergent self. She was critical of what she called the contemporary 'forcing system' of education whereby young girls were 'crammed with knowledge and accomplishments'. In its place she would rather have something that approximated to her own experience, in which what is learnt by living a certain life and experiencing certain things is allowed to be the magnetic centre for all understanding. In other words, she insisted on the centrality of subjectivity and, in particular, of a female subjectivity properly strengthened – not denied – by the cultivation of understanding.

The value she put on the experiential made it difficult for Anna Jameson to be a moralist. Harriet Martineau disparaged her 'sentimental philosophy' but Harriet Martineau did not share Anna Jameson's commitment to the experiential nor her easy relationship to her own subjectivity, imagination and emotional spontaneity. (Harriet Martineau would never have published a *Commonplace Book of Thoughts, Memories and Fancies*.) Harriet Martineau's response to the inconvenience of being a public woman in a society which volubly insisted women were private creatures was to insist that there was no problem: 'Whatever a woman proves herself able to do, society will be thankful to see her do, – just as if she were a man . . . I judge by my own case.' For Martineau, education was the means by which women would be able to draw level with men and operate as men did; lack of education was really why women were positioned as they were: 'women, like men, can obtain whatever they show themselves fit for. Let them be educated, let their powers be cultivated . . . and all that is wanted or ought to be desired will follow of course.'[15] The key words are 'just as if she were a man', 'like men' and 'ought to be desired'. Implicit is a rejection and repression of what is deemed 'womanly' and thus unfitted for the 'manly' world. Strategically practical perhaps, this was not the route Anna Jameson chose. In her Introduction to *Characteristics of Women* (1832) she put the following words into the mouth of a fictionalised female author:

> I have endeavoured to illustrate the various modifications of which the female character is susceptible, with their causes and results. My life has been spent in observing and thinking; I have had . . . more opportunities for the first, more leisure for the last, than have fallen to the lot of most people. What I have seen, felt, thought, suffered, has led me to form certain opinions. It appears to me

that the condition of women in society, as at present constituted, is false in itself, and injurious to them, – that the education of women, as at present conducted, is founded in mistaken principles, and tends to increase fearfully the sum of misery and error in both sexes; but I do not choose presumptuously to fling these opinions in the face of the world, in the form of essays on morality and treatises on education. I have rather chosen to illustrate certain positions by examples and leave my readers to deduce the moral themselves, and draw their own inferences.[16]

It is an impeccable liberal position. It refuses the didactic, and at the same time credits women (her assumed readers) with an independent judgement that mirrors her own. To construct such an image of the reader was a bold move if we remember that she was writing at a time when ideologies of womanhood represented women as beings in need of constant guidance and instruction in the secluded spaces of home. These domestic interiors were both literal spaces of privacy and also symbolised protection from knowledge in its broadest sense: knowledge of the random nastiness and delights of the world beyond. From the point of view of moralists, women's knowledge was best given to them in carefully curtailed segments, airbrushed and gift-wrapped to preserve such 'womanly' qualities as ignorance, innocence and purity. The not-knowing that resulted from such regimes was signified by a willingness to be told by others; by a deference to authority which was the exact opposite of observing for yourself and finding out and – most importantly – having informed opinions. The mixture of emphatic assertion with the apparent refusal of emphatic assertion in this passage from *Characteristics of Women* is typical of Anna Jameson's writing. She goes on to have her character say that she wouldn't dream of writing a book maintaining the superiority of women or 'speculating on the rights of women – nonsense! Why should you suspect me of such folly? It is quite out of date.' Such playful sophistication allows her to have it both ways. As in her comments on popular education, she is resistant to all talk of 'systems and methods, institutions, school houses, school masters, schoolmistresses, school books; the ways and means by which we are to instruct, inform, manage, mould, regulate, that which lies in most cases beyond our reach'.[17] In the teaching of children and adults she is opposed to rule, dogmatism and prescription. She champions a different principle: the pursuit of an authentic, independent self fed freely by the multiple and unpredictable richness of the world.

In paying due attention to her inspirational role, feminist history is kinder to Anna Jameson than literary history which affords her the barest of walk-on parts. Neither a dramatist, nor a novelist, nor a poet, how is she to be given an appropriate place within our categories of the literary? Her literary criticism, of which the extract from *Characteristics of Women* above is a sample, is as preoccupied with social questions as with literary issues. *Characteristics of Women*

is a study of the female characters in Shakespeare, but this is in large part a
vehicle for an examination of the condition of women in England. Nor is this
an accident, since for Anna Jameson questions about literature were also
questions about the social mores which produced and reproduced it. Her
ability to mix in literary circles in Germany (where her work, especially the
work on Shakespeare, was treated with enormous respect) and in Italy, and
to translate and write about the literature and art of those countries, is a
measure of her understanding of societies as constructs, open to observation
and interpretation by individuals prepared to make the necessary efforts. In
a less exalted way, she was also opportunistic, seeking subject-matter that had
a quality of exoticism, that depended on specialist knowledge – languages,
especially – and in which there was consequently relatively little competition
in the market-place. But just as her *Handbook to the Public Galleries of Art in and
near London* was useful and enabling, so she sought to provide useful materials
for the study and discussion of the situation of women. One comparative
investigation which she planned but did not fully carry out was outlined to
Ottilie von Goethe in the summer of 1841. She wanted to write a three-
volume study, *Memoirs of Celebrated Female Artists*:

> By Artists I mean all women who have gained a livelihood (une existence) by
> the public exercise of their talents, whether as painters, engravers, Musicians,
> dancers and actresses; considering the whole position of these women as re-
> gards society, how society has treated them, how they have influenced Society,
> their former position in different countries and their present and future (prob-
> able) position. The first volume will contain the female professors of painting
> and engraving in Italy, Germany &c. The second volume will contain musicians,
> singers and dancers, and the third volume actresses.[18]

The book didn't happen, perhaps because the market for such a study was
not assured. We might reflect, however, on the difference it might have
made to young women growing up in the 1850s and 1860s if their teachers
had had scholarly work of this sort to hand. Anna Jameson wrote a great deal
about art, but very little, as it happened, about practising women artists of
her own or earlier times. The essay on the singer Adelaide Kemble (1843)
is one of the few essays in her entire corpus which treats of a woman artist.
The essay is a substantial account of Adelaide Kemble's short but successful
career, much of which was transacted in Italy, written on the occasion of her
retirement from it: 'Adelaide Kemble exists to us no more. She has retired
within the sacred precincts of domestic life . . .'. This elegiac tone dominates
the piece which mingles acceptance of Adelaide Kemble's decision with a
triumphant assertion of her loss to the world and regret for the waste of a
talent honed by years of 'unremitting study'. The 'perfect mastery over those
vocal and mechanical processes through which the ardent mind within was

to make itself heard and felt' had been achieved, only to be immured in a tomblike 'honored and tranquil home'. The singer perfects an art and follows a profession, but this profession also represents a stance towards life, an unconventional way of being which is under constant pressure. The emotional account of Adelaide Kemble's final performance – the weeping, the choking, the suffocation, the acclamation and, at last, the sacrificial victim's anguished cry, 'What! Is it all over?' – offers her to us as one whom the powers of darkness have closed in on, stopping her mouth with the 'funereal silence' of propriety. Her retirement is memorialised, in other words, as a waste of training; a condition which, like the 'untrained' lives of most women, aroused a 'desperate passion' in Anna Jameson. Ardent minds – her own, Adelaide Kemble's – were made for expressivity. Using a discourse of the artist which echoes earlier discourses of genius ('genius has no sex') she laments the loss of self involved when a lifetime of professional artistic training is renounced in favour of domestic retirement.[19]

This opposition, between an authentic expressive self, hard-working, seriously engaged with the public world, and domesticity imaged as a form of entombment, provides the structure for Anna Jameson's most enduring piece of writing, *Winter Studies and Summer Rambles* (1838), an account of her travels in Canada in 1837–8. In this book she employed the strategies that had been so successful in *Diary of an Ennuyée*: first person narrative sometimes in the form of journal entries, sometimes appearing to be letters; a hint of emotional suffering; foreign lands, adventurous exploration; cogent observation; and the romance of study. This combination had worked its magic on many female readers of *Diary of an Ennuyée*, amongst whom was the actress Fanny Kemble. She described her reactions thus:

> I . . . was possessed with a wild desire for an existence of lonely independence, which seemed to my exaggerated notions the only one fitted to the intellectual development in which alone I conceived happiness to consist. Mrs Jameson's *Diary of an Ennuyee*, which I now read for the first time, added to this desire for isolation and independence such a passionate longing to go to Italy, that my brain was literally filled with chimerical projects of settling in the south of Europe, and there leading a solitary life of literary labour, which, together with the fame I hoped to achieve by it, seemed to me the only worthy purpose of existence.[20]

When we ask ourselves what Anna Jameson embodied, what she meant to the thousands of young ladies who idolised her, we can reflect on some of Fanny Kemble's phrases: 'lonely independence', 'intellectual development', 'a solitary life of literary labour', 'fame'. Significantly, Anna Jameson took care that her model of a bohemian existence was a perfectly respectable one, applauded by reviewers and read by earnest Christians up and down the land.

She was known for her deep religious convictions. She published her comments and reflections on sermons she had heard and, in her *Commonplace Book*, included prayers such as the following: 'To trust religiously, to hope humbly, to desire nobly, to think rationally, to will resolutely, and to work earnestly, – may this be mine.' What she projected were fantasies of self-realisation. The fantasies were embodied in autobiographical narratives which invited identificatory responses but which also kept their feet firmly on the ground. *Winter Studies and Summer Rambles* is prefaced by the following epigraph from Spenser's *Faerie Queene*:

> And over the same door was likewise writ
> *Be bold*, *Be bold*, and everywhere, *Be bold*;
> That much she mus'd, yet could not construe it
> By any riddling skill or common wit;
> At last she spied at the room's upper end
> Another iron door, on which was writ,
> *Be not too bold*.

Among iron doors and ambiguous messages about boldness (though even the instruction 'Be not too bold' is an invitation to be bold) the book introduces us to a woman imprisoned inside a house in Toronto because the cold is so severe it freezes the ink in her inkwell. We follow her progress through a difficult winter. She struggles valiantly. She tries to follow a systematic programme of study and has to work to combat the low spirits produced by her dislike of her surroundings and the vaguely indicated difficulties of a personal situation that is never fully spelled out. Her recipe for survival is simple: work, and an interest in the world beyond her frozen window. As she explained to Ottilie von Goethe, 'I write for Englishwomen and to tell them some things they do not know'. Such readers would be informed and improved; they would also be excited and perhaps inspired.[21]

Ostensibly, what Englishwomen 'do not know' in this particular case is the country she describes: Toronto society and, farther afield, the wild, little-explored regions beyond Lake Huron. In summer when she launches forth all alone on her adventurous travels, she pushes back iron doors left right and centre, relishing the delights of independence: canoeing, sleeping under the stars, being free of drawing room protocols and small town tittle-tattle. After a seven-day canoe voyage on which she is the only woman amongst twenty-one men (none of them connected to her) she comments that it was hard to come back to the relative civilisation of sleeping indoors on a bed: 'to sleep on a bed was impossible; I was smothered, I was suffocated, and altogether wretched and fevered; – I sighed for my rock on Lake Huron'. Throughout *Winter Studies and Summer Rambles* she presents herself as feminine but intrepid. The two are allowed to exist together. None of the reviewers objected to the activities she described on grounds of gender (or anything else). Yet we never forget that it's a woman travelling in this way, observing with a full sense of her own entitlement. At one point we are reassured that as a woman travelling alone she had never been in a situation where 'fair words, presence of mind, and money' had not been sufficient to see her through.[22] The sub-text, what Englishwomen 'do not know', is that to be a woman and to do these things is possible.

As always, Anna Jameson's primary interest is in the social condition of women in the different societies she encounters. In Canada, she made it her business to observe the manners and customs of the native Indians, describing her personal encounters with individual Indian women, and relaying oral traditions, stories, histories, descriptions of clothing, food, etc. She makes comparisons between the lives of European women and the lives of the Indian women she meets. She finds the European women do not necessarily come off best. Her central example is the subject very dear to her own heart: work. In Europe, she reflects, there is an ideology which apparently exempts women as women from work. But in fact the ideology only operates for women of a certain class: it exempts middle-class women from work and forces lower-class women to work twice as hard to make up for it. That being the case, she observes briskly, it is hard to see 'what right we have to look down on the barbarism of the Indian savages who make drudges of their women'. She presses the point further, asking, where a woman 'is idle and useless by privilege of sex, a divinity and an idol, a victim or a toy, is not her position quite as lamentable, as false, as injurious to herself and all social progress, as where she is the drudge, slave and possession of the man?'[23]

Anna Jameson taught by example, and what she taught was the importance of exploration and observation, on the basis of which independent opinion was formed. This is the central motif of *Winter Studies and Summer Rambles*. Winter explorations are through books, summer explorations through uncharted territories. Both the mind and the body, the interiors of houses and the great outdoors of the natural world in its most extreme forms of wildness – social and physical – are the proper province of a perfectly proper woman. All travel writing by women to some extent asserts this, but Anna Jameson incorporated it as part of the art and argument of her text. As such, her work opposes itself to the narrowly prescriptive, closed, didactic, instructional moral writings which were commonly directed at women. Just as she doesn't know what she's going to find at the end of her journey, so she doesn't really know what the right answers are to the questions about women's place in the social order. But she knows it is an issue that needs constant investigation.

Throughout her writings, Anna Jameson exhibits a combination of open-mindedness, opportunism and a rock-solid allegiance to her own observing and experiencing self. In making this evident in her texts, it becomes an expression of what she wishes to teach. If she dismisses 'facts, dates and names' as, for example, in *Memoirs of Celebrated Female Sovereigns*, this is not because she is deferring to the view that women are not up to scholarship (though there is enough collateral rhetoric of that sort in her writings to produce irritation in latter-day feminist scholars). Rather, it is because she aims at a larger philosophical framework: the big moral questions of life. It is a way of avoiding the narrowed version of women, promoted by prescriptive writers, whilst at the same time offering herself to women as an appropriate model for emulation. Her works, even the more sentimental, point towards the existential mysteries and insist that women, too, are entitled to humble themselves before them. Being fully human, as opposed to being a woman at a particular historical period, is to be engaged with experience at all levels; it is not to be a passive consumer of somebody else's answers. Book learning, however well-intentioned, does no good if its connections with lived experience are severed.

It is not really difficult to see why Anna Jameson should have been 'the idol of thousands of young ladies'. Not many women of the early nineteenth century offered other women such clear affirmation of the desire to make themselves up and make the world their own. An early, very well-disposed, review of *Diary of an Ennuyée* saw the danger she represented and warned against it: 'With a love of fine arts, our fair countrywomen learn to acquire on the Continent a licence of observation and criticism which we would not see substituted for the retiring sensitiveness of their insular manners.'[24] This licence of observation and criticism was exactly what Anna Jameson achieved for herself and what she offered, by precept and practice, to other women.

NOTES

1. Anna Jameson, *Winter Studies and Summer Rambles in Canada* (1838), 3 vols, vol. 1, p. 5.

2. Martha Vicinus, *Independent Women: Work and Community for Single Women 1850–1920* (1985), p. 7.

3. Ray Strachey, *The Cause: A Short History of the Women's Movement in Great Britain* (1978) [1928], p. 89.

4. Judith Johnston, *Anna Jameson: Victorian, Feminist, Woman of Letters* (Aldershot, 1997); Barbara Caine, *English Feminism, 1780–1980* (Oxford, 1997).

5. See Caine, *English Feminism*, pp. 66–70.

6. Strachey, *The Cause*, p. 90.

7. Biographical information from Johnston, *Anna Jameson*, and Clara Thomas, *Love and Work Enough: the Life of Anna Jameson* (Toronto, 1967).

8. Anna Jameson, *Diary of an Ennuyee* (1826).

9. See Johnston, *Anna Jameson*, p. 156.

10. Anna Jameson, *A Handbook to the Public Galleries of Art in and near London* (1842).

11. *British and Foreign Review* (1842), quoted in Johnston, *Anna Jameson*, p. 156.

12. Thomas Carlyle, *Letters to his Wife*, ed. Trudy Bliss (1953), p. 93.

13. Harriet Martineau, *Autobiography: Volume 1* (1983) [1877], p. 352.

14. Virginia Woolf, *A Room of One's Own* (1975) [1928], p. 28.

15. Martineau, *Autobiography: Volume 1*, p. 401.

16. Anna Jameson, *Characteristics of Women* (1832), vol. 1, p. 7.

17. Anna Jameson, *A Commonplace Book of Thoughts, Memories and Fancies* (1855), p. 117.

18. *Letters of Anna Jameson to Ottilie von Goethe*, ed. G.H. Needler (Oxford, 1939), p. 131.

19. Anna Jameson, *Memoirs and Essays Illustrative of Art, Literature, and Social Morals* (1846), pp. 69–121.

20. Frances Ann Kemble, *Records of a Girlhood* (1883), p. 124.

21. Jameson, *Letters to Ottilie von Goethe*, p. 101.

22. Jameson, *Winter Studies and Summer Rambles*, vol. 3, p. 340.

23. *Ibid.*, vol. 3, pp. 311–12.

24. *Monthly Review* (1826), pp. 414–26.

CHAPTER FIVE

Barbara Leigh Smith Bodichon: Feminist Leader and Founder of the First University College for Women

PAM HIRSCH

As the leader of the Langham Place group, Barbara Leigh Smith Bodichon (1827–1891) was at the centre of feminist agitation for at least thirty years. This took many forms: she campaigned to change laws which affected women, she led a campaign to gain the vote for women long before the suffragettes, and she always considered that useful work for women was part of citizenship. I have tried to do justice to her many-faceted activism in my biography of this remarkable woman.[1] Here, I will concentrate specifically on her educational projects, although this is an artificial distinction as she saw education as a key component of her liberal and feminist politics.

What empowered her to be an effective leader? Briefly it was a peculiarly progressive education and an unusual amount of financial independence for a woman of her time. On the paternal side she was born into one of the first families of dissent. Her grandfather William Smith (1756–1835) had been one of the leaders of the movement for the abolition of slavery, for the reform of Parliament and for the removal of religious disabilities. Barbara's father, Ben Smith (1783–1860), followed in his father's footsteps as MP for Norwich, and was similarly Unitarian in religion and reforming in politics.

Barbara was the eldest of Ben Smith's five illegitimate children, whose mother, a milliner, had died when she was seven. Largely ignored by the extended and powerful Smith family, the children were brought up by their father with the help and influence of various remarkable women, including Ben's youngest sister, Julia, and Anna Jameson.[2] Ben Smith was on the management committee of the Infant School Society, a Whig group founded by Lord Brougham, to enquire into educational innovations. In 1818 the committee visited New Lanark in Scotland, where Robert Owen had set up an experimental infant school for the young children of his mill-workers. Employed there as teacher was an ex-weaver, James Buchanan, a Swedenborgian who believed that children were spiritual beings possessing earthly bodies (and therefore senses) who were engaged in a lifelong training of the soul to be ready for truth. Although the committee brought Buchanan to London they soon decided he was too much of a queer fish for them to deal with. Ben Smith, however, at his own expense, established a purpose-built infant school in Vincent Square, Westminster, with Buchanan as its head. It was a poor area; the parents of the children paid a penny a week to Buchanan and Ben matched each penny with another penny. As well as education, food and warm baths were provided, and even clothes-mending was attended to within the school.

When in London, the Leigh Smith children attended the school; Barbara Leigh Smith's vision of what education should be was strongly marked by Buchanan's example that stimulating the imagination was at the heart of all teaching. Every day he read aloud to the children 'from the three sacred books – the Bible, The Arabian Nights and Swedenborg'. Describing to her friend Florence Davenport Hill the impact of her first visit to Westminster Infant School, Barbara Leigh Smith wrote of the poor children 'clustring on him like hiving bees, all trying to caress him'.[3]

Barbara Leigh Smith's secondary education was at a Unitarian school run by the Misses Wood in Upper Clapton in London, from about 1838 to 1841. She did not enjoy this school. A description by Elizabeth Whitehead (who was later to become Principal of Barbara's Portman Hall School) makes it clear why this should have been so. Although the Misses Wood were 'kind and good women who tried to make their pupils happy', unfortunately 'teaching as an art was then and there so little understood':

> Learning by rote from poor text books was the method employed; there was no explanation, no illustration, no attempt to awaken the mental faculties. Sums were given out to be done mechanically, not the most elementary principle was laid down. You puzzled over them, the answers were looked out by the teacher in a book, if wrong you were sent back to your desk to puzzle again![4]

It seems no wonder that she went off to school clutching her beloved copy of *The Arabian Nights* as a touchstone of all she (and Buchanan) believed. In 1853, just before opening her own school, Barbara wrote to Buchanan's daughter, 'I think the daily religious conversation with him in all our games together had an effect in making me wish to do some good in the world . . . Education seems to me now to be of more importance than Politics; the first is of eternal interest, the second temporary.'[5]

When she reached twenty-one, her father gave Barbara Leigh Smith a portfolio of shares which provided her with an independent income of between £250 and £300 a year. Westminster Infant School had closed in 1839 when Buchanan emigrated, so she decided to found a school that would be, as she put it, 'the child of Robert Owen's child of James Buchanan'.[6] She researched by visiting a variety of British Schools (for Dissenters), National (for Anglicans), Catholic, ragged and industrial schools, studying their methods and noting with particular concern the poor quality of the teachers. In 1849 she studied with a tutor from the dissenting College of Preceptors John Stuart Mill's *Political Economy* and glossed his opinion that 'No remedy for poverty can succeed which has not in mind to raise the standard of learning' with her own comment, 'In a word – to improve the people, to give them some intellectual necessaries, indeed *education* seems to me to be the only remedy.'[7] Her tutor, as well as influencing her broad philosophical position, had also pointed out to her the importance of an appropriate relationship between the Principal of a school and its Master. He lamented that often 'Instead of being, as it ought to be, a relation of friendship and of cooperation in the noblest work upon earth, the training of the youthful mind for usefulness, for earthly happiness, and for heaven, this relation is degraded to the same level as that between master and servant.'[8] This was an idea which Barbara Leigh Smith took on board and she firmly intended to establish an ideal relationship between herself as Principal and her chief mistress. Through Unitarian networks, a governess, Elizabeth Whitehead, heard that Barbara Leigh was looking for a chief mistress for a new, experimental school. As Elizabeth Whitehead wrote later, 'having settled together the principles which should underlie our work, Barbara left me with utmost freedom to carry it out'.[9]

The first matter to be taken care of was to find the best available training. Barbara Leigh Smith paid Elizabeth Whitehead enough money so that she could give up her governessing job in order to study the writings of educational innovators and to observe in elementary schools in London. Elizabeth Whitehead studied at one of the Birkbeck Schools, founded by William Ellis (1800–1881), a political economist keen to promote a national system of secular education, for the children of the artisan and tradesmen classes.[10] The ethos of the schools was to teach 'useful' knowledge, and to learn by enquiry rather than by memorisation. Ellis trained his own teachers, so Elizabeth Whitehead attended his weekly lectures, and, five days a week, observed and practised in the Birkbeck school in Peckham, opened in 1852 under the headship of William Shields.

1854 was an auspicious year to open the Portman Hall School as it was the year that the Royal Society of Arts organised the first national Education Exhibition ever to be held in Britain. Patronised by many public figures, including Prince Albert, it aimed to be a showcase for new ideas and experiments in education. Children's work from many schools was displayed and prominent educationists gave public lectures. Madame Ronge, for example, gave a lecture and demonstration of Friedrich Froebel's system stressing the harmonious development of children's abilities through play which was strikingly similar to Buchanan's methods. Elizabeth Whitehead attended a lecture by the University College Professor of Mathematics, Augustus de Morgan, which delighted her, although, as she wrote to Barbara Leigh Smith on 20 July 1854, she thought it would have been 'rather startling to the Peckham people – for he urged upon teachers the necessity of training the imaginative, equally with the reasoning powers of the child & reminded them that the nations most famed among the ancients for mathematical inventions had likewise produced the finest poetry &c'.[11]

Barbara Leigh Smith rented rooms in Carlisle Street, a rather poor neighbourhood near the Edgware Road, not far from her home in Blandford Square. The rooms were used in the evenings for meetings of temperance societies, and the largely Anglican committee took some persuading to let the rooms to Unitarians. They issued 2000 prospectuses in the neighbourhood which included such details as their intention of copying Mrs Buchanan's practice in Westminster Infant School of using part of the school day as a time for teaching good plain sewing put to the immediate practical use of mending their own clothes. Barbara Leigh Smith argued that the physical well-being of children was an important part of education and deplored the constraints of girls' physicality. Elizabeth Whitehead wrote telling her of one of her observations:

> I have been to the Professor of 'Rational Gymnastics' since I wrote to you – seen some of the exercises & practised a few – much to the amusement of 2 of my sisters, who caught me, they say, making unaccountable movements without any apparent cause. The worthy Professor teaching gymnastics, & nothing else, urges very properly the importance of what he teaches but declares scholars should practise these movements for at least 2 half hours every day. We cannot find this possible, I fear, but I shd. think the gymnastics might soon become popular 'plays'. How charming it would be to organise a regiment of stay-less, free-breathing, free-stepping girls! I must stop! My imagination runs on, & pictures school-girls like Grecian water-carriers – but I check it – I fear the sins of the mothers will permit no great amount of grace in English girls of this generation? If we make them abjure stays, it will be doing much for the next at least! . . . By the bye – the Professor of Gymnastics agrees with you in thinking it essential the children shd. have backs to their seats.[12]

Portman Hall School opened on 6 November 1854 with over a hundred pupils. Barbara Leigh Smith's aim, unlike the Birkbeck schools, was to mix social classes. Her school was progressive in the sense that it educated young boys and girls together, which, although a common practice for working-class children, was not generally considered acceptable for middle-class children. Children of professional parents, children of tradesmen and children

of artisans all attended the school. In addition, an international or cosmopolitan atmosphere was encouraged; children of various nationalities were
welcomed as pupils there.

Barbara Leigh Smith considered that the teaching of religion in schools
was 'utterly useless' and should in any case be left to churches, chapels,
synagogues or mosques.[13] The great importance of secular schools, in her
view, was that 'children of different denominations being together, they learn
toleration, forbearance, and charity'.[14] At morning assembly, therefore, she
asked that there should be a reading of a poem, a parable from the Bible, or
a story of some heroic deed.

Like the Birkbeck schools, the ethos of the school was to develop intellectual
skills by stimulating children's curiosity rather than by inculcating feats of
rote learning. However, where it differed was that great emphasis was placed
on developing the children's aesthetic sensibility. This was not surprising
perhaps, in view of the fact that Barbara Leigh Smith was a professional
artist.[15] The main room at Portman Hall had a raised platform on one end of
the room with a swing-slate and music-board. On the sides of the hall were
displayed the best maps, pictures and diagrams and art objects they could find.
Sometimes Elizabeth Whitehead found the best value for (her Principal's)
money in 'Catholic shops'. In a letter of 1 September 1855 Elizabeth told
Barbara of her plan to purchase a statue of the Virgin Mary found in one
such shop:

> a sweet young figure with simple flowing drapery falling from the shoulder – a
> fine lovely face – the serpent lies at her feet but it is not disagreeably prominent
> ... I should like to have this very much. It wd. be one type of womanhood –
> very beautiful for our girls and boys to love ... Some day I should like to have
> a Michael Angelo type of woman in the school – as a contrast to the lady of
> grace.[16]

The Principal herself was especially involved in taking the children on trips
out of school, visiting museums and art galleries to widen their range of
cultural experiences, and to 'reward' children for their efforts.

As the school's popularity grew, a Miss Watson was taken on to help with
the 'junior' department of the school, who had been trained at Combe's
school in Edinburgh.[17] By August 1855 it was decided Miss Watson was un-
suitable and Barbara found another governess, Ellen Allen, to replace her.
Elizabeth Whitehead reported to her Principal on 1 September that she had
'taken to her work splendidly [though] she finds our children very different'
from the well-behaved French children she had been governessing. She was
quite strict with her monitors, the older girls who instructed younger children in reading, writing and arithmetic, having 'no toleration for slovenly
teaching in those things she has taught'.[18] It seems surprising that they used

Fig 5.1   *Her self-deprecating cartoon 'Barbara Leigh Smith in the pursuit of Art, unconscious of small humanity' reveals her characteristic sense of humour and lightness of touch. Although ambitious in her career as an artist, nevertheless she was also fully engaged with the educational needs of children.*

a monitorial system at all, as it had been one of Owen's radical moves to abolish that system in his school. Presumably it was a pragmatic decision to keep costs down, and perhaps also, because good teachers were so hard to find, it was deemed better to have a cascade effect from the excellent chief mistress via the monitors, than to employ inadequate mistresses.

One of Elizabeth Whitehead's sisters, Alice, was a monitor in the infant section of the school. Like Elizabeth she professionalised herself, in this case by attending Saturday classes at Johannes Ronge's kindergarten in Hampstead. Ronge and his wife, Bertha, were German refugees who had come to London in 1849 and set up the first English kindergarten in 1851. Elizabeth Whitehead proudly reported that:

> Alice is a delight with her little children – & I think she has succeeded well so far. The children enjoy themselves exceedingly in the room upstairs all to themselves. A is full of the right feeling & spirit about them. We have long talks night and morning in our walks, about her charges, & she is undertaking it with so much zeal and anxiety to fulfil it in the very best way . . . [Mr Ronge] said he wished he cd. educate a thousand such as Alice as teachers.[19]

As well as the paid mistress and her assistants, the school had help from lady volunteers who came to give lessons. This aspect of the school was considered by Barbara Leigh Smith to be extremely important. When asked to make a submission on her experience to the Commission on Popular Education (1861), she wrote:

> I believe that much good can be done by ladies of culture giving a few hours a week to teaching in schools, and I most earnestly recommend the commissioners to open an examination and give certificates to volunteer lady teachers . . . The corps of volunteer teachers at Portman Hall School is unique, and the most successful part of the school. Some children come many miles to school, and when asked why their parents sent them so far (from Tottenham Court Road to Paddington), answered because the parents thought the lessons on physiology and laws of health so good. These lessons are taught by a volunteer. The same might be said of many other lessons . . .[20]

Certainly a most remarkable group of women were volunteer teachers at Portman Hall. The volunteer who taught 'physiology and the laws of health' was Jessie White, whom Barbara Leigh Smith had met in Rome in the winter of 1854 and had recognised as a kindred spirit, someone to whom liberal politics were part of the air she breathed. As a result of this meeting, when Jessie White brought one of Garibaldi's children, Ricciotti, for treatment in a London hospital, he attended Portman Hall. Although crippled, he was more active on his crutches than most children with two good legs, and frightened the little children by leap-frogging wildly around the room. Jessie White was devoted to the cause of the Risorgimento and had tried (unsuccessfully) to train as a doctor in order to serve the Italian cause. She went on to become embroiled in one of Mazzini's unsuccessful attempted coups. Although she claimed that she was a political *reporter*, not an actor, it seems likely that she acted as a courier, bearing documents to an Italian underground group. In 1857 she was imprisoned in Genoa for four months with another 'conspirator', Alberto Mario, whom she married after their release in December 1857. When the war of independence against Austria began, Jessie was involved in nursing Garibaldi's redshirts in makeshift battle hospitals. She spent the rest of her life reporting national developments in Italy for various Italian and foreign periodicals. Another volunteer was Octavia Hill, who gave French and drawing lessons. Her own parents had run a pioneering infant school in Wisbech, Cambridgeshire, based on similar Pestalozzian principles to Owen's school in New Lanark. Octavia Hill had been trained as an artist by Margaret Gillies and she later earned her living as a copyist for John Ruskin, before going on to work in the improvement of housing in slum areas of London, and ultimately founding the National Trust. Two years before Portman Hall started, Octavia's mother, Caroline Hill, had founded a cooperative crafts workshop for unskilled women and girls. Aged only fourteen, Octavia had been in charge of the 'toymakers', a group of girls from a ragged school whom she trained to earn a living by making doll's furniture out of wire and chintz. In short, the volunteers at Portman Hall were all remarkable and unconventional women, who must have lent some excitement and glamour on the days they attended. Barbara Leigh Smith, her sisters Bella and Nannie and another professional artist, Eliza Fox, all gave drawing lessons.

Inevitably, however, the major responsibility fell on the chief mistress, Elizabeth Whitehead, who, despite her enthusiasm for the great experiment and despite attempts by all of the Leigh Smith family to give her refreshing holidays, suffered from a breakdown in her health, although she retained the inspectorship of the school throughout the school's existence. There were also some disappointments. A Miss Carmichael was taken on, but she proved entirely unwilling to undergo the training which Elizabeth Whitehead had undergone. Barbara Leigh Smith was disappointed that some of the women she appointed seemed to have no desire to professionalise themselves, but seemed to regard teaching as a stop-gap enterprise before marriage. The final blow was the loss of Ellen Allen in marriage to a Catholic gentleman who did not want her to be involved with a 'pagan' school. In a letter to her friend Marian Lewes (the writer George Eliot) on 2 August 1863 Barbara confessed that

> this marriage is a great up-rooting of one of my interests in life because it has made me give up the school; I know no-one I can trust to carry it on and so it is wiser to stop. It is the individual that makes the work and I have no faith in

Schools, institutions, &c., unless there is a soul in them. It is absurd of people
to say they will do good and establish this and that, the great thing is to find a
good worker with good head, good heart, and sound health, and then just be
contented to help them to do what they best can without any fixed plans of
your own which only shackles the real worker . . .[21]

Elizabeth Whitehead was by this time married to Frank Malleson, a Unitarian, related to the Courtauld and Taylor families. Elizabeth was saddened by
Barbara's decision, although she concurred in her opinion that, with Ellen
Allen's departure, none of the existing staff were capable of the task of
leadership. Her letter of 21 August 1863 commented:

The more I think of the school passing away from us – of there being no
'Madame Bodichon's school with all that it implies – with no results that man
can estimate (though deep down in many a heart are results wh. one can
estimate – it seems more & more heart breaking . . . It is true that no school can
depend on any one labourer other than its teacher or teachers – no committee
could make a fine school with a Miss Carmichael, or only a Miss Croyden as its
head – a school is the incarnation of its teacher – & no one outside can help or
save if the spirit is wanting within . . . I do uphold that tho' I have not been able
to teach in the school for at least 2 years – I have been able to give all that was
needed while Ellen was teacher – I've been able, as it seemed, to comfort her
on dark winter days – to rejoice with her on bright days – to hold in your
absence that slender thread necessary to hold things together . . .[22]

Elizabeth accepted the demise of the school, however, and turned her thoughts
to another educational enterprise, which she envisioned as a sister institution
to the Working Men's College, in order to provide (secondary) education for
teachers, shopgirls and servant maids. The Working Men's College had been
founded in 1844 by F.D. Maurice, the leader of the Christian Socialists, and
was supported by several of Barbara Leigh Smith's friends, including Dante
Gabriel Rossetti, who was on the committee, and the Rev. Llewelyn Davies,
whose sister Emily Davies was to become Barbara's partner in a later educational experiment. The college also exploited gentlemen volunteers: Rossetti,
for example, taught the advanced art class there from 1855 to 1861, and
Ruskin gave lectures on art history. Elizabeth wrote to Barbara asking her if
she would consider being the Principal of this new college, but, receiving a
discouraging reply, wrote again:

You gave me a heart's blow in yr. letter about the Working Women's College
. . . You know how necessary & precious yr. sympathy is to me – & how as you
first set me to work educationally & my proudest thought for public work, is to
work with you, it pains me to the heart that you shd. not be quite with & for this
really great idea – wh. you once bade me carry out – & for which I believe the
time is quite ripe . . .[23]

Indeed, eight older girls of Portman Hall School were among those who had already put their names forward for classes. But, once Barbara Leigh Smith had unequivocally declined the role of Principal, Elizabeth Whitehead settled instead on a council of teachers, which included Octavia and Miranda Hill, with Elizabeth herself as Honorary Secretary and her husband as Treasurer. Barbara offered the new college any of the equipment from Portman Hall which could be useful to them and also gave some money. The College for Working Women opened in 1864.

Barbara Leigh Smith declined Elizabeth Whitehead's invitation for two reasons. Firstly, it was clear that Elizabeth Whitehead and her husband Frank Malleson did not need her. They were fully capable of getting on with the work themselves. Barbara Leigh Smith wanted to turn her attention to another educational problem, the lack of suitable 'secondary' education for middle-class girls. The Royal Commission on Popular Education of 1858 had broken new ground by inviting twelve women to give their expert opinion for the first time. In August 1859 Barbara (now married and known by her married name of Bodichon), as the Principal of Portman School, was invited to con-tribute. Even at this stage, she took the opportunity to deplore the lack of properly trained women teachers, especially for girls' schools, blaming fathers for not wishing to invest money in their daughters. Her analysis made clear that the poor quality of schools for girls was symptomatic of a wider social malaise: 'I believe', she wrote,

> the laws and social arrangements affecting the condition of wives in England, to be one of the causes why good teachers cannot be found for girls' schools, and why girls' schools deserve the bad character the Rev. J.P. Norris so truly gives them. I believe that, until the law gives a married woman a right to her own wages, and an independent legal existence, some control over her chil-dren, and social arrangements admit a woman's right to more liberty of action, that the education of girls will be miserably neglected . . .[24]

One of Barbara Bodichon's attributes as a leader was that she had sharp instincts for recognising and taking advantages of opportunity. When in 1857 Lord Brougham, an old friend of her grandfather and father, set up the Social Science Association as an open forum for progressive middle-class ideas, she persuaded him to open it to women. She herself contributed a paper on 'Middle-class Schools for Girls' to the fourth annual meeting of the Social Science Association held in Glasgow in 1860. Although the papers were published in the Association's *Transactions*, in 1858 Barbara Bodichon founded the *English Woman's Journal*, to, in effect, educate women them-selves. In her article on middle-class schools for girls, she points out the difficulty of collating reliable data, as 'it is exceedingly difficult to visit such establishments; they are *private* and I have found the mistresses exceedingly jealous of inspection, most unwilling to show a stranger (and quite naturally) anything of the school books, or to answer any questions'. She had also referred to the inequity of endowments for boys and girls of the middle class, and had expressed her desire that the rich would be persuaded to give money for an equivalent provision for girls to the boys' grammar schools. Her argument was that 'giving education, the very means of self-help, is the safest way of being charitable'. She further argued that the education of middle-class girls *relative* to boys of the same class was wider than the gulf between the education of working-class girls and boys, because of the gulf which widened between the genders when middle-class boys went to public schools, followed by Oxford and Cambridge.[25]

Part of her reluctance to commit to the Working Women's College was her long-held dream to establish a university college for women. As she wrote to Helen Taylor much later, 'ever since my brother went to Cambridge I have always intended to aim at the establishment of a college where women could have the same education as men if they wished it'.[26] The nearest thing to college life Barbara had been able to achieve was to enrol at Bedford College when it opened in 1849 to study drawing with Francis Cary, the Professor of Drawing at the Ladies' College, in Bedford Square, Bloomsbury. Maurice and the Governesses Benevolent Institution had founded Queen's College, an Anglican establishment, in 1848 to provide training for governesses, and this was helped by several of the lecturers at King's College. Elizabeth Reid, a Unitarian, had set up a non-sectarian college and so looked for her support mainly from lecturers at University College in London, which had itself been founded to award degrees to Dissenters.

Barbara's aunt, Julia Smith served as a member of the Council for one year, and as a Lady Visitor for five, of The Ladies' College in Bedford Square. It was non-residential and largely concentrated on making up for deficiencies in earlier education, thus being closer to secondary than tertiary education today. Some of the students, however, were attending a full-time four-year course to obtain certificates of general proficiency for teaching, and this professionalisation of women teachers was relatively new. There were also 'ladies' attending courses for brief periods, the income from whom kept the college afloat in its precarious early years. The three Leigh Smith sisters, Barbara, Bella and Nannie, all attended art classes in this capacity.

Her time at Bedford College was an important part of Barbara Bodichon's career both as an artist and as an educationist. In 1859 she was one of the campaigners involved in the fight to persuade the Royal Academy Schools to admit women. In her will she left Bedford College £1,000 and in 1896 they named their art studio after her, as they regarded her as 'possibly the most distinguished of Bedford College students in the ranks of Art'.[27] At the college she met women who were being trained to teach, but as they were coming into college daily it was almost impossible in those circumstances to create the kind of intellectual community that she had witnessed at her brother's Cambridge college. The possibility of providing an environment for women, offering full-time study and independence from family duties, flickered more strongly in her imagination.

After her marriage in 1857 to a French physician and philosopher resident in Algiers she spent half of each year abroad, so it became vital that she had comrades-in-arms to carry on the good work when she was away. In 1858 she met Emily Davies, and, immediately recognising her determination and desire, introduced her into the Langham Place circle. Emily too had suffered a sense of personal injustice when her brothers went to Cambridge, and with the promise of Barbara Bodichon's money felt they could create the opportunity for women in the next generation to enjoy what they had missed. The first stage on the way towards the establishment of a university college for women occurred in 1857 and 1858 when Oxford and Cambridge respectively established a 'local' or 'middle-class' examination designed to provide boys' secondary schools with standards for their graduates (serving roughly the same function as our own day's A-level examinations). In the summer of 1862 Emily Davies, as Secretary of the London Schoolmistresses Association, had made informal enquiries to both universities about the possibility of extending these examinations to girls. From Oxford she had received a polite but unmistakable rebuff but Dr Liveing of the Cambridge Local Examination Syndicate could see no objection *in principle* to the examination of girls. This chink in the armour was the signal for the formation of a committee in October 1862 consisting of Social Science Association members committed to the higher education of women. This committee, which included both Emily Davies and Barbara Bodichon, organised a petition to the university for the formal opening of the local examinations to girls. In February 1865 Cambridge officially opened local examinations to girls. From this small beginning, all else followed, in a long slow struggle towards women finally being acknowledged as full members of the University of Cambridge, which was finally achieved in 1948.[28]

Both Barbara Bodichon and Emily Davies had leadership qualities, although they had very different leadership styles, and different roles. Emily Davies was an excellent committee woman, having the patience and tenacity to attend to the tiniest nuts and bolts of business, essential in any long and difficult campaign. She was not, however, a leader who inspired people by the force of her personality; rather she overpowered people by sheer force of purpose. Barbara Bodichon, on the other hand, was what the French call an *enthousiaste*, and her presence inspired almost everyone with whom she came into contact. Unless (and it is very unusual) all of these attributes are found in one person, both kinds of leaders are necessary for long campaigns. Barbara Bodichon's personality was important in three main areas: she was good at persuading people to give their money towards founding the projected college, in a kind of development officer role. She was also vital as a mediator with the early students when Emily Davies's authoritarian attitude made the students mutinous. Finally, her abundant warmth and charm meant that she was so different from the *Saturday Review* stereotype of the dried-up old spinster bluestocking that her glamour held out a kind of promise that intellect in a woman did not automatically mean a lack of what the nineteenth century saw as womanliness. This was reassuring both to doubtful supporters and to the students themselves.

In August 1867 Emily Davies went down to Barbara Bodichon's Sussex home, where the two women spent the whole month undertaking some detailed planning of the projected college, both in terms of its building and its curriculum. There were two areas where they did not see eye to eye – the first was the religious allegiance of the college and the second was the issue of the young women's physical well-being. The Smith family had always put their money into secular educational institutions – Ben Smith into Westminster Infant School, Barbara's uncle, Octavius Smith, into University College, London, and Barbara herself into Portman Hall School. Emily Davies, however, was an Anglican, and she wanted to persuade Barbara that they would have a better chance of being accepted by the Cambridge establishment if they were nominally Anglican, although no student, in practice, would be obliged to attend Anglican services and instruction. Barbara was unhappy about it; every fibre of her own political instinct, and the agenda of her family over three generations, had been to remove religious disabilities from public institutions. It was ironical that Barbara Bodichon found herself in the more conservative Cambridge camp. Naturally Emily Davies tended to coopt other conservative women such as Mrs Russell Gurney and Lady Stanley onto committees whereas Barbara would probably have been more comfortable within the more liberal Newnham camp.[29]

Barbara Bodichon was also concerned about the possible toll on women's health if Emily Davies persisted in her insistence that *no* concessions were to be given to women students that were not given to men, despite the fact that they both knew that young women would be handicapped by inadequate secondary education. On her American honeymoon tour in 1857–8 Barbara had been impressed by the sense of physical well-being she had perceived in the young women studying at Eagleswood School, New Jersey. She considered that if parents were to allow their daughters to leave home to study, the college must regard itself to some degree *in loco parentis* and assume responsibility for the health of the young women in its care. Consequently, although Barbara pledged £1,000 to the projected college, she wanted to make it a condition of her donation that her friend the first woman doctor, Elizabeth Blackwell, should hold a Professorship of Hygiene. She made her position crystal clear in a letter to Emily dated 31 October:

> A danger of working too hard exists always for young women if they have to do things in a given time I think. I give you permission to express my intentions where you can do it fully. I desire to see some one in power who has made the physical constitution of women a study and if I give my £1,000, as I am not rich, I must be sure it is used in accordance with my best judgement of what will really promote the great object we have in view, the ennobling, morally, intellectually and physically one half of humanity. . . . We must do this well if we do it at all. My whole heart is in the idea.[30]

Barbara Bodichon was also committed to the college being built in the centre of Cambridge. Emily favoured renting a house in Hitchin, which was some 35 miles from London and 27 from Cambridge as, at this stage, it was not clear whether Cambridge or London would be the sooner to 'adopt' the little sister. Barbara strongly objected to establishing a college out of the reach of museums and libraries, or where even clean tap water, gas lighting, decent roads and a railway station were to be relied on. Nor did she think 'a hired house . . . good husbandry'. Nevertheless, in 1869 Emily Davies arranged to rent Benslow House in Hitchin, and the college at Hitchin opened its doors on 16 October to five pioneers. They undertook exactly the same course as Cambridge undergraduates (the Little-go followed by the Tripos) in the same time-scale (ten terms) as the men. On 10 December 1870, the five pioneers took and passed their *viva voce* examinations. *Punch* recorded this unique event in its own inimitable style, under the headline 'The Chignon at Cambridge':

> At the examination lately held at Cambridge, a number of students from the Ladies' College at Hitchin passed their 'Little-go', the first time that such undergraduates ever underwent that ordeal. It is gratifying to be enabled to add, that out of all those flowers of loveliness, not one was plucked. Bachelors of Arts are likely to be made to look to their laurels by these Spinsters . . .[31]

During the Hitchin years, Barbara Bodichon frequently visited, sent paintings and books, invited the hardworking young women for country holidays in Sussex and arranged parties for them at her London home (where the young women also sat their entrance examination). She also, briefly, served as Mistress.

Barbara Bodichon continued to press for the permanent college to be built in the centre of Cambridge but only achieved a compromise. A sixteen-acre site was found in open fields near Girton village, at the junction of the Girton and Huntingdon roads about two miles from Cambridge. Emily Davies regarded Barbara Bodichon as a 'perfect treasure' as Chair of the Building Committee. She was in her element, interpreting her brief widely, and interested in every detail, right down to the route of the coal carts to the basements

and the siting of the hot water furnace, tiles, material for curtains, the planting of trees and obtaining gifts of books for the college. Consultations with
the architect, Alfred Waterhouse, continued all through 1872. It was built
in the currently fashionable Gothic revival style: as Emily Davies said, 'as
we cannot have tradition and association, we shall want to get dignity in
every other way that is open to us'.[32] The difficulty was in achieving dignity
economically. Economy, for example, dictated the choice of long corridors
(wings), rather than a staircase system as in the medieval men's colleges.
The college was built solidly with 16-inch-thick walls out of 'best red kiln
burnt' brick from Haverhill, pointed in 'black ash mortar'.[33] Barbara and
Emily were agreed in wishing to provide each young woman student with
a set of two rooms, a bedroom and a sitting room with wide double doors
between. Barbara, true to her early concerns about women's health, was
insistent on the provision of a gymnasium, although it was not built until
about a year after the college was occupied, when money became available.

At the beginning of September Barbara Bodichon and Emily Davies spent
some frantic days at Girton trying to make sure that the windows opened
properly and arranging curtains and blinds, and ordering blue carpets for
the students' sets. However, in October 1873, when the nine Hitchin students and six new ones arrived at Emily's and Barbara's embodied dream,
the actuality was a long way from the vision. The building was hardly finished;
builders' rubble littered the space between the Huntingdon Road and the
college, carpenters' tools littered the corridors. Emily Gibson, writing home
to her parents, described Girton College as 'a red raw building among bare
fields with windows and doors still being fitted into their frames'.[34] The lone
building standing naked and exposed in flat windswept fields without any
trees, lawns or flowerbeds to offset the bleak effect can hardly have lifted the
spirits of the young women entering it. Money was so short that the permanent buildings had to be added on one piece at a time. Barbara visited with
her friend the garden designer Gertrude Jekyll and they drew up plans for
the gardens, although there was not enough money for them to be laid out
until the 1880s.

Barbara Bodichon's enormous delight in the foundation of Girton College
continued unabated. Writing to a niece on printed college paper in April
1877, she imagined herself as the eponymous heroine of Tennyson's poem
The Princess, describing herself as 'in the College for 3 days resting in my own
Palace! Certainly it is very delicious & our 35 students & their 35 little houses
very jolly.'[35] She visited students in their rooms, joined them at lunchtimes
and watched them working with their microscopes in Girton laboratory. She
was full of joy that the long-held vision had been brought down from the
clouds and made a material reality. Shortly afterwards, she suffered a stroke
which left her a semi-invalid for the rest of her life, and which led to the

Fig 5.2 *Barbara Bodichon, co-founder of Girton College, dressed in a costume which echoes the academic gowns worn by male scholars, indicating a desire for equivalent dignity.*

memory of her crucial role in the early days of Girton fading fast. In 1884 she gave another £5,000 to Girton and formally donated all of her paintings and her books that she had brought to Girton over the years. When she died in 1891, she left Girton a further £10,000, thus establishing the first university college for women free from debt and able to expand and flourish. Her contribution to education, and to that of women's education in particular, is perhaps her most lasting legacy.

NOTES

1. Pam Hirsch, *Barbara Leigh Smith Bodichon: Feminist, Artist and Rebel* (London, 1998).
2. See Norma Clarke's essay in this collection.
3. William Smith Papers, Cambridge University Library (Add. 7621).
4. Elizabeth Malleson, *Autobiographical Notes* (printed for private circulation, 1926), p. 36.
5. *Buchanan Family Records*, ed. B.I. Buchanan (Cape Town, 1923), pp. 24–5.
6. William Smith Papers, Cambridge University Library.
7. Abstract, Bodichon Papers, Girton College, Cambridge.
8. Philip Kingsford, *Two Lectures Upon the Study of Political Philosophy* (1848).
9. Malleson, *Autobiographical Notes*, p. 73.
10. William Ellis, *Education as a Means of Preventing Destitution* (1851).
11. Barbara McCrimmon Papers, Fawcett Library, London Guildhall University, 7/BMC/F11.
12. *Ibid.*, 7/BMC/F12.
13. 'The Portrait of a School', *Journal of Education* (1 Sept 1886), p. 358.
14. 'Report of the Commissioners Appointed to Inquire into the State of Popular Education', *Parliamentary Papers* 21 (1861), pp. 103–4.
15. For an account of Barbara Bodichon's artistic career, see Pam Hirsch, 'Barbara Leigh Smith: artist and activist', in Clarissa Campbell Orr, ed., *Women in the Victorian Art World* (Manchester University Press, 1995), pp. 167–86.
16. Elizabeth Blackwell Collection, Butler Library, Columbia University, New York.
17. George Combe (1788–1858): see his *Remarks on National Education* (1846); *What Should Secular Education Embrace?* (1848).
18. Elizabeth Blackwell Papers, Columbia (mistakenly purchased on the assumption that they were letters from Blackwell to Bodichon).
19. *Ibid.*
20. 'Report', *Parliamentary Papers* 21, pp. 103–4.
21. George Eliot and George Henry Lewes Collection, Beinecke Rare Book and Manuscript Library, Yale University, New Haven.
22. *Ibid.*
23. Barbara McCrimmon Papers, 7/BMC/F13.
24. 'Report', *Parliamentary Papers* 21, pp. 103–4.
25. Barbara Bodichon was also a co-founder of the National Health Society, one sub-group of the Social Science Association. Its work was taken over in 1948 by the National Health Service. One of their campaigns was to secure the opening of school playgrounds during evenings and school holidays.
26. August 1869, Mill-Taylor Papers (ref. 12/50), London School of Economics.
27. Report of the Council of Bedford College, 1895–6.
28. See Rita McWilliams Tullberg, *Women at Cambridge* (Cambridge, 1998) for a full account.
29. See Gillian Sutherland's essay in this collection on the founding and early days of Newnham College.
30. Emily Davies, *Family Chronicle* (Girton College, Cambridge), pp. 540–1.
31. Barbara Stephen, *Emily Davies and Girton College* (London, 1927), p. 239.
32. Hester Burton, *Barbara Bodichon* (London, 1949), p. 164.
33. Prudence Waterhouse, *A Victorian Monument* (Cambridge, 1990), pp. 12–13.
34. Daphne Bennett, *Emily Davies* (London, 1990), p. 146.
35. Hcox 1/239, Girton College, Cambridge.

CHAPTER SIX

Anne Jemima Clough and Blanche Athena Clough: Creating Educational Institutions for Women

GILLIAN SUTHERLAND

Anne Jemima Clough, born in 1820, was the first Principal of Newnham College, Cambridge, one of the first two colleges for women in the University of Cambridge, serving from 1871 until her death in 1892. Blanche Athena Clough, born in 1861, was the fourth Principal, serving only from 1920 to 1923 but a power in the college long before that. They were aunt and niece. Anne Jemima's brother, Blanche Athena's father, was Arthur Hugh Clough, favourite pupil of Dr Arnold of Rugby, poet, whose loss of faith attracted much attention, yet another of those worn out in the service of Florence Nightingale, and who died aged 42, three months after Blanche Athena was born. Both Anne Jemima and Blanche Athena had to learn to live with an icon.

The family connections are intrinsically fascinating and provide a route into some of the major concerns of the high Victorian intellectual elite, the 'lights of liberalism', as Matthew Arnold, Arthur Hugh Clough's close friend, was to call them.[1] The lives and work of the two women also provide a way of exploring another major theme of the nineteenth and twentieth centuries – also among the preoccupations of the lights of liberalism[2] – the transformation of education for women and the grounding and securing of that transformation in institutional forms. Anne Jemima played an important part in challenging the model of education for women prevailing at the beginning of the nineteenth century, one which may be called the 'domestic' model. Blance Athena carried this work forward, both in the creation of an embryo institution, Newnham College, but also in the re-positioning of this institution to face outwards, preparing to take a full part in the collegiate federation that is the University of Cambridge.

It was a powerful orthodoxy in late eighteenth- and early nineteenth-century England that the education of 'ladies' – that is, those girls and women who had attained or who aspired to gentility – was best conducted in a domestic setting. Much of the theorising about the education of ladies stressed the centrality of moral education and the distinctive contribution of moral standards and sensibility that the well-bred wife brought to her home and its conduct. In a determinedly Protestant society the convent option was not available. The conclusion therefore was that, ideally, girls should be educated at home by their own mothers. This kind of thinking helps us make sense of the apparent disjunction between Anna Barbauld's practice and her theory: she ran a school for boys but wrote that the education of girls should take place at home.[3]

In practice, of course, it was by no means always possible for this to happen. As late as the 1830s at least a quarter of English children could expect to have to cope with the death of one or more parents.[4] In households where both parents survived and were seemingly well-equipped for the task, pressures of other responsibilities sometimes led to daughters as well as sons being packed off to school. Such was the experience of the little Jane Austen at the age of seven, in 1783 – and then again at the age of nine.[5] Increasingly schools for girls began to proliferate but many of them emphasised their domestic character, the home-like nature of their establishments, relatively small, intimate, shaped by the personal influence and example of the schoolmistress and her family. The rhetoric was of the school as home.[6]

The rhetoric found both reflection and reinforcement in the general perception of schoolkeeping as an activity which would allow a group of sisters or widowed mother and daughters to support themselves without loss of gentility. The Byerley sisters, great-nieces of Josiah Wedgwood, adopted this strategy, as did Mary and Rebecca Franklin, daughters of a Coventry Baptist minister. Their schools, respectively near Stratford-upon-Avon and in Coventry, were to educate Mrs Gaskell and George Eliot.[7] The priorities which should govern the education of ladies and all the difficulties of finding the appropriate vehicle for its delivery are beautifully explored in Anne Brontë's novel *Agnes Grey* (1847), which drew on Anne's own experiences, not only in the Clergy Daughters' School at Cowan Bridge but also subsequently as a governess. Agnes, Anne's heroine, experiences great problems as a governess in households where the mother does not set appropriate moral standards. When, after Agnes's father's death, she and her mother both have to earn their bread, her mother proposes they should start a school. 'Thanks to my having had daughters to educate, I have not forgotten my accomplishments . . . I will exert myself and look out for a small house commodiously situated in some populous but healthy district, where we will take a few young ladies to board and educate.'[8]

At first sight Anne Jemima Clough appears a most unlikely challenger to such rhetoric and such a model, for she had been entirely educated at home by her mother. In 1822, when she was two, the whole family crossed the Atlantic, to Charleston, South Carolina, where her father hoped to build up his fortunes in the cotton trade. Mrs Clough was a retiring woman and this move intensified the isolation of mother and daughter, the more so as James Butler Clough travelled extensively in an effort to drum up business. Anne's three brothers were sent back to school in England as soon as they were considered old enough and they spent their holidays mostly with a succession of relatives. Anne and her mother remained based in Charleston until 1836. Looking back on her childhood at the beginning of the 1860s Anne recalled the sharp contrasts between her parents and conveyed vividly the precepts and example of her mother's teaching.

> My father was very lively, and fond of society and amusement. He liked life and change, and did not care much for reading. He had a high sense of honour, but was venturesome and over sanguine, and when once his mind was set in anything, he was not to be turned from it, nor was he given to counting consequences. My mother was very different. She had no love of beauty, but stern integrity was at the bottom of her character. She loved what was grand noble and enterprising, and was truly religious. She early taught us about God and duty, and having such a loving earthly father, it was not difficult to look up to a Heavenly one. She loved to dwell on all that was stern and noble. Leonidas at Thermopylae, and Epaminondas accepting the lowliest offices and doing them as a duty to his country; the sufferings of the martyrs, and the struggles of the Protestants, were among her favourite subjects. There was an enthusiasm about her that took hold of us and made us see vividly the things that she taught us. But with this love of the terrible and grand she was altogether a woman, clinging to and leaning on our father.[9]

On their return to Liverpool, Anne, now aged sixteen, settled into a conventional pattern of visiting the poor and assisting at local day and Sunday schools. Cotton prices continued to fall and her father was not a good businessman. In 1841 he suffered a second and final business failure. This financial crisis led Anne to try keeping a small girls' school on a more systematic basis.[10]

The contrast between Anne's educational experiences and those of the brother to whom she was closest, Arthur Hugh, was extreme. He had gone from his preparatory school to the hothouse of Arnold's Rugby and then on to Balliol College, Oxford. After graduating he was elected Fellow and Tutor at Oriel College, Oxford. Anne took an intense interest in every stage of this; and Arthur in turn encouraged her in a growing preoccupation with the processes of teaching, how done well, how done badly.[11] In 1849, with his help, she spent a precious three months in London, as an observer at the Training Schools attached to the Borough Road and Home and Colonial colleges for teachers. She would have liked to stay in London; but her mother summoned her back to Liverpool and once more she tried to work with a small informal group of middle-class pupils. Then in 1852 they moved to Eller How, just outside Ambleside in the Lake District; and there Anne established a more substantial school with a group of pupils, both boarding, like Mary Arnold, the future novelist Mrs Humphry Ward, and day.

Mrs Clough's death in 1860 and a legacy from an uncle brought Anne a measure of freedom. However only a year later another kind of family duty appeared to beckon when Arthur Hugh's early death in November 1861 left his widow, Blanche Mary Shore Clough, with the care of three small children, the youngest of whom, Blanche Athena, had been born only the preceding August. In 1862 Anne left the Lake District and went to live with her sister-in-law, to help with the children.

Blanche Mary Clough was a fussy woman, with a considerable capacity to irritate people.[12] The family circle was also an affluent one and well supplied with servants and nurse-maids. Anne Clough found herself under-employed and less than happy. However the family circle was also a very well-connected and actively progressive one. Blanche Mary was a cousin of Florence Nightingale; and the great cousinage of Smiths, Nightingales and Bonham Carters brought Anne into contact with the ladies of the Langham Place set, the group who in the 1850s and 1860s began to campaign to improve the position of women.[13]

These contacts brought Anne at last fully on to the public stage. In 1865 she was one of the signatories of the women's Memorial to the Schools Inquiry Commission, chaired by Lord Taunton, inviting them to investigate the state of girls' schools as well as that of boys. She submitted to the commission a note of suggestions for action, which in 1866 she expanded into a short article for *Macmillan's Magazine.* In this article she acknowledged the power of the traditional arguments for educating girls at home or in home-like little schools but contended that there was 'always a need for superior guidance and the excitement of collective instruction and companionship to call forth the higher intellectual powers'. She argued for educating girls with their peers, stressing the importance of higher intellectual powers as well as moral tone. She stressed the benefits rather than the dangers of large group-ings, going on to propose that to raise standards and mobilise resources economically schools might combine to share specialist teachers. She suggested that these local networks might also arrange courses of lectures by distinguished visitors, 'as a means of creating a taste for higher studies and collective instruction'. This is an argument for girls' schools unashamedly functioning as institutions, playing a role distinct from that of the family, whether core or extended.[14]

In 1867 Anne Clough chose Liverpool, the English city she knew best, as the base for a pilot project on these lines. The girls' schools already in

existence were not confident or well-organised enough to form an association of schools; but the scheme for specialist lectures open to adult women
as well as adolescents commanded considerably more support and not simply
in Liverpool. The North of England Council for Promoting the Higher Education of Women, which she helped found, brought together local associations in five cities, Liverpool, Manchester, Sheffield, Leeds and Newcastle.
This enterprise proved to be a seed-bed not only for provision for women but
also for University Extension Lectures for both men and women.[15]

Meanwhile in 1869 Anne Clough had been invited to become head of a
new school for middle-class girls, which it was hoped to start in Bishopsgate,
in London. Adequate funding was not forthcoming, however, and this left
her free to consider an invitation of a different kind. Supporters of women's
education in Cambridge had organised a series of lectures on the North of
England Council model there and the first lectures in 1870 attracted 80
women. Demand from those who lived too far outside Cambridge to travel in
daily immediately made itself felt, although the local committee were uncertain how strong this demand would prove. On his own initiative, therefore,
the philosopher Henry Sidgwick, one of the leading activists, leased a house
in which these students might stay. In 1871 Anne Clough agreed to take
charge of it and the first five resident students.

The demand for a base in Cambridge proved far more buoyant than the
committee had dared hope. After a series of moves the decision was taken in
1874 to form a limited company, to raise funds and build on land leased
from St John's College at Newnham on the edge of the town. Newnham Hall
opened its doors to some 30 women students in the autumn of 1875. In 1879
the Newnham Hall Company merged with the Association which had originally been formed to run the lecture scheme, to become the Newnham
College Association, still technically a limited company, and in 1880 they
opened their second building. In 1879 they had built a chemistry laboratory
and in the early 1880s adapted a former Nonconformist chapel for use as a
biology and physics laboratory.[16]

Building a building and making an institution are not of course at all the
same thing. Bricks and mortar and numbers of persons are necessary but not
sufficient. An institution requires also the development of organisational
patterns, ways of doing things not entirely plastic to the impact of individual
personalities, dependent on the dynamism – or whims – of founders. Physical
growth came quickly to Newnham, rules and simple bureaucratic structures
more slowly.

Anne Clough herself faced both ways. Although she had begun to make
the case for institutions, her own personal style was reminiscent of the older
pattern of girls' schools. She was passionately interested in the welfare of every
student, waited up for them, paid them little attentions and compliments,

sometimes fussed but with a concern that was patently genuine. Her manners were and remained very homely, too homely, some people thought, for the enterprise Newnham had become by her death in 1892. She found neither committees nor rules easy and had a talent for beginning arguments in the middle; yet because she could and did apologise handsomely – to students as well as colleagues – whenever she got things wrong, she succeeded in working with both committees and rules most productively.

The varied and often limited educational backgrounds of the early Newnham students also made it harder to make rules about admissions and courses, although this variety was a key element in a distinctive Newnham approach to the higher education of women. The earlier dominance of the 'domestic' model of girls' schools meant that in 1871 not much in the way of systematic and structured secondary schooling for girls existed in England – this had been one of the grounds for the Memorial to the Taunton Commission in 1865. The great push to create girls' secondary schools of a kind the twentieth century might recognise – that is, not educational 'homes' – began only at the end of the 1860s. The Endowed Schools Act of 1869 gave the Statutory Commission it created powers to remodel endowments to create schools for girls as well as for boys. When the commission's life ended in 1874, 27 schools had been created and another 20 schemes were in the pipeline. By 1903, the Charity Commission, which inherited their powers and responsibilities, had added another 45 girls' schools. Simultaneously concerned local groups were making use of the limited company model to found proprietary schools for girls. The very earliest were the North London Collegiate School and Cheltenham Ladies' College, both founded in the 1850s. However in 1872 the Girls' Public Day School Company was formed and by 1880 already it had opened eleven schools in London and eleven elsewhere in the country.[17] All of this activity, however, coincided with rather than preceded Newnham's early years. Many of the Newnham students of the 1870s and 1880s had little or nothing in the way of formal schooling behind them and even when well read and cultivated, they might be ill-equipped to go straight into a regular Cambridge course of study.

The strategy adopted to deal with this by the other women's college beginning to grow in Cambridge at the same time, Girton, proved an elitist one. Emily Davies, Girton's founder, was determined that equality for women could only be secured and be seen to be secured if women did exactly the same course as men, taking the same time over it. Therefore Girton students had to commit themselves to courses and fees for three years, to take the same entrance examination as the men, the 'Previous' or 'Little-Go', including compulsory Greek, and then degree-level examinations at the end of three years. Only a privileged few had both the resources and the prior training to cope with this.

Anne Clough set her face firmly against such an approach. She knew all too well how imperfect the education of many girls was and she also knew all about problems of straitened family resources and the immense demand from women who wanted to be teachers in order to help their families. In this she was supported by Henry Sidgwick, who in addition considered the requirements of the 'Previous' old-fashioned and educationally limiting.[18] Therefore the early Newnham students could come for as little as one term; they were not required to take Tripos, that is, degree-level examinations, but if they wished to they were allowed extra preparation time. If their ambitions and resources led them in this direction, the preferred entrance requirements were the newly invented Higher Locals, antecedents of Advanced Level, devised initially for women only.

The two policies are plainly reflected in the early Girton and Newnham student populations. In the eleven years 1869–80 113 students entered Girton; in the nine years 1871–80 more than double that number, 258, entered Newnham. The ages on entry of approximately half the students of each college are known. The great majority were aged between 15 and 25 when they arrived. However, six of the Girtonians were aged between 26 and 30 and two were in their thirties; seventeen Newnhamites were aged between 26 and 30 and a further seven were in their thirties. Diversity of age and experience and rapid turnover did not help the setting of patterns or the establishment of any kind of discipline.

The vast majority of these early students went into teaching. Seventy-one of the 113 Girtonians are known to have been employed, 63 of them in some form of teaching. Of the 258 Newnhamites, 171 are known to have been employed, 167 in teaching. Many of them went to staff and to head the expanding network of girls' schools and thus to improve the formal schooling of the next cohorts to come to Cambridge: the two processes fed off each other. By the 1890s the profiles of the students of Newnham and Girton more closely resembled each other: more Newnhamites took the Tripos and the spread of ages had been significantly compressed.[19]

The growing homogeneity of the Newnham student population was both powerfully expressed and reinforced by a second major burst of physical expansion at the end of the 1880s. Blanche Athena Clough, who first came to Newnham in 1884, looked back on the changes in 1924:

> When I came up there were thirty-seven students in Old Hall [the first building] and forty-eight in Sidgwick Hall [the second building] . . . The dining-hall of Sidgwick Hall . . . was our largest room and there we had our debates and danced on Thursdays . . .
>
> When Clough Hall was built in 1888 and we had another fifty students and a real College Hall which would hold us all, the College began, as it seems to me, to be a good deal more like what it is now. Three Halls seem much more than

two, and when there was a common meeting place the whole thing was drawn together and became clearly one community. Up to that time we had to have our Commemoration dinner and speeches in two parts, though we met afterwards and danced in Sidgwick Hall. The supper on trestle tables in the new Hall on the evening after it had been opened by the then Prince of Wales was our first real College Feast.[20]

Having begun with five, Anne Clough was presiding over some 130 students at the time of her death in 1892. Her successor as Principal was Eleanor Sidgwick, née Balfour, Henry's wife, an administrator *par excellence* and a superb financial manager.[21] By this time Blanche Athena Clough, known to her family and friends as Thena, was also making an organisational contribution. After a few years of semi-formal schooling, at Miss Metcalfe's school in Hendon, she came up to Newnham in 1884 intending only to stay a year, and stayed three. Then in 1888 she became her aunt's secretary and her support was vital to Anne's last years. Used to the comfortable affluence of her mother's family, domestic management on a shoestring came as rather a shock to Thena. Although in public she was comical in her recollections of her early efforts, which included miscalculating the number of rooms needed for new students, in private, in her notebooks, she complained bitterly of the drudgery involved.[22]

Fig 6.1   *Anne Jemima Clough surrounded by the Newnham staff in 1890. Her niece, Blanche Athena, at this time serving as secretary and helper, stands behind her, notebook in hand.*

Thena Clough became very good both at drudgery and at larger administrative tasks. She always began her arguments at the beginning and her clear, economical draughtsmanship is immediately recognisable in minutes, memoranda and letters. She became a Vice-Principal in 1896 and was the person invited by the College Council to become Principal in 1911, on Mrs Sidgwick's retirement. After much agonising, she declined, propelling forward her great friend Katharine Stephen.[23] She played a leading role, however, in launching an initiative that year which ultimately helped complete the transformation of Newnham from large-scale country house, inhabited by a sprawling extended family, to collegiate institution. This was the decision to seek a royal charter and statutes from the Privy Council. Girton only began on this process ten years later and the Oxford women's colleges were later still.

The significance of a charter and statutes, which took five years to secure, is difficult to exaggerate. They brought key changes in the structure and governance of the college. No longer was it a limited company, with shareholders. The teaching staff, formerly the company's employees, now formed a self-governing academic corporation.[24] In addition these changes carried an important message for the rest of Cambridge, and indeed for Oxford too, signalling that women could make and had made a college like men's colleges, one facing outwards into the wider university.

The full resonances of this act become clearer if we explore the early relations between Newnham and Girton and the University of Cambridge. At first women students who wished to take University examinations had to arrange to do so by private treaty with each examiner. However in 1881, with unexpected ease, they secured a blanket permission to take these examinations – although provision was made for a class or results list separate from that for men.

It took a little time to consolidate this gain. Thena Clough remembered the Newnham of the 1880s as essentially inward-looking, impinging little on the general University consciousness:

> We didn't think ourselves at all an important affair, and we had no great ideas of what ought to be, but we were a very lively buzzing community, pushing along our way, very much amused with ourselves and very little noticed by the world at large. We had no part or lot in University societies except the Ladies' Discussion Society and I think C.U.M.S. [Cambridge University Music Society] . . . in any case the University generally were (*sic*) hardly aware of our existence.[25]

The ultimate objective of the women and their supporters, however, was admission not simply to examinations but to degrees and the full membership of the University community and share in University government that that brought. Achieving that would involve forcing the University to acknowledge not simply their existence but also their academic good standing. Girton and Newnham differed somewhat on tactics but neither was under any illusion that the process would be a straightforward one.

Some events in these years brought entirely positive publicity. In 1887 Agnata Ramsay of Girton was the only person placed in the first division of the first class of the Classical Tripos; and in 1890 Philippa Fawcett of Newnham was ranked above the Senior Wrangler (the top-ranking man) in the Mathematics Tripos. Newnham enjoyed having the new building of 1888 opened by the Prince of Wales, accompanied by the Prime Minister, Lord Salisbury, who just happened to be Mrs Sidgwick's uncle. 1897, however, brought a serious setback. Supporters of the two colleges had taken to the Regent House a proposal to give women simply the titles of degrees – not the rights and privileges. This was resoundingly defeated, by 1707 votes to 661, amid extraordinary scenes. The fact of defeat and the misogyny so openly and widely expressed were bad enough; but even more alarming was the violence which accompanied the undergraduate celebrations of that defeat. The celebratory bonfire in the Market Square did hundreds of pounds' worth of damage.

The women did not choose to expose themselves to this kind of public rebuff again before 1914. However, to seek a charter and statutes was to begin to re-position oneself for the next time, saying to the rest of Cambridge, 'our structure is like yours: we too are a self-governing academic community'. Some of the Newnham teaching staff, notably the classicist Jane Harrison, had already begun to think on these lines in 1897, in the debate which preceded the vote. By 1911 enough of her colleagues were convinced to encourage Thena Clough to launch the process.[26]

The issue of membership for the women was faced again in both Cambridge and Oxford at the end of the First World War. The catastrophic loss of fee income brought about by the war led the two universities to seek government subsidy for the first time. The price of this was a royal commission, chaired by H.H. Asquith, the former Prime Minister. Since the government which established this commission had also enfranchised women over 30 in 1918 and passed a more general Sex Disqualification (Removal) Act in 1919, there was some hope that pressure from outside might be brought to bear on the two universities to fall into line with every other university in the United Kingdom. Thena Clough found herself uniquely positioned to try to influence this process. She had accepted appointment to the royal commission, as the token Cambridge female member; and in 1920 finally, reluctantly, she allowed herself to be drafted into the Principalship of Newnham by the newly constituted governing body, exercising its right to elect the Principal under the new statutes. She had refused to stand as a candidate originally; and only when the governing body, unpractised at managing these affairs, deadlocked over two other competing candidates did she finally accept nomination and resolve the deadlock. Everyone was conscious that any public sign of disagreement or disarray at such a critical juncture would be very damaging.[27]

In the course of 1920, Oxford, which had already disfranchised its non-resident MAs, voted to admit women to full membership. In Cambridge, however, where non-resident MAs were still entitled to vote in the Regent House, their votes helped to defeat a similar proposal. Various alternative schemes were then formulated and discussed while the supporters of Newnham and Girton debated amongst themselves the appropriate timing for an appeal to the royal commission. The summer of 1921 marked the fiftieth birthday of Newnham and Thena Clough was to be seen presiding with style and composure over a grand Jubilee garden party, while the dealing and the caballing continued behind the scenes. However the most the negotiations within the University could achieve was half a loaf, the titles of degrees but not the substance, the proposal that had been so roundly defeated in 1897; and this was confirmed by a vote in October 1921. Again the rebuff to the women was celebrated with violent enthusiasm by the male undergraduates. This time they brought their destructive capacities to Newnham, charging up Newnham Walk with a handcart, which they used as a battering ram against the handsome bronze gates erected as a memorial to Anne Jemima Clough in 1894.

Thena Clough fought on. With the sole Labour member of the Asquith Commission she signed a note of dissent to the Final Report in 1922, contending that public funds should not go to an institution which discriminated against women. The majority of the commission sat on the fence: their Report included a sentence of memorable confusion: 'we desire strongly that Cambridge should remain mainly and predominantly a "men's University" though of a mixed type as it is already'.[28] Supporters of the women raised the issue when the Report was debated in the Commons, but to no avail. Titles of degrees were all that Cambridge women were allowed for the whole of the inter-war period. Although they were recognised teachers and could sit on faculty boards, they had no share in University government and could neither speak nor vote in Senate or Regent House on any matters.[29]

Thena Clough, now in her early sixties, knew she was not the woman for another long-drawn-out-campaign. In 1923 she stepped down as Principal, retiring to her beloved New Forest, although continuing by letter and visit to give strong support to Pernel Strachey, her successor and good friend.[30] She lived long enough, however, to see the University of Cambridge grant full membership to women in 1948. Having played her part in the creation of the institution and had the frustration in the 1920s of seeing it trapped on the threshold of University membership, she could at last see Newnham taking its place within the walls. Her grandmother, although she loved 'the terrible

Fig 6.2 *This drawing of Blanche Athena Clough was commissioned by old students shortly after her retirement from the Principalship of Newnham.*

and grand', had clung to and leaned on her husband.[31] Blanche Athena Clough and her college were no-one's dependants.

NOTES

1. Christopher Harvie, *The Lights of Liberalism. University Liberals and the Challenge of Democracy 1860–86* (1976); for an excellent short account of A.H. Clough's life see Anthony Kenny's 'Biographical Introduction' to his edition of *The Oxford Diaries of Arthur Hugh Clough* (Oxford, 1990); and for Clough's relationship with Matthew Arnold see Ian Hamilton, *A Gift Imprisoned: The Poetic Life of Matthew Arnold* (1998). The essay that follows is drawn from work for a double biography of A.J. and B.A. Clough.
2. Gillian Sutherland, 'The movement for the higher education of women: its social and intellectual context in England, c.1840–80', in *Politics and Social Change in Modern Britain: Essays presented to A.F. Thompson*, ed. P.J. Waller (Brighton, 1987), pp. 108–10.
3. See Mary Hilton's chapter above.
4. Michael Anderson, 'The emergence of the modern life cycle in Britain', *Social History* X (1985), p. 78.
5. Claire Tomalin, *Jane Austen. A Life* (1997), ch. 4, 'School'.
6. The physical expansion of provision is chronicled by Susan Skedd in her unpublished 1996 Oxford D.Phil. thesis, 'The Education of Women in Hanoverian Britain c.1760–1820'. The ideology is explored in Christina de Bellaigue's unpublished 1996 Cambridge Part II dissertation, 'The Rise and Fall of the Domestic Model of Girls' Schools 1780–1820'. I am indebted to Christina for continuing fruitful discussion of these themes.
7. Gordon S. Haight, *George Eliot. A Biography* (Oxford, 1968), pp. 10–21; Jenny Uglow, *Elizabeth Gaskell: A Habit of Stories* (1993), pp. 34–46; P.D. Hicks, *A Quest of Ladies* (n.d. [1949]).
8. Anne Brontë, *Agnes Grey* (1847), ch. xix, 'The Letter'.
9. *Letters and Remains of Arthur Hugh Clough* (1865, privately printed), p. 9.
10. Biographical information about Anne Clough is taken from B.A. Clough, *Memoir of Anne Jemima Clough* (1897) unless otherwise indicated.
11. See the letters exchanged between them in *The Correspondence of Arthur Hugh Clough*, ed. F.L. Mulhauser, 2 vols (Oxford, 1957), I.
12. See for example her correspondence with Benjamin Jowett 1861–7, Balliol College, Oxford, Phillips 292.
13. An excellent account of this group can be found in Pam Hirsch, *Barbara Leigh Smith Bodichon: Feminist, Artist and Rebel* (1998), ch. 11, 'The Reform Firm'.
14. Anne J. Clough, 'Hints on the organization of girls' schools', *Macmillan's Magazine* XIV (1866), pp. 435–9.
15. Bodleian Library, Oxford, Bryce Papers, 159, ff. 167–8. Anne Clough to James Bryce, Spring 1867, ff. 189–92; same to same, 4 Nov 1867, ff. 204–5; same to same, 13 Nov 1867; James Stuart, *Reminiscences* (1911, privately printed), ch. v.
16. Paula Gould, 'Women and the culture of university physics in late nineteenth-century Cambridge', *British Journal for the History of Science* 30 (1997), pp. 127–49, and Marsha L. Richmond, '"A lab of one's own": The Balfour Biological Laboratory for Women at Cambridge University, 1884–1914', *Isis* 88 (1997), pp. 422–55.
17. Sheila Fletcher, *Feminists and Bureaucrats: A Study in the Development of Girls' Education in the Nineteenth Century* (Cambridge, 1980), Appendix 3; Josephine Kamm, *Indicative Past: A Hundred Years of the Girls' Public Day School Trust* (1971), Appendix II.
18. The disagreement and all that flowed from it is explored in Rita McWilliams Tullberg, *Women at Cambridge* (2nd edn, Cambridge, 1998). The account of relations between the two institutions and between them and the University of Cambridge in what follows is based on *Women at Cambridge* unless otherwise indicated.
19. Sutherland, 'Movement for the Higher Education of Women', pp. 100–4.
20. Newnham College Roll, *Letter*, 1924 (Cambridge, privately printed, 1924), quoted in *A Newnham Anthology*, ed. Ann Phillips (2nd edn, Cambridge, 1988), pp. 28–30.
21. Janet Oppenheim, 'A mother's role, a daughter's duty: Lady Blanche Balfour, Eleanor Sidgwick, and feminist perspectives', *Journal of British Studies* 34 (April 1995), pp. 218–24.
22. *Letter*, 1924, p. 30; British Library Additional MSS, Clough–Shore-Smith Papers, 72830B, ff. 4–5.

23. *Ibid.*, 72830E, ff. 38–42.

24. Newnham College, Cambridge, *Council Reports 1897–1912*, pp. 228, 244, 259 and 274; *Annual Reports*, Principal's Report for 1914–15, pp. 30–1; Principal's Report for 1916–17, p. 25.

25. *Letter*, 1924, pp. 28–9.

26. Clough–Shore-Smith Papers, 72830E, ff. 34–8.

27. Newnham College, Cambridge, *Minutes of Governing Body Meetings*, 28 Nov 1919–21 June 1920, pp. 62, 66–9, 77–8, 80–1, 83, 85, 87, 92–3.

28. *Report of the Royal Commission on the Universities of Oxford and Cambridge*, 1922 Cmd 1588 x, pp. 254–5, 245.

29. The frustrations of this experience are explored in Gillian Sutherland, ' "Nasty forward minxes": Cambridge and the higher education of women' in *Cambridge Contributions*, ed. Sarah J. Ormrod (Cambridge, 1998), pp. 93–8.

30. Clough–Shore-Smith Papers 72828, ff. 102–4: Pernel Strachey to Thena Clough, 24 Aug 1930, ff. 105–6: same to same, 1 Nov 1931; British Library Add. MSS, Strachey Papers 60728, f. 170, Pernel to Pippa Strachey 5 May 1935; f. 205, Pippa to Pernel Strachey, 15 December 1934; f. 206, same to same, 17 Dec 1934; ff. 226–7, same to same, 14 July 1937.

31. Above, p. 103.

CHAPTER SEVEN

Clara Collet's Dissenting Inheritance and the Education of Women

JANE MILLER

I wrote a chapter about my great-aunt Clara some years ago and called it 'An Odd Woman': a title I meant to be paradoxical in ways I shall try to explain. The chapter was in a book called *Seductions*[1], and I used Clara as great-nieces may use once formidable great-aunts: to explore the way in which women – and I included myself as well as her in this – are seduced by male traditions, ideas, writing, perhaps by actual men, even as we work and write on behalf of women. I thought of such seductions as inevitable for women, part of what feminism has always had to recognise and contend with, though the seduction itself, and the reasons for women consenting to it, will have been differently experienced in different settings and at different times.

Clara Collet died in 1948 when she was 88 and I was 15 and still putting up some resistance to seductions of many kinds, including hers. She had no chance, therefore, to agree with me about seduction or to demur. She did not suffer fools gladly, especially fifteen-year-old ones, and she'd have thought my metaphor of seduction a bit overheated, to say the least. She was born in 1860, in Crouch End in North London, the fourth of the five children of Collet Dobson Collet and his wife Jane, who owned and ran a laundry. The Collet family had effectively been Unitarian since the end of the seventeenth century in their principled opposition to the Trinity (though it was only later that they began to call themselves Unitarian)[2], and while there had been returns to Anglicanism amongst her father's generation (several of his deserting siblings settled in New Zealand), Clara and her brothers and sisters were brought up as Unitarians. My father, who grew up in the house owned by Clara and her brothers and sisters, described his family as middle middle class, because they had always had one servant, but never more than one. Clara's father, Collet Dobson Collet, sang professionally in the chorus at Covent Garden and was a friend and occasional publisher of Karl Marx. Towards the end of a long life, when he was already in his eighties, Dobson Collet wrote a history of the centuries-long campaign to abolish taxes on

115

newspapers.[3] The history he wrote began with Milton, recorded the struggle to get rid of newspaper tax by the Chartists, with which he had been involved in the role of secretary, and ended with the campaign's eventual success in 1855.

Clara and her two sisters went to North London Collegiate School, opened in 1850 by Frances Mary Buss, and offering a wider and more modern curriculum by the time Clara was a schoolgirl there in the 1870s than almost all boys' schools of the day. Clara left the school when she was just 17 to take up a post as assistant mistress at the newly opened Wyggeston High School for Girls in Leicester. She taught there for seven years, mostly the older classes, while working to pass the two parts of her London BA as an external student and to gather a teaching qualification at the same time. Miss Buss sent her a postcard in 1880 to congratulate her on becoming at 20 North London's first graduate.

Much later, Clara assembled and edited her diary entries between 1878 and 1885, presumably for publication, as 'Diary of a Young Assistant Mistress'.[4] In it she wrote about walks and friends and tennis and holidays and other

Fig 7.1   *Clara Collet aged twenty-one, when she was an assistant mistress at Wyggeston High School for Girls in Leicester.*

teachers. There were incipient love affairs which sadly came to nothing and an offer of marriage which she rejected and suffered over. There are regular entries about her pupils' examination results, and a moment of anxiety and subsequent depression as she contemplated humiliating failure teaching a test lesson at her old school as part of the 'teacher's exam', to be watched by Miss Buss. This test lesson, which she passed of course, was almost certainly taken under the aegis of the Council of the College of Preceptors. Miss Buss, as the council's first woman member, persuaded them in 1870 to start training classes for graduate secondary school teachers. Predictably, these classes were taken up with a good deal more enthusiasm by women teachers than by men. Clara wrote of school inspections, staff meetings, disagreements and expeditions. She mentioned her salary when she started at seventeen (£80 a year) and the fact that it had risen to £160 after seven years. She wrote about sermons and Unitarianism (she spent a lot of her free time with young men and women from local Unitarian families), and she wrote about her reading, which took an uncharacteristic turn for the worse (she wrote of 'inspissated gloom') as she dolefully made her way through the writers on education of the day, like Bain and Arnold and Fitch. She never quite lets us see her in the classroom with her pupils (very few women teachers ever do), but the sense that her role there was oddly uncomfortable is conveyed by several allusions to 'the worry of school' and by her comment – not long before she left teaching more or less for good to study for an MA in Moral and Political Philosophy at University College London (where she was the first woman to do so) –

> My views on every subject are growing more and more unpopularly unorthodox and I doubt very much whether I shall be able to teach children much longer; what I care about no one wants taught and I do not know other subjects well enough to hold my own as a first-class teacher.

Clara had enjoyed her own schooldays. She appreciated the teaching of Miss Buss herself and her staff of clever and committed women. She always managed her homework in less than the time allotted for it, and was inclined to regard as 'duffers' any girls who didn't. She had accepted that her only way of getting a chance to develop her own intellectual interests lay in becoming a teacher. Sometimes she longed to go to Girton, but her father wasn't rich enough, and she had always known that she would need to earn her living as soon as possible. So teaching it was, and she was not surprised to realise that the studies she pursued while she was teaching had the effect of distancing her from the classroom rather than strengthening her work within it.

Clara's life's work was not finally in women's or girls' education, but in women's employment. She is best known nowadays as an early woman civil servant, who rose to characteristically ambiguous heights in the Board of

Trade as an expert on women's work and pay. She did return to teaching
very briefly after finishing her MA, but then became a pioneer social researcher (another interesting area of professional development for women
in the 1880s). Her professional interests were as broad as those of many men
who went to the top of the Civil Service: she was an economist, a statistician,
a social researcher and an expert on policy and pay and working conditions.
In addition, she reviewed books and wrote articles, lectured, served on committees and wrote one book, *Educated Working Women*,[5] which was published
in 1902. She also read widely and with an eye for what a book or an author
might have to say to and about 'the female portion of the world'.

In addition, she indulged a private passion for her family's history and for
what the letters and diaries she found and organised revealed about women's
education in Dissenting families during the eighteenth and early nineteenth
centuries. She published some of this material privately and she left a good
deal of other material in a publishable state, though she presumably got cold
feet or was rebuffed when it came to actual publication.

By 1887 Clara was working on Charles Booth's survey of the London poor,
writing longish chapters on subjects like the range of school provision for
girls in the city and, at almost the other end of the spectrum, the conditions
of women workers across a whole range of trades, in small factories and
workshops or as piece workers at home. This meant visiting their homes and
workplaces, and though I cannot imagine her striking the women or the
employers she interviewed as grandly patrician, she must have seemed to
some of them to have come from another planet. She is free with expressions
of exasperation and dismay at the impossible situations in which these women
worked and brought up their children, and not above blaming the women
themselves occasionally for incompetence, ignorance and so on. But her
reports are wonderfully detailed, and she was scrupulously sensitive to the
differences between the women and their situations – economic, social and
individual differences – and to the undeniable usefulness to them of having
skills, however poorly rewarded. The strength of her reports lay in their sense
of these women's multiple vulnerabilities in the market place to husbands,
fathers and employers, so long as limited experience and education made
them reluctant to take responsibility for what they produced or for what they
were paid. She reported with feeling and knowledge from the front line, and
again and again she came back to the importance of education. And the
education she believed these women needed was always practical and moral
in about equal proportions. Here she is at the end of a long survey of
women's trades published in 1889:

> The something which should be done is to some extent being done already by
> quiet workers among the East End working girls, who, coming in contact with

them in their clubs, their evening classes and social gatherings and in their homes, know well that improvement in the condition of these girls is identical with improvement in their moral character. What is needed for working women in general is a more practical education in the Board Schools; greater facilities for the exercise of thrift, and definite instruction in the advantages and best methods of saving. If the women and girls will not go to the Post Office Savings Bank, is it quite absurd to suggest that the Post Office Savings Bank should go to the women and girls? And lastly, and not least, trade union is wanted; not union against employers, but union with them; a recognition on the one side of the need and advantage of having good organisers whose exceptional ability makes them worth an exceptional reward; and acknowledgement and acceptance on the other of the responsibility which lies with everyone whose position, talents, or advantages have made him his brother's keeper. The question of wages is trivial compared with the question of regularity of employment and kind and just treatment.[6]

The work Clara did for Booth's London survey earned her a place as a reporter on women's home work for the Royal Commission on Labour set up in 1891. From there she went to the Board of Trade, where she stayed until 1917, becoming eventually Senior Investigator for Women's Industries in the Commercial, Labour and Statistical departments there. She was that extremely rare bird for the time: a woman civil servant, who worked with men, in institutions organised by and for men and according to male traditions of professional behaviour and procedures. Yet her specialism was women's work, women's education and training and women's pay. Her professional life was constructed out of and also split along gender lines. She seems to have managed it all superbly, though an entry in her diary of 1910 records that she threatened to resign in order, as she put it, 'to speak freely about the way in which the women's side of the Labour Exchanges is being organised, capable women being subordinated to men who know nothing and care nothing about women's interests'. It was a rare outburst, and she was persuaded to stay.

Clara had a personal, practical and professional interest in education. Her research for Booth led her back to the need to improve schooling for working-class girls, though she was insistent that for the most part this should be matched to their domestic and social futures, that it should not be unduly academic and should focus on areas like child care, hygiene and family economy. She was also insistent that it should do more than this:

But the intellectual education of the factory girl and the child-nurse should not be neglected even for these more imperative and immediate wants; and that education can best be obtained through the medium of good literature. If these children are backward in everything else, in a knowledge of all that is termed 'life' they are only too precocious. They know evil so well in too many

cases that in offering them of the tree of knowledge we are but introducing
them to the good and helping them to discern it. We need not fear to put into
their hands, or to give them the key to the works of the great novelists and
essayists whom we have recognised as our greatest teachers and our best friends.[7]

Clara also maintained a lifelong interest in women teachers, and wrote up
some detailed research about what variously qualified teachers earned and
how they spent their money on rent, clothes and holidays.[8] She thought
and wrote with feeling about unmarried women and work and about poor
married women who *had* to work, and about the kinds of help government
and/or charity might offer such women. She occasionally wrote in a language
of neat platitudes – 'a boy's education is civic, a girl's domestic' or 'the rather
above the average woman is quite on a level with the average man' – which
are curiously empty of her own experience and that of her sisters and friends
and colleagues. Yet she had an abiding interest in the history of women's
education and in the contemporary need for a whole range of training and
education for girls and women.

Clara's background and schooling provided her with a broad culture. She
was well aware that few women of any class in England at the time could
equal that experience, and she was not above the occasional patronising
sarcasm at the expense of 'wives' and other women who were less serious and
knowledgeable than she was. However, she had also grown up believing that
an education must be put to work: to earn a living and to contribute to
society's improvement. She was contemptuous of what were often thought of
as 'accomplishments', and she was determined that a rational translation of
her own experience into the provision of education for all girls and women
should only be thought of and measured in terms of its usefulness and
relevance to present and future domestic and work possibilities, particularly
in the case of single women or widows.

It is possible to see her position on education as more than an aspect of
her own nature and her specialised professional interests. In some sense, it
was her Dissenting inheritance, learned as part of her own family's history of
educating girls and women. It is an inheritance she thought herself *formed* by,
and which interested her for other reasons as well. Two sets of letters that she
came across among her family papers supplied her (as they supply us) with
material for thinking about that inheritance, and particularly the form in
which beliefs about the education of women were often expressed. Both sets
of letters consist of men giving advice to women, on how to be women and
mothers and then, of course, on how to bring up their sons. This was not,
after all, a frivolous matter in Dissenting families, for the men from such
families continued to be denied entry to university until at least the 1820s.
And if fathers were the ideal educators of their sons, it was also accepted
that sons could be helped by having intelligent, knowledgeable mothers and

sisters. Clara could be dryly ironic about some of the formalised advice given by men to women, and there is no doubt that she would not have taken kindly to the sort of non-stop counselling her grandmother and great-aunts must have come to regard as a perpetual accompaniment to their every endeavour. Clara also had experience of her own Dissenting home, with its expectation that women were to be educated to be earners, for they were quite likely not to become wives and mothers. Both her father and her brother Wilfred (my grandfather) were able to make belated use of the access on offer from the 1820s onwards to University College, London – to take external degrees, in Law, in both their cases. And Clara was, as I have already pointed out, to profit later from the new access available to women in the 1880s to take an external BA and then her MA.

In 1933, Clara pruned and privately published the letters her grandfather John Dobson had written to his cousin Eliza Barker during the four years before their marriage in 1810. She called the volume, with characteristic edge, *The Letters of John to Eliza. A Four Years' Correspondence Course in the Education of Women. 1806–1810.* John's letters survived, presumably because Eliza kept them. Hers to him did not, though some that she wrote to her sister Mary later in life do still exist. Sometimes, John's letters read like love letters to the eighteen-year-old cousin he is preparing for marriage to him, though they are somewhat uneasy love letters, for he clearly wondered occasionally whether his future bride was quite good enough for him. He writes as a hopeful young businessman of twenty-seven, trying to establish himself in shipping and overseas trade. His sermon to this young woman is a good deal more practical and down-to-earth than James Fordyce's 'Sermons to Young Women',[9] in which young women are advised to remember that their 'business chiefly is to read Men'. As John writes to Eliza, with his own brand of delightfully egotistical logic, 'it is only in the event that you can avail yourself of opportunities to cultivate your mind, that I can rationally hope to make you permanently happy'.[10]

John, as it happens, is writing to a young teacher; for Eliza and her sister Mary, who was four years younger, worked as assistant teachers at Miss Devall's school in Sloane Street, Chelsea. This does not, however, encourage him to regard Eliza as in any way his equal, and he is not reticent in offering his advice on virtually every facet of her life: on shoes and hats and dresses; on health and the benefits to it of walks and dancing; on grammar and style and usage and what she ought to read to keep them in good repair; on travel and the miracles of inoculation and on how to negotiate a pay rise without looking greedy. He assumes that she will have a globe or atlas as well as a dictionary by her side at all times, and particularly while she is reading his letters. It is her duty to teach the children in her school and his, as he sees it, to teach her. His letters may be read, as his granddaughter Clara suggests, as a textbook, and Eliza seems sometimes to have found them wearisome. They come accompanied by books and papers and magazines – *The Edinburgh Review* and *The Weekly Messenger,* for instance – and always there are detailed instructions about how to read and about the good that will come from doing so. He sends her Maria Edgeworth's stories:

> Keep them by you dear Girl, and now and then *when your heart* is so disposed read *one* of them. I send the Popular Tales with them which are also as excellent as the others. I have added two small volumes of poetry by Bowles which you have already seen but which I wish you at your leisure to *enjoy* – do not however in attending to the agreeable, forget the useful – study the Scientific Dialogues with steady and unwearied attention untill you find yourself completely mistress of them. Never take them up when you are not perfectly disposed for them – and never suffer anything to pass until you understand it – *it does not signify how little you acquire at a time provided that be accurately acquired* – do not disturb yourself if you should find you have forgotten what you had once acquired – *it is for a time the case with everybody* – begin again – if you meet with anything you cannot clearly comprehend give me the page and subject and I will try to render it more clear to you.[11]

The pedagogic tone is unrelenting and unacknowledged. John is pleased to think of Eliza becoming a teacher and admits that he would never have the patience to work with children himself, whereas 'it is extremely pleasant to me to think of you as interested about children'. He wants her to dress fashionably and take an interest in her clothes, but he is also certain that 'there is much more Economy in your qualifying yourself to direct the Education of your children should you be blessed with any than there would be in saving the expense of making your new stock of Cloathes'. In fact, they were to have six children of their own. The links between Eliza's current work as a teacher and her future responsibilities as a mother are spelled out as John pictures her surrounded by the children she teaches, and imagines her passing on to them information from the books and newspapers he supplies her with:

> Indeed I do conceive that you might very much increase your powers of usefulness & the interest you would take in many of the articles . . . were you to read them to the children you are fond of. Surely the little Girl who took so much delight in hearing Miss B— talk about Astronomy would love to listen to her – and would you not delight to fill their little minds with truths and drive away those prejudices which you say sometimes disturb you.[12]

Irritated at times by her apparent complacency and by her unwillingness to tell him her innermost thoughts, he sometimes criticises her, for 'ludicrous blunders' in her letters, for using 'get' rather than 'become' and 'that' as an expletive. Quite early in the correspondence he writes frankly of his misgivings:

And to begin – and I will confess to you that I am sensible you are deficient in many of those accomplishments which are universally considered of some importance to a female. You do not sing, or play, or paint, or speak Italian, or write French with fluency – you possess no extraordinary taste in dress – converse very little – are neglectful of the trifling forms & ceremonies which are thought essential in society – and would not shine particularly in cutting up a goose for a large party at the head of your own *table*, nor in doing the general business of it. I am further sensible that although you have read much, it has consequently *hitherto* been but of little advantage to you. I am aware that you are not a perfect beauty – that there are figures much more graceful than yours is. I know that your constitution is indifferent – that it is such as to expect you to be frequently unwell ... I think I hear you almost breathless cry out Stop – and ask me how I ever could have told you 'you were exquisitely dear to me – that I was satisfied with you and that you had more than answered all my expectations?' – I said so, my dear Friend, because I felt it was the truth – and I believe it still.[13]

She seems to have taken the huff, and his concluding sentiment did not let him off. Nor was this the last time he offended her. Eventually he bought a grand piano for her future use, after four years of nagging her to practise, and to practise playing 'good' music rather than bad, indeed 'scientific' music rather than the simple tunes she was used to, by which he seems to have meant the more complex counterpoint of Handel and Haydn. There are harangues on poetry, on taste, on science and mathematics and on being *au fait* with foreign affairs. These were the years of Napoleon's dominion over most of Europe, and John's business took him abroad, most often to Malta. Years later, his granddaughter Clara's pretty sparingly used editorial pencil is wielded to amputate some longish tirades on electricity, magnetism and other modern marvels.

Clara published these letters, I think, out of a double sense of their interest. She used them to illustrate the historical fact that the education of women had been taken seriously in Unitarian families and that it was an education for real life, by and large, rather than for social accomplishments or even intellectual benefit; but she also used them to emphasise the contradictions, as she perceived them, in educating women beyond a certain point if they were to marry and have children. She made it clear that she much preferred her great-aunt Mary to Eliza, who so stubbornly resisted her future husband's efforts to educate her. Mary, who did not marry and lived to the age of 93, was a woman after Clara's own heart, a woman of intellect, sense and spirit. John is gently mocked for his consistently pedagogic tone. Eliza, however, is despaired of for having no real intellectual interests of her own.

Pamela by Samuel Richardson is not one of the novels John recommends to Eliza, though it is hard to believe she did not read it anyway. The peculiar wooing Eliza received might well have provided her with an interpretative strategy for reading Richardson's novel. For in the place of John's unflagging transmission of his own views on matrimony and the role and duties of women, Richardson imagined the woman herself and literally gave voice to her struggle to become the mother and teacher who would be seen to vindicate, through her enchanting (but also enchanted) submission, the limitations set on her own education and the efficacy of a regime organised to produce men and to control the influence women had on them.

That tradition of men advising women on the principles of modern childcare and education goes even further back in Clara's family. More than fifty years before John started writing to Eliza, in 1752 (twelve years after *Pamela* was published and ten years before *Émile* burst upon the world), a great-uncle shared by John and Eliza, called Joseph Collet, wrote three long letters to his future sister-in-law, Sarah Lasswell, apparently in response to her request for his 'Opinion on that most Difficult Subject the Education of Children'.[14] Clara had these typed and must have wanted to do something with them. Neither Joseph nor Sarah had children of their own when the letters were written, so one may presume that experience was not an essential qualification for an exercise of this kind. It seems likely that Joseph (like Richardson's Pamela) would have read John Locke's *Some Thoughts Concerning Education*,[15] and that his own thoughts were influenced by a need to adumbrate a quite different educational regime, which was not intended for Locke's 'young Gentleman', but for the sons of Dissenting middle-class families. The letters suggest that rationality, moderation and good sense are the essential qualities for child-rearing, that education is principally a family responsibility, and that the chief hazards faced by young children are likely to be at the hands of nurses and servants and their mothers themselves. Childhood had not yet been marked out as a separate terrain, requiring a specially trained workforce. But whereas Locke focuses on the figure of the tutor, Joseph Collet regards the family, and especially the father, as primarily responsible for a boy's education.

The letters move through the years of the child's growing up (the child is a boy, of course), so that the first letter takes him to five or six and the establishment of good habits, through kindly persuasion and truthfulness. There will be early formal teaching of the alphabet, numbers, world geography, the reading of moral stories and fables and a persistent focus on children's developing habits of care, accuracy and attention. Punishment is to be avoided. It is clear in a number of ways that this is an upbringing designed for children growing up in the Dissenting middle class of the mid-eighteenth century: it is anti-aristocratic, anti-classical, liberal in some respects, in favour of French and Dutch (the mercantile languages of the period, though an earlier generation of the family put Portuguese before French) rather than

Latin and Greek. These, Joseph insists, are fine for children 'if you design them for Law, Physick or Divinity', but certainly not otherwise:

> I could wish our School learning for young Gentlemen from 10 or 12 years of age to their prenticeships was Carry'd on in a Different manner than it is at present, of what use can be their reading Ovid and many other Heathen authors but to Learn their Superstitions, and what Service can all their non-sense of their Gods and Godesses amours, dissensions, Battles &c. be of but only to fill Children's Tender minds with foolish Ideas, Ridiculous fancys, Idle Superstitions and above all (as they are growing to an age so susceptible of and Inclinable to amorous desires) Their Lewd and Wanton Storys must Infallibly tend to the blowing up the Sparks of Lust and Impurity which it is one great design of Education to damp and extinguish; How much better would it be if some books of Christian morality were read in the place of those heathen authors.

In Joseph Collet's universe, children will be encouraged to show kindness and generosity to the poor, though they must also learn very early on to distinguish the industrious poor from beggars, to whom they should not give money (a principle adhered to with somewhat discomfiting enthusiasm by Clara more than a hundred years later in her support for the Charity Organisation Society).[16] The concentration here is firmly on the education of boys, for it is through boys and then through men as fathers that family order and happiness are to be achieved:

> How Happy is the Father of an Orderly and Well Govern'd Family. He acts as a King in his own house and sees his Laws Chearfully and punctually obey'd, as they are not the effects of meer Arbitrary will and absolute Power but wise, usefull and necessary to the Hapiness of every one of his Children.

By the age of ten or eleven – as the third letter asserts – the purpose of education is premised on a future when the young 'must soon quit their fathers House and go into the wide World, the young men to their prenticeship and the young ladys to be mistresses of familys Themselves'. And these families are the model of order and sense, with the father presiding as inspiration for and regulator of a regime of relative permissiveness. The historian Rosalind Mitchison has reminded us how relative that permissiveness was likely to be, however, in the middle of the eighteenth century:

> Individualism may mean permissiveness. In the reaction to both formalism and puritanism it often did. But it could also mean the expression of the personality of the father at the expense of everyone else . . . The private person with whom Locke's political thought was concerned was an adult male landowner. No one else counted as an individual, certainly not a servant, an employee, a woman.[17]

Joseph Collet was a man of his time who did not altogether ignore the education of girls. A final image might have resonated with Clara's somewhat contrasting memories of her own childhood in North London, reading Shake-speare with her brothers and sisters and the younger daughters of Karl Marx:

> Where there are several young Ladies in a family it is a very Good Method to let
> the Eldest read for an Hour whilst the rest work and then the Second take it for
> another hour and the eldest sit down to work, and so on till each has read Her
> hour, Thus they'll Improve in reading and working at once, and have food for
> the mind as well as Employment for the hands, and when your son is at home
> and can be spared from other Studys or bussiness, Let him read to them (as of
> an Evening) whilst all the Ladies work, The books to be Chosen are such as will
> both divert and Instruct as Telemachus and the Travels of Cyrus, Love makes a
> Man, the provoked Husband, and Cato are the best Romances and plays I know
> of,[18] but I should be very Carefull of these sort of books, Good History, as
> Prideauxs Connection of ye old and New Testamts, Echards Eclesiastical His-
> tory, Rollins Roman and Antient History, Rapins History of England &c. are
> what I should prefer, as giving us a real account of things and not filling the
> mind with foolish Romantick Ideas, without any foundation in truth, but of all
> books for young Ladies I prefer the Spectators Tatlers and Guardians, as soon
> as ever they are capable of understanding them.

Carefully circumscribed and marked out here are the purposes and limita-tions of a woman's education, the uses to which it might be put, its domestica-tion within the family and a sense of reading as accompaniment to useful and profitable activity rather than as an end in itself. There is the separation of the male and female economies of space and time: the time spent (or all too easily wasted) by women is compared with the time used gainfully by men. Even the care of young children, if it is taken seriously and done with a clear sense of outcome, is better performed by men.

It is possible to trace many of Clara's beliefs in the need for a practical and moral education for working-class girls back to this well-developed tradition of educational thinking in the middle of the eighteenth century. It was not an especially religious education, but it was certainly meant to serve as a practical preparation for modern life and for business. Did Matthew Arnold have such 'Protestant Nonconformist' treatises (or at least their contempor-ary versions) in mind when he railed at the narrowness, the provincialism and the philistinism that his *Culture and Anarchy* (1869) was intent on extir-pating? When he wrote there of 'our middle class, the great representative of trade and Dissent, with its maxims of every man for himself in business, every man for himself in religion', he could be said to be reacting to Clara's Dissenting heritage, and to its place in the tradition he blamed so violently for the potential anarchy and cultural confusion of his day, despite the luke-warm interest in religion displayed by Clara's forebears. He was also alluding, presumably, to the grim utilitarianism represented by Dickens's Thomas Gradgrind, that 'man of realities'.[19] Arnold warned against those who 'will try to give the masses, as they call them, an intellectual food prepared and adapted in the way they think proper for the actual condition of the masses'. 'Culture works differently', he wrote:

> It does not try to teach down to the level of inferior classes; it does not try to win them for this or that sect of its own, with ready-made judgments and watchwords. It seeks to do away with classes; to make the best that has been thought and known in the world current everywhere; to make all men live in an atmosphere of sweetness and light, where they may use ideas, as it uses them itself, freely, – nourished, and not bound by them . . . This is the *social idea*; and the men of culture are the true apostles of equality.

It is true that there is not much truck with Matthew Arnold's 'sweetness and light' in Clara Collet's inheritance, and a good deal more of the 'energy, self-reliance, and capital' Arnold warned against. Almost exactly 150 years after Joseph Collet wrote his letters to Sarah Lasswell, Clara registered her own sense of history and change:

> Our pioneers were full of enthusiasm in their journey to the promised land where sex barriers should be removed and sex prejudices die away. Those of us who passed through the gates which they opened for us were (I am afraid it must be admitted) often unpopular among those we left behind and were delighted with the novelty of the country before us. The next generation are coming into the field under new conditions. To begin with, it is realised that work is work; next, that economic liberty is only obtained by the sacrifice of personal freedom; that there is nothing very glorious in doing work that any average man can do as well, now that we are no longer told we cannot do it. The glamour of economic independence has faded, although the necessity for it is greater than ever.[20]

I have found myself looking to women of Clara's generation for solidarity, a sense of historical continuity, even some recognition of what it might look like fifty years after her death. It is possible to feel relief that she avoided the snobberies and grand unrealities of Arnold's *Culture and Anarchy* while also feeling sorry that she could not envisage a time when education for women as well as for men might be thought of as more than instrumental, more than an aspect of social reconstruction. There is a certain irony in considering the opposing voices in this debate of the second half of the nineteenth century at a moment at the end of the twentieth century, when public discourse on education is usually stripped of idealism in the interests of achieving precisely those minimum levels of literacy and numeracy which were being sought then. Yet what a later generation of women undoubtedly shares with Clara are the ambiguities, the experience of change and its surprises, the continuing need to think about girls' education as inseparable from class and economics as well as from families and children. Clara thought and wrote out of a sense of contemporary life and out of her sense of herself as an anomaly, a woman living her life as few women had done before. The privileges and the constraints of her growing-up may have seduced her into a view of public policy on the education of working-class girls, which overrode the excitements of her own intellectual development. There is certainly no triumphalism in anything she wrote and she was not given to utopian visions. There is, though, careful and serious reflection on just how far things had changed and just how much there was still to do.

NOTES

1. Jane Miller, *Seductions. Studies in Reading and Culture* (1990). I have also written about Clara Collet in *School for Women* (1996).

2. Samuel Collet's letters to his brother Joseph on this subject were privately published by Clara in a booklet called *William Whiston's Disciples. In correspondence with each other 1723–1768.*

3. Collet Dobson Collet, *History of the Taxes on Knowledge. Their Origin and Repeal* (1899), 2 vols. Introduced by George Jacob Holyoake.

4. Clara's diaries and other unpublished writings are in my possession. There are copies of most of them in the Modern Records Centre of the University of Warwick Library.

5. Clara E. Collet, *Educated Working Women* (1902).

6. Clara E. Collet, 'Women's Work', in Charles Booth, ed., *Labour and Life of the People. Volume 1: East London* (1889), p. 476.

7. Clara E. Collet, 'Secondary Education – Girls', in Charles Booth, ed., *Labour and Life of the People. Volume II: London Continued* (1891), p. 588.

8. Clara E. Collet, 'The Expenditure of Middle Class Working Women', in *Educated Working Women* (see n. 5 above).

9. James Fordyce, *Sermons to Young Women* (1766), 3rd edn, 2 vols.

10. Clara E. Collet, *Letters of John to Eliza* (1933), p. 22.

11. *Ibid.*, p. 19.

12. *Ibid.*, p. 72.

13. *Ibid.*, p. 15.

14. These are in my possession, in the original manuscript and in the typed version.

15. John Locke, *Some Thoughts Concerning Education* (1693), in James L. Axtell, ed., *The Educational Writings of John Locke* (Cambridge, 1968).

16. For an account of the society's role in the debate see Gareth Stedman Jones, *Outcast London. A Study in the Relationship between Classes in Victorian Society* (Harmondsworth, 1984).

17. Rosalind Mitchison, 'The Numbers Game', in *The New Review* 4:47 (1978).

18. Addison comes curiously out of this recommended reading list: as the author of the 'romantic' play *Cato*, usually thought of as a neo-classical tragedy of a 'stern' kind, and the editor of *The Spectator*, which Joseph Collet sees as suitable for young ladies who might otherwise be tempted by foolish romantic ideas.

19. In Charles Dickens', *Hard Times.*

20. Clara E. Collet, 'Through Fifty Years: The Economic Progress of Women', in *Educated Working Women*, p. 142.

PART THREE

Work and Professional Life for Lower Middle-Class Women

CHAPTER EIGHT

Sarah Jane Bannister and Teacher Training in Transition 1870–1918

WENDY ROBINSON

Tucked inconspicuously away in Barnet Local Studies Centre is a large and impressive portrait in oils of Sarah Jane Bannister, first woman Alderman of the Borough of Hendon.[1] Evoking a genteel and learned presence, it portrays a lone elderly woman with cropped steely grey hair and round spectacles, formally dressed in civic robes, holding an open book against a background of library shelves. Painted to commemorate her retirement from public office in 1939, it once occupied pride of place in Hendon Public Library. Proposed by Hendon Borough Council and funded with private subscriptions, such a portrait clearly represented an uncommon and generous gesture. To the present viewer it suggests that this imposing looking woman, with her piercing blue eyes and firm smile, was, in her time, someone who was much valued and respected. Indeed, it begs a whole host of questions about her career and public life. Now, damaged, dusty and largely forgotten, the portrait has been removed from the public gaze. This sadly neglected artefact provides a fitting historical metaphor for Sarah Jane Bannister and many other women like her, who were once much esteemed by those whose lives they touched in their professional and public capacities, but who have since been largely forgotten and overlooked in official local or educational histories.

For over sixty years Sarah Bannister occupied an important place in the educational world of elementary teacher training, school inspection and local government. She spent many years working with pupil teachers as the only woman principal of one of London's late nineteenth-century pupil-teacher centres before moving on to become principal of an innovative new non-residential training college under the London County Council. She retired from official working life as a Local Inspector of Schools, but soon moved into Hendon's local politics where she continued to champion various educational causes. In 1897 Sarah Bannister was on an influential government committee on the pupil-teacher system and teacher training. Her own evidence on the experience of instructing female pupil teachers, as well as her broader views on the future development of teacher training, was deemed very significant at the time.[2] Whilst she clearly achieved some local acclaim by the time of her retirement, the substance of her professional life and career has been lost to history. This might perhaps be because she was one of many active female educational practitioners whose success was met daily at the chalk face and not in published works, or because the world in which she operated was that socially nebulous and constantly changing one of elementary school teaching.[3] Individual woman teachers as unique individuals with specific personal and domestic as well as professional circumstances remain fairly elusive, shadowy figures to the educational historian. Dina Copelman, in her extensive work on London's women teachers, eloquently expresses this frustration: 'How intimately can we get to know the individual teacher? The sources are fickle, sometimes yielding sharply focused snapshots of life and a personality, other times hinting at deep mysteries but providing little detail, yet other times remaining obdurately silent.'[4] It is likely that there were many other women teachers like Sarah Bannister, who led important and interesting professional lives but who have not as yet caught the attention or the imagination of researchers willing to pursue the faint, patchy or even empty traces they have left behind.

Sarah Bannister's long career, whilst noteworthy in itself, presents an illuminating exemplar not only of how important aspects of elementary teacher training were honed and refined but also how they offered ambitious women teachers excellent opportunities for enhanced professional development. This challenges many of the traditional, negative historical representations of women elementary teachers.[5] At the same time, as this essay uncovers the story of Sarah Bannister's career and educational vision, it will be seen that both her aspirations for herself and for trainee and serving women teachers exposed certain educational, professional and moral tensions which turned upon critical aspects of social class and gender. She was steeped in the elementary school world infamous within a class-ridden and class-segregated system for its narrowness, low standards and dominance by the working class.[6] It was also a highly feminised world, dogged with low expectations and low status. As she strived to broaden and elevate the prospect of elementary school teaching, whilst at the same time improving her own professional position, Sarah Bannister had somehow to find a way through those pervasive social class and gendered constraints. For her, and for many other teachers of her ilk, politicians and educationists, the answer for elementary school teachers lay in upward social mobility through a more advanced educational, social and cultural outlook. The injection into the profession of teachers drawn from higher social class backgrounds was also welcomed. Ultimately, this idea was to shape the development of educational policy which envisaged a different and much closer relationship between secondary education, teacher training and higher education. Ironically, whilst this has traditionally been celebrated as a natural and positive development in the history of the elementary teaching profession, it was to compromise the accessibility and openness of the profession to children from working-class backgrounds, as well as the importance of the practical component of professional training. Moreover, with the eventual decline of the pupil-teacher system in the early years of the twentieth century in favour of a more college- or university-based approach, the education of intending teachers was placed under much firmer central control and supervision with the gradual exclusion of serving practitioners from the process. This alienation has had lasting implications for the development of teacher training and for the professional status and autonomy of the teaching profession.[7]

Very little is known of Sarah Bannister's early life or family background other than that which can be gleaned from her birth certificate. Indeed, for the whole of her life, only tantalising snippets of her personal family circumstances can be glimpsed.[8] Born in 1858 in Somerset, Sarah's father was recorded as a journeyman mason by trade. By the time of Sarah's marriage in 1881, her father was recorded as a builder. This briefest of records suggests that her socio-economic origins were originally located in the skilled, artisan working class. It is a strong possibility that Sarah became an apprentice pupil teacher before entering Tottenham Teacher Training College.[9] Even at a young age, Sarah must have demonstrated her aptitude for the teaching profession. On completion of her own teacher training she was appointed by Tottenham College as a resident lecturer, where she remained for two years until her marriage. Aged 23 she married Henry Bannister, a widowed schoolmaster fifteen years her senior. Henry's own father, John Mugford Bannister, was also a schoolmaster, suggesting not only that Sarah might have married into an established teaching dynasty but also that her marriage was an affirmation of her own rising social status to upper working- or lower middle-class professional respectability.

Marriage to Henry possibly gave Sarah an opening into the work of the London School Board (LSB). He himself was involved in an experimental evening school project, working with pupil teachers and uncertificated assistants. In January 1882, Sarah Bannister was appointed by the LSB to teach physiology and domestic economy at the William Street and Sumner Road evening classes for pupil teachers.[10] At the same time she was also appointed as an inspector for the Bradford School Board. It is unclear whether she was required to relocate to Bradford for this purpose, or whether she remained in London and travelled to Bradford on a regular basis. What is clear is that right from the start of her marriage, she continued to actively develop her own career, combining marriage, motherhood and professional life. Sarah and Henry had one daughter – Winifred Katherine. Quite how Sarah found the management of this potentially conflicting lifestyle is unknown but it cannot have been an easy balancing act, particularly when social mores and expectations were unsympathetic towards working wives and mothers.[11]

1884 marked a significant and exciting turning point in Sarah Bannister's professional career. At the relatively tender age of 26 she had already built an impressive range of professional experience working with trainee teachers, pupil teachers and inspecting ordinary elementary schools. Now she was to become a practical pioneer in the transformation of the pupil-teacher system. This system, originally introduced in 1846, was a predominantly school-based, apprenticeship model of initial teacher training for the elementary profession, which formed the backbone of training and supply for over sixty years. During the 1880s and 1890s specialised pupil-teacher centres were developed in which all the pupil teachers in a town or region would come together for systematic academic and some professional instruction. Eventually pupil teachers spent up to half their time in the centres, as pupils, and the other half in their practice schools, as teachers. The centres, which have been largely overlooked in histories of education, worked together with the local practice schools to hone and refine their novice teachers and significantly raised academic and professional standards.[12]

The LSB, renowned nationally for its progressive reforms, was one of the leading authorities in the development of the pupil-teacher centres. Both Sarah and Henry had worked on an early scheme which offered additional instruction to pupil teachers at evening classes. In 1884, recognising that better trained pupil teachers would ultimately raise overall academic standards within its elementary schools, the LSB was set to launch a new and more radical scheme which was designed to offer pupil teachers half-time instruction in central classes held during normal school hours. Sarah and Henry were chosen to pilot this innovation in London's first official centres. Sarah Bannister was appointed as headmistress of a centre for girls in a school room under the Lycett Memorial Chapel, Mile End Road, and Henry Bannister as a headmaster of a centre for boys based in the East End's famous university settlement, Toynbee Hall.[13]

As a result of their pioneering work, eleven, and subsequently twelve, new centres were established. Sarah Bannister remained London's only female centre principal, at Stepney's Centre for Girls, until it closed in 1908. As well as managing a full staff of assistant teachers, liaising with local schools which her pupil teachers attended for the teaching side of their training and reporting to the LSB, she also maintained an active teaching presence and was responsible for the instruction of reading, recitation, French and needlework. During the early years of her headship at Stepney, she also found time to further her own academic education. Having enrolled for a part-time correspondence degree course with the University of St Andrews, the first university to offer women the opportunity of acquiring near-degree status, she was awarded an LLA. Interestingly, Henry's subsequent career development appears to have been less eminent than Sarah's. When the LSB properly organised its centres across London, he became an assistant, not headmaster, at the Hackney Centre.[14]

Sarah Bannister's position as headmistress of the Stepney centre opened up a whole range of important professional and social connections which were to exercise a profound influence not only in the progression of her own career but also in the development and refinement of her particular vision for the training of teachers. Perhaps one of the most fundamental of these connections was her association with Canon Samuel Barnett and his wife Henrietta at Toynbee Hall. The Barnetts had magnanimously hosted the first centre at Toynbee Hall under Henry's headship and from then on maintained a deep interest and commitment in the broader intellectual and cultural education of London's pupil teachers. It was Sarah and Henry Bannister who formed the linchpin of this activity and who also became good friends of the Barnetts.[15]

Toynbee Hall became the home of the London Pupil Teachers Association (LPTA), established in 1886 with a debating society, reading circle and large competitive athletic and rowing associations. With an impressive upper- and middle-class patronage, the LPTA became an essential and integral part of the social scene of London's centres.[16] Amongst its patrons were a number of leading political and educational figures including Sir Lyon Playfair, Dr Montagu Butler, The Hon. Alfred Lyttelton and Dr Gladstone. Links were forged with the Universities of Oxford and Cambridge when Canon Barnett formed a scholarship committee, committed to raising funds to send a few of the very best male pupil teachers to these universities. In 1890 a girls' association was established with Philippa Fawcett as president, later followed by Mrs Henrietta Barnett. As with the boys' section, the girls' association attracted the patronage of a number of influential society ladies, as well as leading women educationists such as Miss Buss, Miss Clough and Miss Wordsworth. Each of the London centres had a branch and weekly or fortnightly 'five o'clock tea' meetings were held sometimes in the centre or, more commonly, at the houses of the lady associates. Activities for girls included the reading of books and plays, music recitals, outings, tennis parties, swimming galas, amateur dramatics, fancy work classes, games clubs and simple lectures on art and social subjects.[17] The nucleus of the girls' association were the Stepney pupil teachers and Sarah Bannister was recorded as never having missed a meeting or social gathering.

Clearly, the LPTA afforded pupil teachers hitherto unrealisable social and cultural opportunities and exposed them to people and places outside their normal social circles. It was officially acknowledged and applauded for its commitment to elevating the culture and tone of pupil teachers and was held up as a model to centres across the country. By exposing pupil teachers to the good influence of highly educated and cultured men and women and encouraging good citizenship, team spirit and fair play, the LPTA hoped to improve the overall tone and bearing of future elementary school teachers.[18] At the same time, the LPTA offered centre teachers the opportunity to socialise and engage with influential society men and women whose social positions were clearly much higher than their own. Employment as a centre teacher was not merely a job – it was a way of life in which the day-to-day mundane aspects of educating future elementary teachers became suffused with a systematic programme of social and cultural enhancement, to the mutual benefit of students and staff alike. The involvement of middle-class reformers and philanthropists in the social life of pupil teachers raises a whole range of important questions relating to social class conflict, culture and the socialisation of the elementary teaching profession, some of which have been addressed in the work of Dina Copelman.[19]

Perhaps because of her connections with the Barnetts and Toynbee Hall as well as the fact that she was becoming an established woman educationist, Sarah Bannister was invited to join a prestigious and influential Departmental Committee on the Pupil Teacher System which was appointed in January 1897 to investigate the working of the pupil-teacher system and to recommend any improvements. She was one of three women on a committee of twelve, which was mainly represented by leading HMI, clergy and training college principals. She was actively committed to her position on the committee which met twice weekly from January to June 1897 on Monday afternoons and Thursday mornings to hear evidence from witnesses. She only missed one of thirty such sessions and presumably had to attend many more committee meetings for the assessment of the overall findings and writing of the final report. As well as giving her own evidence as a witness, she pursued a clear agenda in questioning other witnesses, contributing to nearly every session. It is from her evidence and questioning that much of her vision for teacher training, discussed below, can be drawn. In essence the 1898 Departmental Committee was unable to condone the long-term future of pupil teaching and recommended that intending teachers should be relocated into the secondary sector where greater emphasis would be placed on their academic rather than professional preparation. The pupil-teacher centres were criticised for their professional and social narrowness and for subordinating educational aims to pressure of examinations. Part of its vision was for the perceived educational and cultural 'narrowness' of the elementary school sector to be bolstered and enhanced by the injection of intending teachers from more cultured and higher social class backgrounds. This vision resonated with Sarah Bannister's own outlook on the future of pupil teaching and was one which was also publicly promoted by Toynbee Hall.[20] She was not afraid of stating her position on the pupil-teacher system – a position which for its extremity was at odds with that of her colleagues as well as her employer. So incensed were many of her fellow London centre principals at her evidence to the 1898 committee that they submitted an official complaint to the LSB. She was accused of exaggerating the extent to which overwork and overstrain amongst female pupil teachers was a problem as well as the extent to which probationers were appointed before they reached the age of fourteen years.[21] Faced with such evidence it is difficult to assess whether Sarah Bannister, for the overall sake of pupil teachers, exaggerated her dissatisfaction, or whether she presented a true picture. Whatever the answer, it can only be inferred that this difficult situation must have been awkward for Sarah's husband in his position at the Hackney centre.

In the decade immediately following the 1898 Departmental Committee Report, Sarah Bannister continued with her work at Stepney, but a radical transformation of the pupil-teacher system was afoot. In line with the Departmental Committee's recommendations, the Board of Education introduced a range of policy initiatives which were to lead to the ultimate demise of pupil teaching and the centres. New regulations for pupil teachers were introduced in 1903 to enable intending teachers to spend four years in attendance at a secondary school prior to taking up their apprenticeship at the age of sixteen years. The practical aspects of the pupil teachers' curriculum were gradually eroded and in 1907 the introduction of the bursar scheme offered a revolutionary alternative to the traditional method of pupil teachership and dealt the final death blow to the centres. Existing centres closed down and no new centres were given recognition. By this time, school boards had given way to local education authorities, with all of their powers to provide local elementary, secondary and teacher training provision.

London's Stepney centre closed on 4 May 1908. One day later, Sarah Bannister, '. . . well fitted by qualifications and experience', was appointed principal of a new London County Council (LCC) teacher training initiative – a non-residential day training college at Moorfields for 312 women.[22] Before fully launching herself into her new role she secured permission from the LCC to take an extended leave of absence. She wished to visit a number of similar educational institutions on the Continent to broaden her experience and to inform her practice at Moorfields. Whilst at Moorfields she continued to promote the social and cultural education of her students. As well as evening socials and soirées becoming a regular feature of college life, Sarah Bannister worked hard to create a congenial and cultured college environment, with the purchase of new furniture, paintings and books.[23] Moorfields was not a long-lived venture and was only ever housed in temporary buildings. As a war measure in 1915 Moorfields closed and its students dispersed amongst its sister LCC colleges at Greystoke Place, Furzedown and Avery Hill.[24] For the remainder of her professional working life, until she retired from the LCC in 1919, Sarah Bannister served as an assistant inspector of schools.[25]

At the end of the war she retired from professional work and was invited by the Hendon Women Citizens' Council to offer herself for election to the then Hendon Urban District Council. She was duly elected and served without interruption until 1938, when she finally retired. When Hendon became a borough in 1932 Sarah Bannister was one of the first aldermen to be elected and the only woman to receive that distinction. She served on almost every statutory committee of the council, as well as on many subcommittees. The bulk of her work, however, lay with the Education Committee and she was the prime mover in the founding of the Hendon Free Library. At one time she was the Council's representative on the National Association of Education Committees and on the Assessment Committee for Central Middlesex. She was also Council representative on the Garden Suburb Institute Council, on the governing body of the Henrietta Barnett School and the Hendon County School.[26] To mark twenty years of service to the civic life of Hendon, Sarah was presented with a portrait of herself in oils at a special ceremony in the Town Hall in March 1939. Sarah died of cancer aged 83 on 16 March 1942 attended by her only daughter, Winifred.

This brief outline of Sarah Bannister's career, which spanned almost a century of change and continuity in education as well as the world at large, clearly does little justice to the full richness and depth of her personal life story. Yet it does demonstrate a remarkable consistency in terms of the development of her professional and public service and suggests a life driven by a particular vision of education as both personally and socially transformative. Indeed, it would be fitting to say that Sarah Bannister was a practical visionary in the fullest sense of the term. Her ideas about education and the training of teachers for the elementary profession were not just of a cerebral or philanthropic nature – they were rooted in years of professional service in schools, with trainee and serving teachers. From the time that she completed her own training for the teaching profession in the late 1870s until a few years before her death in 1942 she was actively dedicated to educational practice. Moreover, her own life exemplified the very personal development and social improvement that she envisaged for the elementary teaching profession as a whole.

In essence, her educational vision was for an intellectually, socially and culturally empowered elementary teaching force which in turn would bestow the benefits of its wisdom and experience upon the nation's children. In her

Fig 8.1   *Sarah Jane Bannister was justifiably proud of her position as Alderman of the London Borough of Hendon and sent out this photograph as her 'Christmas Wishes' in 1935.*

practice, her dealings with her employers, her professional and social associations and her contribution to the 1898 Departmental Committee, she honed,
developed and expressed this general principle. Her vision was not, however,
unproblematic. Rather, as she sought to promote her ideas about teacher
training and suitable women candidates for the profession, she struggled
with a fundamental dilemma which not only exposed difficult social class
tensions but also raised the spectre of an elementary teaching force rich in
its own personal, social and cultural education but practically unable to teach.
Significantly, this dichotomy between on the one hand securing a highly
educated, intellectually rigorous teaching force whilst on the other ensuring an equal capacity in practical teaching power has long haunted initial
teacher training and is arguably still not fully resolved at the present time.
Sarah Bannister's particular focus was upon the education of girls and women,
possibly because of the range of her own teaching experience and because of
the dominant female presence within the elementary teaching profession.
She extended her vision at two levels: to female pupil teachers who would
form the bulk of the future profession; and to serving women teachers whose
conditions of service and opportunities for career development were deserving of closer attention.

Firstly, to consider Sarah Bannister's position on female pupil teachers:
she had been actively involved in improving the education and training of
pupil teachers from the start of the centre movement but, by the time she
gave her evidence to the 1898 Departmental Committee, she appeared wholly
disenchanted. She felt hampered by what she perceived as a relentless round
of examinations and curriculum pressures on pupil teachers, all of which,
despite the best efforts of enlightened centre teachers, served to encourage
mechanical, unthinking and unreflective learning. She was genuinely concerned at the arduous nature of a pupil teacher's working life – time being
split between their personal and professional education in the centres and
their practical teaching in London's elementary schools. She also had misgivings at the relative youth of candidates for pupil teachership, some of
whom entered the centres as probationers before their fourteenth birthdays.
She felt that pupil teaching, because it demanded such commitment at an
early age and because it entailed such a frenetic lifestyle, failed to attract the
best possible candidates. The sort of girls coming forward in her view were
'. . . often girls with very little in them; they are nice girls so far as they go,
but then they go such a very little way'.[27] As a result, the elementary teaching
profession ran the risk of being dominated by teachers who were incapable
of rising to the high standards required for the proper education of the
nation's children. She would have preferred to see more girls admitted to
her centre who had themselves completed a secondary education and who
came from more socially advantaged homes.

Through her involvement with Toynbee Hall and the LPTA, Sarah Bannister had witnessed the broadening of her students' all-round education and experience, through a systematic yet voluntary programme of intellectual and cultural reform. She wanted a wholesale extension of this type of educational activity – for novice teachers to experience a more liberal, humane education which would enable them to develop the skills of independent learning and thought. She feared that the centres, which relied too heavily on grants earned by external examinations such as the South Kensington Science and Art certificates, advocated a narrow approach to learning which was overly examination-oriented and which ultimately resulted in woeful ignorance.[28] One of her most insistent lines of enquiry in the 1898 Departmental Committee was to push her view that the minimum age of admission to pupil teachership should be raised. The only way she could envisage reform was if all intending teachers were funded to complete a proper course of secondary schooling followed by a shortened two-year apprenticeship in a specialised centre when they had reached the age of sixteen. Her solution inevitably raised questions about the social class origins of elementary teachers, who traditionally, like herself, had largely been drawn from working-class homes. Convinced that public elementary education would benefit by the admission of a higher class of pupil teacher, she was open to the possibility of the profession being made more attractive to candidates drawn from higher social class backgrounds. The following quotation embodies the nub of her argument: 'I think a person with a cultured mind and a liberal education is bound to have a better influence than the one who knows no life outside the elementary school. He may not be so skilled in producing results – he probably would not produce such good results as far as results can be written down on papers and worked out as a percentage, but I have no doubt that his influence would be felt in far more valuable ways and would be an advantage.'[29]

There was, however, a certain tension in her vision which evidently worried her and which she was unable to resolve. Her vision did not exclude the value of some sort of pre-training pupilage or apprenticeship for intending teachers but she couldn't quite square the cost of a more liberal education to the actual practice of teaching. This has to be understood in relation to the particular context within which Sarah Bannister was operating – at a time when a proper mechanism for providing a subsidised full-time secondary education for all intending teachers was not yet a reality. She was clearly concerned about how much theory of teaching, school method and management lectures pupil teachers should receive and how this could be balanced with their own academic education.[30] Some years after the 1898 committee reported, she was still deeply exercised by this question. Now with the weight of her reputation behind her and with the ear of some influential educationists she wrote, on the recommendation of Sophie Bryant, a letter to the President of the Board of Education which stated that, 'The question of the moment seems to be how to secure for the future teachers in elementary schools a training in teaching which will be of real value and yet will not be such as to make of no effect the greatly improved opportunities now within their reach for carrying on their own education.'[31] Restating her position that she wanted pupil teachers to complete their own academic education as well as being able to demonstrate their capacity for teaching, she proposed that the interval of eight or nine months between the date of taking the examination qualifying for admission to a training college and the actual date of entering college would be most profitably spent by the ex-pupil teachers in carefully selected schools of excellence under close supervision. Significantly, whilst the Board of Education raised serious objections to her proposal on financial grounds it recognised the educational value of such a plan. The bursar and student-teacher schemes which in 1907 replaced pupil teaching were very much in keeping with her idea.

In the meantime, Sarah Bannister knew that her proposals for reform, along with those of the 1898 committee as a whole, would not take any immediate effect because of financial constraints. She therefore set out to expose some of the other defects of the system which she felt hindered the progress of many girl pupil teachers. One particular bone of contention for her was the excessive load imposed on pupil teachers by an overweighty centre syllabus. Indeed, she directly criticised the LSB for its short-sightedness in this respect. She would have preferred to see fewer subjects on the syllabus and for pupil teachers to concentrate and excel at some of the basics in preparation for more advanced and less repetitive study at the training colleges. When she had tried, however, to experiment with a lightened syllabus at Stepney, '. . . the Board would not allow me to continue it; they forced my hand and exposed me and told me that I was leaving out what I ought to have been doing'.[32] She thus insinuated that the LSB was far more concerned with making the centres pay than offering a genuinely good education. Female pupil teachers in particular had also to cope with the additional burden of perfecting the art of needlework. Sarah Bannister proposed some fairly radical and pragmatic suggestions for the reduction of needlework-associated pressure and argued that the needlework syllabus should be remodelled. She expressed her irritation with teachers who over-emphasised the value of close work and excessively fine stitching which went far beyond the basic government requirements. She was not ashamed to admit that it was her practice to encourage her girls to do as little as possible to satisfy government standards. She also did not enter her students into the LSB's annual needlework exhibition, preferring such prizes to be sacrificed to time better spent on physical recreation. She recommended that the sewing machine should be used as much as possible to kill the craze for elaborately worked garments, and to save time she suggested that girls should be encouraged to use ready-made, cheap paper patterns.[33]

Sarah Bannister's fears for the mental and physical well-being of female pupil teachers whom she considered overworked and strained to the point of total exhaustion featured in her dealings with the LSB and in the 1898 Departmental Committee. She painted a particularly bleak picture of the daily routine of London's female pupil teachers who were often away from home for over ten hours at a time, without substantial sustenance and rest before returning home to domestic chores and more private study. She also stressed the difficulties faced by girls whose families, because of their own social status, were unable to take any real intelligent interest in their work. Whilst she insisted that she did everything in her power to check her girls' tendency to overwork, particularly when doing evening homework, she emphasised that it was the system as a whole which was to blame for overworking pupil teachers. 'I have tried my hardest, but the Board overruled my judgement when I relieved some of the weakest from a part of their work.'[34] She had clearly taken issue with the LSB over this contentious issue of overwork on a number of occasions.

The second thrust of Sarah Bannister's educational vision concerned the careers, opportunities and conditions of women teachers in general. In 1912 when she was principal of Moorfields Training College she featured on the front page of the widely read journal *Woman Teacher's World*.[35] In her brief address, Sarah Bannister clearly identified herself both professionally and personally with women teachers and talked in zealous terms of a crusade to elevate and improve their work and status. As part of her overarching ambition for a revitalised and empowered elementary teaching force, she was preoccupied with three major issues. These focused on improved career prospects and higher education for women teachers, the attraction of suitable candidates into the profession and better conditions of service. These concerns can be seen as a logical extension of her vision for pupil teachers.

Sarah Bannister promoted the appointment of women teachers to positions of power and authority over educational institutions above the normal woman's realm of kindergarten or domestic science colleges. In order to secure such positions, women needed access to improved higher education. She herself had worked hard to enhance her own academic qualifications whilst progressing up the career ladder. Whilst in 1912 she was pleased to find that '. . . every year women are being entrusted more and more with positions of greater responsibility and authority, positions in which they not merely carry out conditions already in existence and prescribed for them, but in which they are called upon to give shape to new conditions, better adapted to the newly recognised needs', she was anxious that such progress should continue. Integral to this was the question of single-sex or mixed education – an issue upon which Sarah Bannister held firm views. She felt that girls' educational, social and moral needs were much better met by women teachers. In her own experience, women were only allowed to head educational institutions which were single sex and by promoting single-sex centres was staking a claim for women to access future positions of responsibility and headships within single-sex institutions.[36]

When thinking about which type of women were suited to teaching, Sarah Bannister once again faced the same sort of academic versus professional and social class dilemma she encountered in her vision for pupil teaching. This was particularly the case in the context of the staffing of pupil-teacher centres. By the end of the nineteenth century, a small number of women teachers who had not themselves been trained in the elementary school system found their way into the pupil-teacher centres. Comprising university-educated women whose experiences of teaching and schooling had been confined to the prestigious girls' high schools, these 'intellectual ladies', as they were referred to by school boards, were often appointed for their superior educational, cultural and social credentials. In practice, however, because they were unused to the longer hours, greater workload and, in particular, the different social class of students found amongst pupil teachers, such women teachers were unsuited to the centres and as a consequence either suffered mental or physical breakdowns or returned to the secondary school sector.[37] In her evidence to the 1898 Departmental Committee, Sarah Bannister drew attention to the growing preference for centres to employ women teachers from more 'cultured' and highly educated backgrounds and stated that she believed this to be a move in the right direction. Nevertheless, whilst she felt that staff who combined higher degrees with an elevated social background would in turn attract a higher class of pupil teacher into the centres, she was unsure about their value in training pupil teachers in the art of teaching. Ultimately, she required centre staff to have passed through a teacher training college and to have proved their ability as classroom teachers. She qualified this judgement with the following statement: 'We often find that graduates offer themselves for vacancies at the pupil teacher centres but they are nearly always thrown out because they can give no guarantee that they are able to teach.'[38] Her own experience of non-elementary trained teachers in the centres varied and she recommended that if centres were going to employ such teachers extra care should be taken in the selection procedure. A period of probation in which the new type of teachers could prove themselves capable of withstanding the pressures of centre life was recommended as a solution.

In terms of elementary school teaching in general she argued for better working conditions and deplored the same tendency towards the overwork and exploitation of women teachers as afflicted female pupil teachers. Not only did she think that 'school boards must become a little more human in their treatment of teachers than some of them are now', but she also advocated a greater concern for the welfare of young teachers straight out of training college.[39] Too often had she seen young teachers in their first full-time appointments lose their enthusiasm and vigour for the job out of sheer exhaustion and disillusionment. She recommended a properly supervised probationary year for young teachers and much better provision of support and encouragement by experienced practitioners. It was not only young teachers who were exposed to the dangers of overwork and unrealistic expectations. From her own experience of the pupil-teacher centres she had witnessed a number of breakdowns amongst experienced centre teachers due to the pressures of overwork and of maintaining certain high standards. In a letter to the LSB she wrote: '... it seems a standing condition of our work, that we are always trying to do more than can possibly be done well, and this, with the inevitable examinations always close at hand, drives the teachers to adopt expedients which cannot be defended on educational grounds, and keeps both teachers and students alike in a state of nervous tension which is not only bad for them physically, but which is also fatal to any expansion of original thought, or the pursuit of any subject a step further than is required for examination purposes'.[40] Whilst Sarah Bannister fully endorsed and promoted the need for teachers to set and maintain high standards by example, she did not condone them being overworked and exploited.

Without inferring too much from these limited insights into Sarah Jane Bannister's professional life it has been possible to get some sense of her as an active woman educational visionary. Unfortunately, the difficult question of just how representative she was of other women teacher trainers from similar social and educational backgrounds cannot be answered at the present time, because the stories of such women have as yet to be fully recovered. Yet it can be argued that it has been worth telling Sarah's story, albeit in its very partial form, even if it does stand alone. Not only has it afforded valuable glimpses into the patterns of professional life encountered by such a woman, but it has also highlighted important issues of social class and gender which transcended her own highly personal experiences into the much bigger educational picture of the time.

Sarah Bannister herself embodied the very essence of what she envisaged for the teaching profession as a whole – a wider education, broader cultural outlook, independence of thought, professional integrity and a proven teaching ability. An able and ambitious woman, she worked herself through the elementary school system to the top of its professional hierarchy before going on to do the same thing in Hendon Borough Council. As a teacher trainer she earned the respect of London's ordinary teachers, her own colleagues and students, and whilst she comes across as having been a rather stern, formidable and persistent character, there is evidence that she was highly respected and well-liked.[41] Sarah Bannister earned her rising professional and social status but was determined not to be tainted by the very negativity from which she sought to escape. She, along with many other teachers who worked in the pupil-teacher centres, evening schools, higher-grade schools and teacher training colleges, wanted more for the elementary teaching profession and for women teachers. In order to realise such an ambition she had to be seen to have risen above the perceived narrow social, cultural and educational expectations of the elementary school world and in order to maintain such a position, had to promote such a rise for the rest of the teaching profession. That this might have been done to the possible cost of its professional autonomy, social class consonance and practical skill could not have been fully envisaged by Sarah Bannister at the time, but these questions clearly exercised her in some way. What she lived out in her teaching career spoke to the heart of some very pressing professional and educational concerns which faced the elementary teaching profession at the time and which ultimately might have influenced the direction of professional preparation, training and status which even today has not been fully resolved.

NOTES

1. I am most grateful to the archivists at the Barnet Local Studies Centre for their interest and assistance in my research.

2. *Departmental Committee on the Pupil Teacher System*, 1898 (hereafter cited as 1898 Departmental Committee).

3. For background reading on the development of the elementary teaching profession see L.G.E. Jones, *The Training of Teachers in England and Wales: A Critical Survey* (Oxford, 1924); R.W. Rich, *The Training of Teachers in England and Wales During the Nineteenth Century* (Cambridge, 1933); A. Tropp, *The School Teachers* (1957); P.H.J.H. Gosden, *The Evolution of a Profession* (Oxford, 1972); H.C. Dent, *The Training of Teachers in England and Wales 1800–1975* (1977).

4. D.M. Copelman, 'Women In the Classroom Struggle: Elementary School Teachers in London 1870–1914' (PhD thesis, Princeton University, 1985). See also Copelman, *London's Women Teachers: Gender, Class and Feminism 1870–1930* (1996).

5. See for example, G. Partington, *Women Teachers in the Twentieth Century* (Windsor, NFER, 1976); B. Bergen, 'Only a Schoolmaster: Gender, Class and the Effort to Professionalise Elementary Teaching in England 1870–1910', *History of Education Quarterly* 22.1 (1982), pp. 1–21.

6. The negative stereotype of the elementary school teacher was, for example, apparent in the Royal Commission on Secondary Education (Bryce Commission) vol. 1 p. 70: 'The master in an elementary school may sometimes be too mechanical; he may sometimes be lacking in general cultivation, and in appreciation of literature – and therefore in fitness to teach it; his efficiency as a teacher may also be limited, in some cases, by the narrow range within which his knowledge of his subjects is confined.' The vexed question of the anomalous and ambiguous status of nineteenth-century elementary school teachers is an important theme in Tropp, *The School Teachers*, pp. 26–43.

7. Herbert Ward discussed the gradual erosion and decline of teacher involvement in the training process in 1928 in J. Dover Wilson, *The Schools of England* (1928). Ward's solution was the unification of theory with practice through institutional partnership. The movement towards partnership schemes in teacher training today is discussed in J. Furlong, C. Whiting, L. Barton,

G. Whitty, S. Miles, 'School Report to Government' in *Times Higher Education Supplement*, 7 February 1997, p. 11. For a fuller discussion see M. Booth, J. Furlong and M. Wilkin, eds, *Partnership In Initial Teacher Training* (1990) and J. Furlong, T. Maynard, S. Miles and M. Wilkin, *The Secondary Active Mentoring Programme: Principles and Processes* (Cambridge, 1994).

8. Sarah's birth, marriage and death certificates as well as her will have been traced at the General Register Office and provide crucial information.

9. For a brief history of Tottenham College see G. Handley, *The College of All Saints: An Informal History of 100 Years* (1978).

10. London Metropolitan Archives (hereafter cited as LMA) London School Board (LSB) Minutes of Proceedings 12 January 1882, p. 188.

11. For a detailed discussion of London's married women teachers see Copelman, *London's Women Teachers*, ch. 8.

12. For a detailed account of the history of the pupil-teacher centres see W. Robinson, 'The Pupil-Teacher Centre in England and Wales in the late Nineteenth and early Twentieth Centuries: Policy, Practice and Promise' (unpublished PhD thesis, University of Cambridge, 1997).

13. LMA LSB (archive for SBL) Minutes of Proceedings 18 December 1884, p. 189.

14. LMA SBL 734 1 February 1886, p. 256.

15. See S.A. Barnett, *Canon Barnett, His Life, Work and Friends*, vol. 1 (1919), p. 347.

16. 1898 Departmental Committee 1 March 1897, p. 137.

17. For particular information on the Girls' Association see: Manchester Central Library, M50/4/6/1–2; also Barnett, *Canon Barnett*, pp. 345–7; LMA SBL 734 11 June 1886, p. 354; LMA SBL 739 4 June 1894; LMA SBL 747 19 May 1903.

18. Royal Commission on the Working of the Elementary Education Act Third Report 24 May 1887, p. 233, and 24 May 1887, pp. 233–4.

19. Copelman argues that by the end of the nineteenth century, London's pupil teachers were able to participate in a range of social activities in the company of a strong peer group. Nevertheless, Copelman questions their ability fully to enjoy these activities because of the burden of their work, studies and domestic duties. For female pupil teachers in particular, initiation into the culture and society of middle-class reformers was further burdened by specifically middle-class notions of appropriate female behaviour, work and leisure. These in turn would contribute to the confusions and contradictions inherent in the professional and gendered identity of women teachers.

20. See *Toynbee Record* vol. IV, 9 June 1897, pp. 108–9, which describes a deputation from Toynbee Hall to the Departmental Committee calling on the raising of the minimum age of entry for pupil teaching and an expansion of secondary education for intending teachers.

21. LMA SBL 742 16 May 1898.

22. LMA London County Council (LCC) Education Minutes 1908, p. 400.

23. LMA EO/TRA/4/14 17 November 1908.

24. LMA LCC Education Minutes 30 June 1915, p. 808.

25. LCC Education Calendar 1916–17: Sarah is listed as an assistant inspector.

26. Aged 77 and vice-chairman of the Hendon Education Committee, Sarah wrote a letter to the editor of the *Times Education Supplement*, 23 February 1935, p. 61, on the issues of the school leaving age.

27. 1898 Departmental Committee 1 February 1897, p. 187.

28. A vital source of additional income for both board or voluntary centres, particularly those outside the large cities, were Science and Art grants from South Kensington. By the 1890s, the London School Board, in seeking to further the work of the centres, stated that they had primarily been established for the training of teachers and that any additional grant earning activities, such as those offered by South Kensington, must be subordinated to this main objective. Nevertheless, it admitted that without the additional income from Science and Art grants, the centres would never have got off the ground.

29. 1898 Departmental Committee 1 February 1897, p. 23.

30. *Ibid.*, p. 17.

31. Public Record Office Kew, Ed 24/429. Letter dated 23 February 1905.

32. 1898 Departmental Committee 4 February 1897, p. 16.

33. 1898 Departmental Committee 4 February p. 17.

34. 1898 Departmental Committee 1 February 1897, p. 17.

35. *The Woman Teacher's World* vol. VIII no. 343 (10 January 1912), p. 1.

36. 1898 Departmental Committee 4 February 1897, p. 19.

37. See for example: LMA SBL 742 29 March 1897 which reported that Miss Rolleston, educated at Oxford High School and Newnham College, was forced to resign from London's Marylebone centre because '. . . she did not feel strong enough to conscientiously fulfil all the duties which devolve upon a woman teacher at a centre'; Surrey Record Office, Kingston Upon Thames, C/ES/89/1 8 October 1900, which reported the case of Miss Hobman, educated at the Mary Datchelor School, who was forced to resign from her appointment at the Sutton centre after only two weeks because she found the work too much of a strain; 1898 Departmental Committee 13 May 1897, p. 404, in which Mr T. Ryder, principal of the Leicester centre, discussed the unsuitability of centre posts for non-elementary trained women teachers. He offered the following illustration of his point: 'We had an application for an appointment from a lady at Cambridge who was a teacher in a secondary school. But she did not exactly want to do the work that we required. She wanted to lecture for an hour or two per day.'

38. 1898 Departmental Committee 4 February 1897, p. 16.

39. See note 29.

40. LMA SBL 738 11 November 1892.

41. This is borne out in Sarah's will which not only makes reference to gifts bestowed upon her by students and colleagues both at Stepney and Moorfields, which she bequeathed to friends, but also to a sense of her having remained in contact with former students and colleagues over a long period of time.

CHAPTER NINE

Mary Miller Allan: The Complexity of Gender Negotiations for a Woman Principal of a Teacher Training College

ELIZABETH EDWARDS

For the first 60 years of the twentieth century, teacher training colleges not only provided clever girls from lower middle-class backgrounds with a vocational qualification, but they also socialized students into the academic and cultural values of the middle class proper. In this chapter, I examine the ways in which Mary Miller Allan, Homerton College's first woman principal, negotiated the discourses of gender and power in her pioneering role as a woman principal. The pervading metaphor of training college life had always been that of the family. In the nineteenth century, colleges had been run on the lines of a mid-Victorian family, in which the paternal authority of the principal was undisputed. With the coming of women principals in the early years of the twentieth century, the family metaphor shifted towards matriarchal rather than patriarchal governance. But the role of women principals was always problematic. If the college was organised as a family, the principal, as its head, must of necessity take on the role of a strong authoritative father. But this paternal role was always intersected and sometimes interrupted by principals' maternal and feminine concerns. Principals attempted to solve this conflict by dividing their lives into public and private spheres. On public occasions they would adopt the role of a powerful authoritative father; privately they could show not only maternal concern for both staff and students but also express their feminine emotional/sexual needs. Miss Allan successfully negotiated most of the pitfalls inherent in her role, using her femininity in the service of, rather than as an impediment to, her masculine public role. Crucially she was able to conduct a homoerotic relationship with her own vice-principal without damage to her public reputation.

'Her rendering of "Stern Daughter of the Voice of God" said it all'.[1] The opening lines of Miss Allan's favourite poem – Wordsworth's 'Ode to Duty' – could well serve as her epitaph. Certainly her students thought the description apt as they gathered around her in the drawing room on Sunday afternoons for poetry reading and discussion on religious and moral topics. These occasions – known as 'Will Speak' – so called because it was always announced that 'Miss Allan will speak'[2] – epitomised the high academic standards and moral probity which Homerton's first woman principal expected from her students.

Miss Allan's predecessor as principal, John Horobin, had died suddenly in July 1902. He had overseen the college's move from London to Cambridge in 1894, and had also administered its transformation into an all-women's institution in 1896. After his death the college was run by Horobin's wife Maud, but this was not a success. The trustees of the college were therefore looking for strong leadership when early in 1903 they invited applicants for the post of Homerton's first woman principal. Their choice of Mary Miller Allan, currently head teacher of the Higher Grade Central School in Leeds, was not without its critics, but Miss Allan was to provide the college with outstanding leadership for 32 years, and to set it firmly on course as the foremost woman's teacher training institution in the country.

Miss Allan had worked her way up from humble origins, via a pupil teachership, to obtaining the Government Teacher's Certificate from Dundas Vale Training College, Glasgow. A lectureship at the Church of Scotland Training College, also in Glasgow, had been followed in 1895 by her appointment, at the early age of 26, to the headship of the Higher Grade Central School in Leeds. The lecturers at Homerton – some of whom had university degrees – were disappointed that Miss Allan's academic standing was not higher. She had however obtained the LLA (Lady Literate in the Arts) certificate from St Andrews University.[3] But this qualification had a somewhat equivocal reputation[4] and in a town like Cambridge the comment of the college's HMI was not unexpected: 'The degree she holds will not be considered of any value in Cambridge society.'[5]

Miss Allan's concern that Homerton, and particularly the behaviour of its students, should be acceptable to the academic and middle-class conservatism of Cambridge society was one of the central themes of her principalship. From her earliest days at the college she was to confound all her critics. A woman of outstanding ability and determination, by her forceful and strict leadership she soon brought 'all the work of the college under her personal control'.[6] Her aim was quite simply to make Homerton the best and most respected teacher training college in the land. Former students bear witness to her formidable qualities:

> Miss Allan had a very strong personality, awe-inspiring, rather unapproachable. She was dignified, just and a disciplinarian.[7]

> She held Homerton in her hand. A very strong character both mentally and physically she never allowed any misdemeanour to go unchecked – she

criticised her students' accents, the way they walked, and always expected us to behave with dignity and a sense of our vocation as teachers.[8]

She was much feared by all the students. We knew, to our peril, that any slip in behaviour or work would bring forth a tirade of criticism. Nevertheless, she doubtless had the good name of Homerton and her hopes for our futures at heart.[9]

The family model was an important element in the organisation of students. Each first-year student was allotted her own 'mother' from among the second-year students. Mothers supervised their 'daughters'' socialisation into college life, and generally acted as their mentors and friends. Similarly, when daughters entered their second year they in turn became mothers to the next generation of students. Miss Allan was quick to recognise that corporate loyalty could be enhanced by extending the college's metaphor of the family to include former students – grandmothers. Before her appointment former students had met informally in London and elsewhere. The principal not only transformed these informal gatherings into a formal Homerton Association – the ancestor of the present Homerton Roll – but by creating the annual Whitsun Reunion, which was held in college, she gave the newly formed association both a focus and a corporate tradition.[10] She well understood the importance of the association in promoting Homerton's reputation: 'She often spoke of her pleasure in, and the value of the Homerton Association, for members had in their hands the status and reputation of the college.'[11]

Miss Allan was one of the first training college principals to guide and monitor what I have called a 'culture of femininity'[12] in women's training colleges. This culture translated the social practices and family organisation of the middle-class home into a new institutional setting. Girls, primarily from lower middle-class backgrounds, were socialized into the mores of the middle class proper. In addition the training college experience enhanced the culture by imbuing students with the academic, educational, and cultural values of the liberal humanist tradition, as well as providing them with a vocational qualification.

Miss Allan quickly set out to enhance the academic curriculum at Homerton. Suitable students were encouraged to study for a further post-certificate year, which included the possibility of reading for Part 1 of Cambridge University's Geographical Tripos.[13] The growth of the college's reputation allowed it to attract to its staff university-educated women, whose dedication and high standards forged a residential educational community in which the enhanced culture of femininity could flourish. Miss Allan personally interviewed applicants to the college, although she sometimes delegated this task to her vice-principal and partner, Edith Waterhouse. This allowed the principal to keep tight control over the quality of Homerton's students. Miss Allan also conducted students' voice and speech training herself. This was an interesting combination of masculine and feminine discourses in the principal's role. The acquisition of a good, clear, minimally accented voice was essential vocationally for teachers in training – but it was also an essential quality of the middle-class culture of femininity:

> Our first morning 'lecture' was a meeting with Miss A. She told us to stand round the room with our backs to the wall. Each student had to read a poem from 'Oxford Book of English verse', but first to give our names. It was uncanny how she pin-pointed the exact part of the country we each came from – Cockney, Welsh, Norfolk, Cornwall, Bradford, etc. Quite an ordeal for most of us.[14]

The principal's involvement in the academic education of students was not confined to the narrow demands of the curriculum:

> Miss Allan took Senior Year Students once a week for English Literature and poetry not covered by our syllabus (e.g. Browning, Meredith, Rossetti) and stimulated our interest in the subject, through which I was able to obtain a Distinction in English.[15]

Miss Allan's purpose in devoting time to enhancing students' knowledge and appreciation of literature went beyond a desire to improve their academic achievement. For she believed that the moral and spiritual values of great literature would guide students throughout their lives. Learning poetry by heart was a way to achieve this aim:

> She was very fond of poetry – especially Browning, and held Browning evenings each week to which all seniors were welcomed. Miss Allan encouraged us to learn poetry by heart, for which I am everlastingly grateful now that I am registered as blind and still have memories of some of the loveliest poems ever written.[16]

Homerton's location in the university town of Cambridge gave students and staff, at least in theory, access to the best of high culture. Miss Allan's attitude to the university was deeply ambivalent. She was well aware of the college's marginal position in Cambridge society, and the indifference of the university authorities to the college's existence. Nevertheless she was very anxious that students should benefit, in her own words, from the 'few crumbs which fall from the University table'.[17] Such was the possibility of attending the university's triennial Greek play:

> The Greek play [Oresteia of Aeschylus] was performed and Miss Allan managed to get the Vice-Provost of Kings to explain the plot and background. She was very pleased and stressed that it was a great privilege. She remained on the platform – as she did with all visiting lecturers.[18]

It was entirely consonant with the principal's public role that she should chair this major cultural event in the life of the college. But her determination to monitor and control every aspect of college life could sometimes reveal a maternal 'fussing' which was an interruption of the masculine discourse of her public role. By the 1930s students were beginning to notice this. Miss Allan's 'fussing' centred on students' behaviour, and the public's perception of it:

> Miss Allan was always very keen that students upheld the reputation of the College. I remember her denunciation of students who went . . . to buy cakes and pastries. She said she'd seen a succession of students coming along carrying confectioner's bags which must give near-by residents the impression that we didn't get enough to eat at College.[19]

Another student related an anecdote when Miss Allan's over-scrupulous concern with students' dress for country dancing in the college grounds was perceived as being absurd, even undignified:

> We usually wore white dresses for these occasions and light stockings. One evening I was wearing lighter stockings than usual and apparently Miss Allan wondered if I had dared to attend the dancing without any! So she asked someone to come close enough to me to find out. (I was very amused when I heard about this afterwards). Miss Allan was very strict on etiquette and suitable dress, as this little story illustrates.[20]

Miss Allan's political astuteness and her ability to persuade and convince all those who were concerned with the work of the college were, however, never in dispute. She was always able to exercise strong paternal authority both with the college's trustees and with the Board of Education, nor did she let difficult parents get the better of her.[21] Her dogged determination not to be intimidated by opposition was revealed in her long campaign in the 1920s to get the University of Cambridge to take over responsibility for the final academic examination of Homerton students. For in 1926 the Board of Education had announced that it was proposing that local universities should take over this responsibility from the Board. Oxford and Cambridge universities, however, were exempt from this obligation because they were deemed to be 'national' rather than 'local universities'. Miss Allan described her anxious and difficult campaign to persuade Cambridge University to make an exception for Homerton, in her report to the trustees a year later:

> The absorbing question still is the approach to the University with regard to the Final Examination of the Students. The matter was first mooted in December 1925, and was discussed first with the Vice-chancellor in February 1926 – but still there is little progress to report, indeed but for the kindness and assistance of the Master of Trinity Hall there would have been none. Since I last reported to you on the matter Dr Cranage has formally brought the subject before the

Extra-Mural Board . . . The decision come to was 'that no action be taken at
present' . . . Dr Cranage unofficially advised that a direct appeal should be made
to the Council of the Senate. The Master of Trinity Hall kindly arranged that
I should meet a member of Council, who advised my again seeing the Vice-
Chancellor, with whom, I had a long interview on the 10th inst. Finally he
advised that a careful memorandum should be prepared on the matter and
signed by some influential members of the University, both Governors of this
College, and others interested.

A year later Miss Allan's long and patient campaign eventually bore fruit,
and in 1928 the university's Local Examinations Syndicate signalled that they
were 'prepared to undertake the work'. The Examinations Syndicate kept
the responsibility for examining Homerton students for twenty years, until it
passed to the newly created Cambridge Institute of Education in 1950. The
link with the university proved of very great advantage to Homerton. As Miss
Allan herself reported to the Trustees in 1930:

> There is little doubt the standard of the examination has been raised since it
> has been taken over by the Examinations Syndicate. The syllabus being much
> more clearly defined, and the external examiners being in touch in almost
> every case with the actual work done.[22]

Homerton was an undenominational college, in spite of its origins in the
Congregational church. Miss Allan herself was a regular attender at Emmanuel
Congregational Church in Cambridge,[23] but inside the college she 'maintained
an unobtrusive religious atmosphere which was entirely undenominational'.[24]
Very unusually for a woman principal she supported the Labour Party, and
in 1918 she signed the nomination papers for Cambridge's first Labour
parliamentary candidate.[25] Miss Allan's unusual party political affiliation has
not yet been fully researched, but, although she did not 'parade' her political
views, either within college or outside it, her more general concern for the
working class was on public record.

> She told us of her growing conviction that the roots of the nation are fixed in
> the working classes whose children we teach.[26]

These words were delivered soon after Miss Allan had taken leave of absence
during 1919 and 1920 for a world-wide tour, which included participating, as
its only woman member, in the Commission of Inquiry into Village Education in India. Her first vice-principal and obituarist extolled the value to Miss
Allan of this 'special' experience:

> She came up against some of the big world problems . . . and met far more
> interesting and important people than most of us may hope to see in a life-time
> . . . it added to Miss Allan's stature in thought and wisdom, giving her a back-
> ground of ideas on newer and far older civilizations than our own.[27]

I would argue however that in spite of this ecumenical experience, Miss Allan's total absorption in her principalship, and her overwhelming concern that the college should be acceptable to the academic and middle-class conservatism of Cambridge society, precluded any real widening of her horizons. During her principalship, tentative links were established with Cambridge University. The Mistress of Girton became the first woman trustee in 1916, and other members of the university acted as external examiners.[28] Nevertheless her concern for Homerton's respectability was made more acute by the college's marginal position in Cambridge society. Cambridge was a town dominated by the male values of its university, which barely tolerated its own women students, let alone those in an obscure teacher training institution. The university's misogyny had been underlined by a privilege which it had only been forced to relinquish as late as 1894. This was its right to imprison women walking in the town – who could well have been Homerton students – whom it suspected of being prostitutes.[29] It is in this context that Miss Allan's legendary annual homily to her students on the importance of avoiding sexual encounters with undergraduates needs to be understood:

> Miss Allan gave us a lovely little lecture about the 5,000 youths who are coming up in 3 weeks' time. She says she's proud to say that Homerton girls have never behaved badly and she's sure that none of us will. She says if we've any friends (already) at the Varsity we can go out to tea with them but we must'nt make friends. It's not done.[30]

> It was Miss Allan's proud boast that for years she had had two hundred women students among four thousand men and had never had any trouble.[31]

Miss Allan's concern about students' sexual behaviour was understandable in the context of the earlier years of her principalship, but towards the end of her service, in the early 1930s, her 'fussing' became increasingly irksome to students. Her obsessive concern with respectability seemed old-fashioned, even absurd:

> In those far-off days males were all suspect. I was reported one Sunday morning for being seen walking with a young man. I had to see Miss Allan and had to explain to her that my companion was a great friend from Home. We went to the same Congregational Church at home. When we were seen together in Cambridge we were walking back from a Morning Service. Miss Allan listened to my explanation, but I had to write home for a permissive letter from my Mother.[32]

> I was called to Miss Allan to be asked whether I thought it was a good idea to see my friend from Emmanual so often. This interview shook me severely: what kind of an institution had I come to.[33]

Homerton College's archive is fortunate to have obtained at the end of the 1980s some 80 replies to a questionnaire sent to Miss Allan's former students.[34] Her students are unanimous in bearing witness to her formidably stern and authoritarian public persona and to her overwhelming concern with their academic progress and social and sexual repectability. But what was she really like underneath this public persona?

> Strong – seemed very unbending, but could do so if you were in trouble, or at Prefects Teas – on the rare occasion. She wasn't the kind of person who would get alongside the student, but she could be gracious. I was terrified of her in my first year, but understood her better in my second, when I was a prefect. I held her in high regard.[35]

Being gracious to students on informal college occasions was an extension of the principal's public role. Miss Allan was always motivated in her actions by her concern for the well-being of the college as a whole and I would argue that her help for students in difficulties was driven more by this concern, than by a feminine sympathy for students as individuals.

> She had a strong sense of self discipline and expected this in the students. She resented any thing such as illness, which was a hindrance to their progress.[36]

Another student drew a warmer picture of the principal, drawing attention to her sympathy with poorer students and, interestingly, using a maternal metaphor to describe her behaviour:

> Sympathetic to students whose opportunities in education had been halted after the General Strike of 1926 . . . Understanding and directive of personal problems. Did not suffer fools gladly. Tolerant to youth's exuberation and mistakes. Encouraging to all efforts. Quick in correction. A Mother figure when sickness confined one to the Sanatorium.[37]

Not everyone agreed about Miss Allan's tolerance:

> I found her completely devoid of the milk of human kindness. She did her best to suppress any liveliness or gaiety in her students, you had to be serious and dowdy to win her approval.[38]

Miss Allan herself, however, was far from dowdy. She was careful to dress appropriately at all times, marking carefully by her clothes the difference between her masculine public role and a more private femininity. Her day-time clothes were chosen to enhance her public dignity and status as head of the college, and were a feminine equivalent of the masculine suit. She wore dark well-cut tailor-made dresses and jackets of good material 'without much attention to current fashion'. She never went out of the college grounds without a hat. When she entered the private sphere however she wore more feminine and stylish attire. For evening supper with the staff, for instance, she wore 'a deep blue mandarin robe',[39] and for her retirement dinner in 1935 her dress was elaborately feminine:

> On the occasion of her retirement... we saw the real Miss Allan, dressed in a beautifully cut gown of black lace with a high Medici collar and a corsage of red roses.[40]

This student's perception of the 'real' Miss Allan as feminine was also evident in Hugh Riviere's portrait, commissioned in 1913.[41] Riviere shows Miss Allan in an embroidered dress, displaying a necklace, bracelet and ring, and with her hands decorously folded in her lap.[42] The perception of the 'real' Miss Allan as feminine by both students and portraitist is interesting. Clearly the principal's 'masculine' public role, however effective in practice, was not seen as an integral part of her personality. Because she was a woman, she had to be 'really' feminine.

Miss Allan's private femininity was crucially expressed in her homoerotic partnership with her second vice-principal, Edith Waterhouse. No fewer than 30 out of the 80 respondents to the questionnaire were aware of the friendship. Here is how two of them described it:

> The only Staff friend, though how friendly one cannot judge, was Miss Waterhouse ('Soda'), who, I think was Deputy Head, and lived in the same block as Miss Allan if I remember rightly. 'Soda' was an odd character, used an ear trumpet, and would fly off at a tangent for the smallest fault, storming away. She could smile though.[43]

> She was very friendly with the Vice-Principal Miss Waterhouse. They were nick-named 'Whisky and Soda' by the students.[44]

Miss Waterhouse's effervescent personality gave rise to her nickname 'Soda' and the coupling together of Miss Waterhouse as 'Soda' and Miss Allan as 'Whisky' (referring to her Glaswegian origins) was emblematic of the successful blending together of the two women's personalities.

The term homoerotic was first used by the feminist historian Martha Vicinus to describe close friendships between women in residential educational communities in England during the late nineteenth and early twentieth centuries.[45] I appropriated the term in a paper which discussed the whole question of homoerotic friendship and women principals.[46] I argued that although these women did not claim a lesbian identity as such, their emotional/sexual bonding with other women, coupled with their refusal of the hegemonic heterosexual discourse, placed them within the lesbian past. Inside the confines of women's colleges, homoerotic friendship was accepted within certain limits – namely that the friendship remained invisible to the outside world, and that the women concerned did not violate standards of respectability by indiscreet behaviour. Principals also faced an additional difficulty in homoerotic friendship from the necessity of reconciling the power discourse of their public role with their own private gender needs.

Fig 9.1   *Although Riviere's portrait was commissioned for the public space of College Hall, the sitter's choice of dress and jewellery draws attention to Miss Allan's private femininity.*

Miss Allan's pursuit of homoerotic friendship was not without its complications. In 1903, immediately after her own appointment, she appointed Margaret Glennie to the Homerton staff. Two years later she gave a temporary contract for one year to Edith Waterhouse, to cover another lecturer's leave of absence.[47] Both these women enjoyed from the first an intimate personal companionship with Miss Allan:

> I believe her closest friend was Miss Waterhouse, lecturer in Education and she had a great affection for Miss Glennie (Science).[48]

That Miss Waterhouse eventually became Miss Allan's closest friend (one former student declared that Miss Glennie was actually 'pushed out'[49]) was due both to differences in the two women's personalities and also to Miss Allan's ultimate preference for the woman who could best serve both her public and private needs. Miss Glennie was described by her obituarist as a 'Christian woman, gifted, beauty-loving and humble' who gave 'forty years of incalculable service to the college'.[50] She was much loved by her students, whose frequent labelling of her as a 'lady' signalled her conformity with middle-class ideals of femininity. Miss Waterhouse was quite different. Her obituarist draws attention not only to 'the brilliant clarity of her mind' which made her a 'great teacher', but also to her 'keen elfin wit' and 'quick effervescent tantrums'.[51] Students were frightened of Miss Waterhouse, as they were of Miss Allan, and dreaded her shouting at them 'Speak up, gel'. (Miss Waterhouse was deaf and used an ear-trumpet.)[52]

Miss Allan was quick to recognise her need to retain Miss Waterhouse's services on a permanent basis. Long before Miss Waterhouse's temporary contract had expired Miss Allan was exercising her considerable management skills. She wrote to the Chairman of the Congregational Board of her desire 'to secure her [Waterhouse's] services' which were of a 'thoroughly satisfactory kind'. She also warned the trustees that Miss Waterhouse was 'applying for another job'. So keen indeed was Miss Allan to keep Miss Waterhouse that she went so far as to write to several members of the board privately to secure their support. Nevertheless, although Miss Waterhouse's appointment was made permanent, she left Homerton in 1907 to take up the post of Mistress of Method at Avery Hill College. A year later she was appointed Avery Hill's vice-principal. Miss Allan revealed in coded official language the loss which she, as well as the college, had sustained:

> I cannot adequately state my appreciation of Miss Waterhouse's work. Her post will be very hard to fill.[53]

I do not think it was without significance that in the same year that Miss Waterhouse became vice-principal of Avery Hill, Miss Allan, perhaps reckoning that she had 'lost' Miss Waterhouse, appointed her own vice-principal from among the existing Homerton staff. Miss Varley had been on the Homerton staff, as lecturer in Mathematics, since 1902, before Miss Allan was appointed principal. She was to take on the post of acting principal when Miss Allan was abroad in 1919–20. Nevertheless Miss Allan was determined to lure Miss Waterhouse back to Homerton, even if she could not offer her the post of vice-principal, and four years later, in 1912, she informed the governors that she was retaining Miss Waterhouse's services on a part-time basis as a supervisor for School Practice. This proved the thin end of the wedge, and by the end of the year Miss Waterhouse was back at Homerton with a full-time lectureship in education.[54] It is difficult to believe that Miss Waterhouse would have taken such a seemingly backward step in her career, unless she had a compelling personal reason to do so. Certainly the rivalry between her and Miss Glennie now became visible in college,[55] and a year later Miss Glennie was given leave of absence for unstated reasons. The power struggle between the two women was finally resolved ten years later in 1922, when Miss Varley was appointed principal of nearby Saffron Walden College. Saffron Walden was a domestic science college, of inferior status to Homerton. We can only speculate if Miss Allan had a hand in this appointment. So at last Miss Allan was able to appoint Miss Waterhouse as her vice-principal; Miss Glennie was given the consolation prize of resident tutor. Miss Allan showed her skill in managing a situation which could have caused great friction in the college. She ensured both women's continuing loyalty to herself and the college, by bracketing their names together in a public appreciation of their services:

> Great care must be taken to secure the services of women of as fine calibre and earnestness of purpose as those who retire and who have done so much to maintain the reputation of the College. I am very fortunate in retaining the services of able and responsible members like Miss Waterhouse and Miss Glennie.[56]

Miss Allan chose Miss Waterhouse rather than Miss Glennie as her vice-principal because she judged that Miss Waterhouse's ability and previous experience as a vice-principal better fitted her for the job. Importantly Miss Waterhouse could also stand up to the principal and not be intimidated by her. But a close working relationship in the public sphere need not of itself have led to a similar intimacy in her private life. Indeed there were very obvious pitfalls in following this course, as the experience of Constance Maynard, founder and first mistress of Westfield College (later to become part of the University of London), showed. As Martha Vicinus has pointed out, the intersection of the discourses of gender and power 'when distance was lost but inequality remained' was always problematic. Moreover emotional overloading when, as Miss Maynard herself recorded in her diary, 'work, friends, pleasure, everything is shared' was an ever-present danger.[57] Miss Allan and Miss Waterhouse were able to overcome these problems by a combination of personal compatibility and flexible role reversal. Miss Waterhouse accepted that her professional role was necessarily subordinate to Miss Allan's authority, and Miss Allan rewarded her loyalty with frequent public tributes 'to her work as vice-principal which I particularly prize'.[58] In the intimacy of their private life together, however, they enjoyed a flexible equal partnership in which, as one of their former students remarked, 'it was uncertain as to who dominated who'. They shared a sense of humour[59] and 'an interest in Gilbert and Sullivan productions'.[60]

> The vice-principal Miss Waterhouse had indifferent health and Miss Allan – may I say – 'cherished' her.[61]

Concern for each other's health was a central and visible site for the expression of the two women's intimacy. Miss Waterhouse lived till she was over 90 years old.[62] Nevertheless her indifferent health was recognised in college and she periodically took extended sick leave including a term spent in the South of France.[63] Miss Allan was able to express her feminine and emotional side in this cherishing of her partner. But at times she could fall victim to that 'emotional overloading' that Constance Maynard had alluded to[64] as an ever-present danger in a relationship between a principal and a member of her own staff:

> (Miss Allan) was always very solicitious about the health of the Vice-Principal. She at times waited outside the lecture room to enquire after Miss Waterhouse's health.[65]

Miss Waterhouse had an altogether lighter touch:

> Miss Waterhouse was vice-principal and was very close to Miss Allan. They were close friends. Miss Allan obviously admired Miss Waterhouse very much and praised her to students. Miss Waterhouse gave warmth to the relationship. I remember one evening when I was due to see Miss Allan in her apartment, I was met by Miss Waterhouse coming out of Miss Allan's bedroom, smiling and signalling me to go away quietly – evidently Miss Allan had gone to bed early and Miss Waterhouse was seeing she was not disturbed![66]

Miss Allan remains a somewhat enigmatic figure. Except for her principal's reports and her contributions to college magazines we have little of her own words. Towards the end of her principalship she was persuaded to write a little about herself in the college magazine. Although she was always careful not to 'parade' any overtly feminist views in public, lest her credibility and respectability (and that of the college) be endangered, she was nevertheless acutely aware of the disadvantages that women suffered in the educational sphere:

> At 18 years of age I went up to Glasgow Normal Training College. But a strange question had to be debated first – Would Glasgow University *that* year open its doors to women undergraduates? But alas two more years were to pass before work was begun there.[67]

I think that Miss Allan's true beliefs were contained in a letter she sent to a London Reunion of former students in February 1920 while she was in India. She names her two deepest impressions as:

1. The quite extraordinary beauty of the world everywhere.
2. (and much harder to express) The extraordinary worth and interest of all man's labour wherever it is free from selfishness. The highest worship of God is the service of Man . . . (This may hardly be coherent stated briefly, and would need to be enlarged upon on Sunday afternoons!)

Miss Allan showed a rare warmth and humour when she was writing this letter far from home to her old students. Homerton was her life and her security and secretly she would rather be at home in the college than representing her country abroad on important business. She expressed these feelings with an emotional intimacy which was far removed from the stern authoritarianism of her public self:

The price one pays for a great experience such as I am having now, is the interruption of the companionship that had made life worth living, of the daily exchange of good offices between those we live with. Some loneliness is inseparable from a Wander-jahr. But how can I thank those of you who banished even this feeling by the cordiality of the greeting which reached me in christmas week . . . I am tremendously proud of your great christmas card, and carry it on all my journeyings. . . . I cannot make you understand how much it meant to me.

Affectionately yours, Mary Allan[68]

NOTES

1. Homerton College Archive (hereafter HCA) Acc. no. 1190, no. 28. Reply to questionnaire on Miss Allan from a student, 1923–25. Note that grammar and spelling in students' replies have been left intact throughout.
2. HCA Acc. no. 1189, no. 7. Reply to questionnaire on Miss Allan from a student, 1918–20.
3. T.H. Simms, *Homerton College 1695–1978* (Cambridge, 1978), pp. 38–47.
4. C. Dyhouse, *No Distinction of Sex? Women in British Universities 1870–1939* (1995), p. 171.
5. Simms, *Homerton College*, p. 46.
6. *Ibid.*, p. 47.
7. HCA Acc. no. 1190, no. 35. Reply to questionnaire on Miss Allan from a student, 1927–29.
8. HCA Acc. no. 1189, no. 7. Reply to questionnaire on Miss Allan from a student, 1918–20.
9. HCA Acc. no. 1190, no. 31. Reply to questionnaire on Miss Allan from a student, 1928–30.
10. *Homertonian* (June 1906).
11. HCA Acc. no. 630. *50 Years of the Homerton Association*, p. 11.
12. See e.g. E. Edwards, 'The culture of femininity in women's teacher training colleges 1900–1950', *History of Education* 22 (1993), pp. 277–88.
13. Simms, *Homerton College*, p. 48.
14. HCA Acc. no. 1189, no. 7. Reply to questionnaire on Miss Allan from a student, 1918–20.
15. HCA Acc. no. 1190, no. 35. Reply to questionnaire on Miss Allan from a student, 1927–29.
16. HCA Acc. no. 1189, no. 4. Reply to questionnaire on Miss Allan from a student, 1915–17.
17. HCA Acc. no. 1190, no. 3. Reply to questionnaire on Miss Allan from a student, 1927–29.

18. HCA Acc. no. 1191, no. 5. Reply to questionnaire on Miss Allan from a student, 1932–34.

19. HCA Acc. no. 1190, no. 44. Reply to questionnaire on Miss Allan from a student, 1927–29.

20. HCA Acc. no. 1191, no. 14. Reply to questionnaire on Miss Allan from a student, 1932–34.

21. HCA Acc. no. ACa 58. Principal's reports 1903–1933, *passim.*

22. HCA Acc. no. ACa 58. Principal's reports, March 1926, June 1927, June 1930; *Homerton News Letter* (1928).

23. HCA Acc. no. 1190, no. 23. Reply to questionnaire on Miss Allan from a student, 1927–29.

24. HCA Acc. no. 807. Reminiscences of a student, 1922–25.

25. HCA Acc. no. 1984. Notes on Miss Allan.

26. *Homerton News Letter* (1923).

27. *Homerton News Letter* (1948).

28. Simms, *Homerton College*, p. 56.

29. E. Edwards, 'The friendly societies and the ethic of respectability in nineteenth century Cambridge', Ph.D. thesis, CNAA, 1987.

30. HCA Acc. no. 888. Letter home from a student, 1928.

31. HCA Acc. no. 1190, no. 39. Reply to questionnaire on Miss Allan from a student, 1925–27.

32. HCA Acc. no. 1190, no. 19. Reply to questionnaire on Miss Allan from a student, 1920–22.

33. HCA Acc. no. 1191, no. 1. Reply to questionnaire on Miss Allan from a student, 1932–34.

34. HCA Acc. nos. 1189–1191.

35. HCA Acc. no. 1190, no. 24. Reply to questionnaire on Miss Allan from a student, 1922–24.

36. HCA Acc. no. 1189, no. 5. Reply to questionnaire on Miss Allan from a student, 1904–06.

37. HCA Acc. no. 1190, no. 13. Reply to questionnaire on Miss Allan from a student, 1929–31.

38. HCA Acc. no. 1190, no. 45. Reply to questionnaire on Miss Allan from a student, 1924–26.

39. HCA Acc. no. 1190, nos. 3, 10, 13, 28. Replies to questionnaire on Miss Allan from students, 1923–25, 1926–28, 1927–29, 1929–31.

40. HCA Acc. no. 1190, no. 22. Reply to questionnaire on Miss Allan from a student, 1925–27.

41. *Homerton News Letter* (1913).

42. The portrait hangs in the Hall at Homerton.

43. HCA Acc. no. 1190, no. 24. Reply to questionnaire on Miss Allan from a student, 1922–24.

44. HCA Acc. no. 1191, no. 18. Reply to questionnaire on Miss Allan from a student, 1932–34.

45. M. Vicinus, *Independent Women: Work and Community for Single Women 1850–1920* (1985), pp. 189–206.

46. E. Edwards, 'Homoerotic friendship and college principals, 1880–1960', *Women's History Review* 4 (1995).

47. HCA Acc. no. ACa. Principal's reports, 3 July 1905.

48. HCA Acc. no. 1190, no. 42. Reply to questionnaire on Miss Allan from a student, 1922–25.

49. HCA Acc. no. 1192. Reminiscences of a student, 1915–17.

50. *Homertonian* (1950).

51. *Homerton Association News* (1962).

52. HCA Acc. no. 1191, no. 2. Reply to questionnaire on Miss Allan from a student, 1932–34.

53. HCA Acc. no. ACa 58. Principal's reports, 1903–33, 9 February 1907.

54. HCA Acc. no. ACa 58. Principal's reports, 21 February 1906, 26 November 1906, 25 February 1907, 30 November 1908, 29 February 1912, October 1921.

55. HCA Acc. no. 1192. Reminiscences of a student, 1915–17.

56. HCA Acc. no. ACa 58. Principal's reports, 9 February 1914, March–June 1922.

57. Vicinus, *Independent Women*, p. 201.

58. HCA Acc. no. ACa 58. Principal's reports, June 1929.

59. HCA Acc. no. 1191, no. 15. Reply to questionnaire on Miss Allan from a student, 1933–35.

60. HCA Acc. no. 1190, no. 16. Reply to questionnaire on Miss Allan from a student, 1929–31.

61. HCA Acc. no. 1190, no. 22. Reply to questionnaire on Miss Allan from a student, 1925–27.

62. *Homerton Association News* (1962).

63. HCA Acc. no. ACa 58. Principal's reports, 19 July 1920, December 1926.

64. Vicinus, *Independent Women*, p. 201.

65. HCA Acc. no. 1191, no. 5. Reply to questionnaire on Miss Allan from a student, 1932–34.

66. HCA Acc. no. 1191, no. 24. Reply to questionnaire on Miss Allan from a student, 1933–35.

67. *Homertonian* (1935).

68. *Homerton News Letter* (1920).

PART FOUR

The Poor Child – Women and the Progressive Challenge to the Elementary System

CHAPTER TEN

'Mrs Roadknight Reports . . .':
Jane Roadknight's Visionary Role in
Transforming Elementary Education

ANNE BLOOMFIELD

This vignette is of Jane Annie Roadknight (1855–1929), who, through her role as kindergarten mistress, teacher trainer and inspector, successfully transformed elementary education in Nottingham, firstly under the Nottingham School Board and subsequently with the City of Nottingham Education Authority until her retirement in 1919. The portrayal, based on reports analysed in the context of the Nottingham period of employment 1885–1919, reveals that Jane Roadknight was an inspirational force in the vanguard of educational change. Her vision extended beyond the mean city streets and formal elementary school room and glimpsed the glories of an educational utopia. Apprenticed as a pupil teacher at the tender age of ten, Jane Roadknight won a Queen's Scholarship, 1st Class in 1873 and went on to complete her training at the Home and Colonial College, London, where she gained a 2nd Class Certificate in 1877, raised to 1st Class in 1888.[1] An accomplished vocal and instrumental musician, she also acquired an award from the London Institute of Needlework.

Jane Roadknight's pragmatism and qualities of leadership became evident as she demonstrated her ability to put her ideas into practice by establishing a model kindergarten at Blue Bell Hill Infants' School. Her reputation soon went beyond the bounds of the neighbourhood school when she was appointed Kindergarten Instructress to the School Board. Subsequently she became a highly respected inspector for the City of Nottingham. During her lengthy career the impact of Jane Roadknight's commitment to educational reform not only came through example, leadership and inspection duties, but also through the provision of training courses for teachers and through the Froebel Society. The great value of joyful experiences in education was recognised as she promoted active learning processes for children whose sombre lives in an industrial heartland were shadowed by the subjugation of a narrow and impersonal system of schooling.

At the end of the nineteenth century, Nottingham was a busy manufacturing town with new factories specialising in hosiery, textiles and lace manufacture, machinery, tanning, brewing, and coal-mining. Industrial artisans and their families lived in sunless enclosed courts or alleys such as Parr's Yard, Knotted Alley, Crossland Place and Narrow Marsh, each packed in close vicinity to the town centre. Further afield, streets of terraced houses, with lace-clad windows and smoke-filled air, were the homes of an ever-increasing child population whose educational needs had to be met. The first Nottingham School Board elected on 29 November 1870 had in its first years filled the gaps left by the voluntary system, but as time progressed, it had taken on an increasingly ambitious role in response to its responsibilities and from 1890 onwards all the children in Nottingham attended elementary school regularly for at least six years. Efforts by the school board to raise standards had proved difficult. Regulations of 1872, which had aimed at a reasonably comprehensive curriculum, did not reflect the type of work currently found in the town's schools which were confined to Religious Knowledge and the basic reading, writing and arithmetic. The curriculum of a few elementary schools had widened and some schools offered 'class subjects' – grammar, geography, English literature, and drawing, which were subjects taken by the whole classes of the senior pupils.[2] But there were serious reservations about the state of infant education. William Abel, Board Inspector, wrote in a highly critical report of 1882:

> The main objection to the organisation of the Board's Infant schools, is that it is not sufficiently bright and intelligent. The majority of these departments remind one of 'forcing houses' rather than 'children's gardens' this state of affairs is now perhaps rather the teachers' misfortune than their fault; but there is happily a prospect of speedy improvement with the introduction of the New Code.[3]

Abel emphasised the limitations of a narrow 'three Rs' curriculum and stressed the need for developmental learning through systematically graduated lessons that would transform what he described as the prison house into the beautiful palace:

> The highest compliment which can be paid to an Infant Teacher is not that she has drilled her little charges to repeat their tables, read, spell, transcribe and overcome the mysteries of addition and subtraction; but that she has made her school a child's palace, instead of a child's prison, by quickening and educating the little ones' intelligence by lessons systematically graduated, and withal so interesting and intelligent that, whilst some new power is constantly being called forth and the various faculties exercised and strengthened, the children are scarcely aware of the expenditure of mental effort.[4]

Abel criticised the 'object' lesson, and stressed the need for an intelligent programme of learning through a series of lessons and objectives that connected the work of classes within the school.

Advocating a deeper understanding about the nature of the child, Abel asserted that teachers could only be successful if they made child nature an all important study, 'and frame their work accordingly'.[5] Abel promoted a sensory approach to learning, emphasising the role of music and play. In good establishments 'this music of the Schools' was not confined to the above subjects but 'ran through the whole of the lessons, the various parts and stages being so harmoniously arranged and blended that the little ones experience no rude jars from the ever new difficulties they have to encounter, but feel their onward projects to be a joyous march, and associate learning with bright and gleesome play'. Abel felt that 'a poor Infant School fails exactly as it lacks music', and attested that the child's curiosity should be met with positive learning approaches brought about through play.[6] William Abel was obviously aware of the revival of the kindergarten idea and its growth under the London School Board, possibly through events encouraged by the Society of Arts or perhaps through association with local politicians, industrialists and educationists as, for example, A.J. Mundella and H.M. Felkin, who, with links in Saxony and Prussia, were strongly influenced by continental trends and actively promoted innovative pedagogy. The Nottingham Board could not ignore his criticism and duly responded.

The Blue Bell Hill Board Schools opened on 30 April 1883. Situated on the hillside to the east of the town, the lofty red brick buildings with a high tower overlooked a valley of terraced streets and factories that cascaded in a south-westerly direction towards the town centre. In *Sons and Lovers* D.H. Lawrence described the mean streets of Blue Bell Hill, with their 'granite cobbles and causeways of dark blue, grooved bricks'. Here, in 1885, Jane Roadknight obtained the post of Special Teaching Staff Kindergarten Teacher and commenced by organising the kindergarten and providing classes for teachers from voluntary, private and other board schools. Her time at Blue Bell Hill provided the opportunity to put her own ideas and beliefs into practice through the establishment of the model kindergarten, bringing continental influences into the Nottingham schools and providing new child-rearing values for working-class children. The first record of this appears in the School Board Minutes, October 1886:

> During the present triennial period a great improvement has been effected in the Infants' Schools of the Board. The Government Code now encourages 'appropriate and varied occupations'; and thus recognises the fact that instruction is most pleasantly and efficiently given to infants in the form of directed play. The music, games, toys, short varied and profusely illustrated lessons, all arranged as parts of one carefully graded system of mental development, attract

into the schools large numbers of young children, who, if left unprovided for, would in most cases, have to spend much of their time in the streets, with all the baneful accompaniments, or in confined home rooms. The constant change of work and play in the Infants' Schools, under skilful guidance, secures for the children of the working classes, many of the advantages of the nurseries of the rich.

The Blue Bell Hill Infants Department has been specially organised as a Model Kindergarten; and the mistress of that school, as the Board's Kindergarten Instructress, conducts a class for the instruction of teachers in the system. 65 Infants' Teachers from both Board and Voluntary Schools are thus being trained in improved methods of kindergarten occupations.[7]

This statement begins to show the changing attitude towards the content and conduct of education and also reflects the infiltration of ideas from continental educators such as Heinrich Pestalozzi (1746–1827) and Friedrich Froebel (1782–1852), both in terms of attitude and content, upon the Wilderspinian and Swedenborgian base of the English infant school system, whose ideas and practices had also informed the philosophy of the Home and Colonial College, where Jane Roadknight had trained. Pestalozzi had believed in organic unity or the coalescent of self-power through the integrative teaching of the *head*, the *heart*, and the *body* and had introduced drawing, writing, model-making, field trips, map-making, as well as singing and physical drill into the curriculum in his model school at Yverdon. Froebel had worked with Pestalozzi at Yverdon before establishing his own educational community at Keilhau. *The Education of Man* (1826) and *Pedagogics of the Kindergarten* (1851) expound his thinking on the purpose and nature of education, emphasising the holistic nature of learning. 'Never forget that the essential business of the school is not so much to teach and to communicate a variety and multiplicity of things as it is to give prominence to the ever-living unity that is in all things.'[8]

Jane Roadknight's understanding and interpretation of Froebel's pedagogy allied with her practical genius were in evidence at Blue Bell Hill Kindergarten and Infants' School. The Inspector's report indicates the atmosphere and ethos within the school. The Rev. F.L. Paul, Vicar of Emmanuel, found the children in the school very well taught and considered that the method adopted of answering questions in sentences, instead of by monosyllables, was calculated 'to produce a degree of intelligence not very often found in such small folks'.[9] The new pedagogy was passed on to teachers through the Kindergarten Examination for Head and Assistant Mistresses of both board and voluntary schools, held at the People's College under Jane Roadknight's direction.[10] The impact of such courses resulted in a groundswell of dissatisfaction against current practice as requests for changes to infant departments were made. Only months following the Examination (14 July 1887), the

Committee had before it a large number of applications for kindergarten improvements, the marking of infants' desks, and marking and widening of gallery ledges in the schools. The Committee recommended 'that the Board authorise the necessary work to be done in some selected cases, namely, Berridge-road, Blue-bell-hill, (*sic*) Carlton-road, Huntingdon-street, Radford Boulevard, St. Ann's-well-road'.

Further endorsement of her work came in July 1887, when F.T. Green, Government Inspector, published his report for Blue Bell Hill Infants' School, showing the growing efficiency and popularity of the school:

> The promise of last year has been well fulfilled, and the school is now in a highly efficient state. No point seems to have been neglected in the teaching, which is bright, intelligent, and thoroughly interesting, to the children. The very crowded state of the babies' room has somewhat interfered with their instruction; but the pleasant manner in which order is maintained reflects great credit on their teacher. The Kindergarten games and exercises are a characteristic feature of the school and care should be taken that so far as the accommodation will allow all the children in each class should be employed in them.[11]

Plans were passed for 375 pupils but despite problems of overcrowding and a special meeting of the Management Committee, Jane Roadknight went ahead with her reforms.

Towards the latter end of the nineteenth century major translations of Froebel's works (between 1885 and 1893) brought his philosophy directly to educators. Froebel believed it was a necessary law of life that the child proceeded from some invisible, unchangeable implicit unity which acted in harmony with a corresponding cosmic unity. The link between the *nature and life* of the child with the *nature and life* of the cosmos was made through his playthings. It was appropriate, therefore, that the playthings assumed certain geometrical forms, and through handling, observing and imitating actions arising from these forms, symbolical and meaningful play would result. Froebelians placed movement and play within a metaphysical context, since the playing of games and the singing of songs did more than exercise the limbs and the voice; they also instilled a sense of humanity and nature.

Froebel used the sphere and the cube, the former representing the material expression of pure movement, the latter of stillness or repose. As the child played with these forms he was able to perceive the 'resemblance between opposites'.[12] Both these forms unite in expressing Knowledge, Beauty and Life, the sphere corresponding with the feelings or heart (affective), and the cube to the thought and intellect (cognitive). The conceptual understanding of geometrical cubic forms occurs through the metaphorical dance in which the child becomes acquainted with surfaces, sides, edges and lines, as represented in Figure 10.1. Froebel asserted that 'these forms could also be called

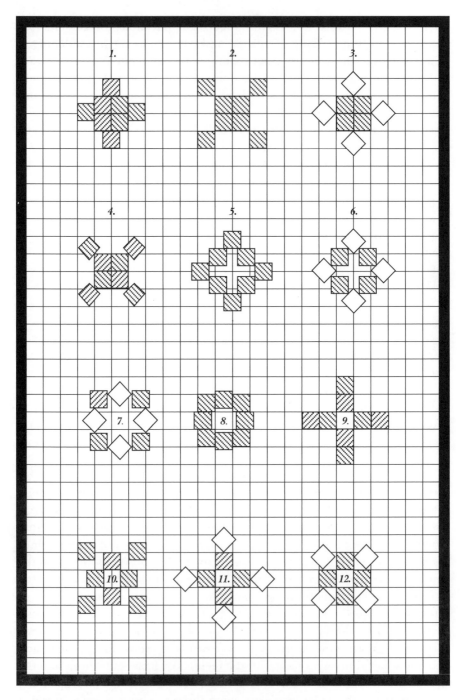

Fig 10.1 *Diagrammatic representation of Froebel's Dance Forms based on the original illustration in F. Froebel,* Pedagogics of the Kindergarten *(New York: Appleton, 1909).*

dance forms as we speak of the dance of worlds, or the dance of seasons, the dance of Nature in general'.[13] By 1888, it was recorded that kindergarten games and occupations were being successfully carried out at Blue Bell Hill. The basic kindergarten 'gifts' used in schools consisted of six woollen balls of different colours, three primary and three secondary; a sphere, cube and cylinder of hard wood; a large cube divisible into eight small ones for constructive exercises; cubes variously divided into bars, smaller cubes, and triangular and quadrangular wood tablets. Jane Roadknight reported that 'a well varied course of instruction has been carried out with intelligence and success, special prominence being given to the kindergarten games and occupations. The elementary subjects, however, have received due attention, and the writing in particular is of exceptional merit.'[14]

Jane Roadknight continued her mission, on the one hand battling against overcrowding at Blue Bell Hill brought about by both popularity and need during a time of high unemployment, on the other hand promoting the kindergarten system in other schools. Her achievements after four years in the post reveal 92.9 per cent 'excellent' awards obtained from board inspections. The Government Code encouraged varied occupations in the form of directed play, including music, games, toys, and short stories read to the children in exemplary fashion by Jane Roadknight and her staff. A report of the three years' work of the board (December 1886–November 1889) noted the progress made:

> The Blue Bell Hill Infants' Department, which was specially organised as a Model Kindergarten is conducted with phenomenal success. The mistress of that school, as the Board's Kindergarten Instructress, has conducted classes for the instruction of teachers in the system with very gratifying results.[15]

The children's physical well-being, both in terms of cleanliness, appearance and exercise, was given more attention as the German form of physical training entered the schools. Although Froebel's own attitude towards physical expression was dramatic, expressive and metaphysical, the system that was adopted by the kindergartens and schools was a derivative of German gymnastics which had evolved in Prussian schools, and used small apparatus, dumb-bells and wands. It was superseded by the Swedish or Ling system.[16] As musical accompaniment enhanced the experience for the children, it was decided to purchase pianos for school use.

Further reports monitor the good progress of infant teaching at Blue Bell Hill, which continued 'to be a model of infant instruction'.[17] Children as young as three and four years old did well and their singing was on a par with that of the upper schools. The Vicar of Sneinton, F.E. Nugee, reported that all the classes were good and 'especially in the four year old class, the teaching is given with much vigour and success and evidently interests the children'.[18] The scripture inspectors were highly impressed with what the children knew and in the manner and conduct of the learning. The Rev. John R. Abel was highly impressed when he inspected the school in 1891:

> I do not wonder that the KINDERGARTEN DEPARTMENT is so popular. Some of the parents have confessed to me that their children would rather be at school than at home. The teachers have no difficulty in gaining attention; their methods of instruction are such as to make the work very enjoyable. They appeal to the natural faculties for acquiring knowledge and the lessons are consequently impressed upon the children's minds. I was much pleased to notice the real interest that was manifested in the welfare of the children. The instruction received under Mrs. Roadknight and her Staff – tempered as it is with so much sympathy and kindness – must have a refining influence upon the children's lives.[19]

The Committee reported that fifty-nine teachers had enrolled as students on a recent course of thirty kindergarten lectures that Jane Roadknight had organised. Forty-eight teachers qualified for examination by regular attendance, of whom twelve presented themselves and eleven passed.[20] The culmination of hard work, visionary zeal and fortitude received national recognition in 1892. Government reports on board schools adopted by the board (14 July 1892) acknowledged the work at Blue Bell Hill Infants' School, stating: '. . . this department is taught in a most zealous and enthusiastic spirit, and is quite a model of what an infants' school of the present day should be'.[21] It marked a turning point in Jane Roadknight's career when her high degree of professionalism was recognised by her appointment as Instructress of Kindergarten and Needlework for the School Board in 1893.[22]

Jane Roadknight continued to dedicate her energies towards developing the kindergarten movement for the school board as well as assuming responsibility for needlework. After a few successful years she was promoted once more, when she became an inspector for the school board. While it was not unusual to have women inspectors at this time, they were mostly found in typically feminine areas – physical training, infant education and in this instance needlework. Travelling to schools around the town she was aware of the home backgrounds and social conditions in which the children lived as well as the economic factors that shaped their lives. Upgrading the standards and value of needlework ran in tandem with improved welfare and education of the young especially as the pupil teachers were taught to draft patterns, cut out and sew garments in order to teach the girls how to make and mend. An initiative to improve the quality of the children's lives was the Children's Guild of Play or 'happy evening' which she started shortly after becoming Board Inspector at Leen Side School, Narrow Marsh, one of the poorest areas of Nottingham where children lived under harsh, substandard conditions.[23]

The project aimed to provide an evening of harmless enjoyment and was hugely popular with an average attendance of three hundred children who went to enjoy the experience of songs, games and fairy-tales. Some, with young babies in arms, were directed off into a large classroom set aside for this purpose and supervised by volunteer workers. The 1898 triennial report of the board recorded that it was a pleasant yet pathetic sight to see hundreds of neglected children, of all ages up to fourteen years, hurrying to the 'Happy Evening' which was one of the brightest hours of their lives. Jane Roadknight desired to extend the scheme to other poor neighbourhoods but declared the work so trying and uncongenial to any but the most zealous that she had not succeeded in recruiting a sufficient number of willing and capable volunteers. Inspector Morgan Owen reported that the '... kindness and patience exhibited by the teachers in dealing with these children, who appear to come from the poorest of homes, deserve the highest commendation'.[24] Through persistence and persuasion, Jane Roadknight enlisted twelve volunteer workers who developed the Guild of Play at Leen Side and made it one of the most interesting and useful branches of the board's work. At Christmas five hundred children 'partook of an excellent tea, consisting of milk and cakes, when the Gilbert Circus Troup also gave, free of charge, the evenings entertainment which was highly enjoyed by the children'.[25]

The overall standard, methods and principles of infant teaching were deemed by the Senior Chief Inspector, the Reverend T.W. Sharpe, to be the most successful part of the elementary school work. Parents thought likewise, evidenced by the large number of infants in attendance below the compulsory age. Organised play had been introduced into the majority of the infants' schools and teachers now took charge of their classes in the playground and joined with scholars in their play. This form of supervision assisted in cultivating habits of orderly play and the growth of politeness in conduct and speech. The best infants' mistresses cooperated with Jane Roadknight, making their kindergarten system an influence pervading all the school work.[26] Conferences were held to promote the understanding that kindergarten methods could apply for older pupils. Jane Roadknight spoke on *Kindergarten in Relation to our Senior Schools* alongside HMI and other practising teachers, reflecting the rising status of the elementary school teacher and their desire to understand and improve practice.[27] Infant mistresses drew up schemes of work for classes in the infant schools in consultation with head teachers of the senior departments who allowed standard I teachers to visit the infant school to observe kindergarten methods. Jane Roadknight expected this would alleviate difficulties encountered when the infant children progressed from the bright sympathetic teaching in infant schools to the more formal work of standard I.

An Education Committee for the City of Nottingham was appointed under the provisions of the Balfour Education Act of 1902 and its powers and duties defined.[28] Mr F. Chastenay, Mr T.H.B. Tallantyre and Mrs J.A. Roadknight were the three inspectors responsible for its implementation. Jane Roadknight's great gift was to bring educational legislation into the realms of practical reality and to transform restricted and narrow methods of schooling into inspirational experiences for children. Although many of her ideas had been formulated at grass-roots level during the latter part of the nineteenth century, it was the Elementary Code of 1904 that allowed greater acceptance of her liberal approach to infiltrate prescribed practice, giving greater substance to her vision. The Code provided the framework for teachers to broaden the constriction of previous practice by offering fundamental work in science, humanities and the arts. Observation, reasoning and thoughtful expression were seen as modes of acquiring knowledge and the Code also recognised the importance of manual and physical education. As changes took place formal teaching methods were replaced by child-centred approaches and the whole ethos of learning for young children became a more pleasurable experience. Timetables began to be restructured to allow for appropriate breaks between lessons and the galleries were removed from infant school classrooms so that more space was created for singing games and play.

'Our set purpose in Infant Schools is to form and strengthen Thought, Power, Imagination, and Individuality', declared Jane Roadknight as she set out to bring about improvements under the new educational regime.[29] Formal reading, writing and arithmetic, now eliminated from the timetables of children below the age of five years, was replaced with kindergarten occupations designed to quicken the senses and develop mental and moral faculties. Sand was utilised for teaching drawing, writing, and modelling. The children drew large objects in coloured chalks on straw boards, on the floor, and on boards placed round the walls, for free and memory drawing. Designing and building were taught by means of the kindergarten gifts – the small wooden bricks, with additional tablets, sticks, thread, rings, shells, beans and seeds. Picture lessons were universally used as a means for the cultivation of observation and language and for the encouragement of intelligent verbal descriptions, while nature lessons were made to vary month by month according to the season of the year. Reading in the upper classes was taught chiefly on the phonetic method and by the use of several interesting and varied narrative and fairy tale readers.

By 1906 all the antiquated galleries from infant schools had been completely removed and now the indoor space was used imaginatively, allowing the child to '. . . get his limbs, and indeed his whole body, into his own power'.[30] No formal drill was taken in infant schools, but only 'rational exercises', for the full development of the body, such as walking, running, jumping, skipping and breathing exercises, movement plays, and kindergarten games which were taken in the playground when the weather permitted. Jane Roadknight and her teachers were making a serious attempt to realise the metaphysical aspect of Froebelian theory, in which free forms of movement, games and dancing were outward expressions of inward action and life.[31] Although the ecstatic enjoyment of the movement plays was derived from a spiritual source, teachers adapted Froebel's ideas in a secular way that reflected their own attitudes and understanding revealed through the demonstrations and concerts of kindergarten children's work that included singing games, skipping, and little plays that the teachers had written.[32] Endorsement for the standards Jane Roadknight had been able to attain came from HMI Hales, and Kenney Herbert (Chief Inspector of the District), who expressed great pleasure in what he had seen.[33] Teachers had taken the fullest advantage of the freedom given to them by the Code and followed a model timetable as a guide. Formal lessons were not given below the age of five years and no lesson was of longer duration than fifteen or twenty minutes, usually to be followed by an interval for rest or play.

Dissemination and application of Froebelian principles in British schools was brought about through the impact of the Froebel Society whose work was being recognised at international and national levels. Membership had increased from 562 in 1899 to 2,600 in 1910. Jane Roadknight realised that the changes she was initiating reflected the recognition of the society's work by the education authority and that achievements at a local level would be strengthened if affiliation to a national organisation could be arranged. The Nottingham Branch of the Froebel Society was founded in October 1905 at a meeting held under the auspices of the Provisional Committee of the proposed branch, under the chairmanship of Councillor C.L. Manning.[34] Jane Roadknight's proposal that a branch of the society be formed in Nottingham was met with unanimous approval and sixty-four names of intending members were submitted at the close of the meeting. Lady Belper agreed to be President and Jane Roadknight was elected to represent the branch on the Central London Council and be chairman of the local committee. The first meeting was held on 24 January 1906 when the membership numbered around 250. A stimulating and informative programme materialised and within three years the membership increased to over 500. It received generous support from the Education Committee and from Nottingham University College. Jane Roadknight reported that the society continued to stimulate in teachers the keenest interest in the principles underlying 'true' education, and was thus developing a wider spirit of cooperation, a broader sympathy, and a happier atmosphere in our schools.[35]

Lectures on curriculum and child development were presented by educational innovators including Cecil Sharp, Margaret MacMillan and Baron D.

Kikuchi, the former Minister of Education in Japan. Jane Roadknight wrote that great interest was being taken by many of the teachers in true kindergarten teaching, that methods were more intelligently understood and that consequently the mechanical repetition had nearly disappeared. Only a few were failing to lift themselves out of 'the old traditional grinding groove'.[36] Her Report for 1907 indicates that methodology for infant teaching was more deeply understood, that teachers were better trained and that status, scholarship and professionalism had increased.

> The natural method from the concrete to the abstract, from the known to the unknown, is now generally followed. The best teachers draw upon the child's own knowledge and gradually, by easy stages, increase that knowledge. They utilise fully the child's powers of observation, its love of questioning and movement. Intelligent teachers note that the natural impulse of a child is to chatter all the live-long day, and that to repress this tendency when the child enters school is to rebel against a fundamental law of mental growth and development. Therefore, they commence in the earlier stages of a child's school life with lessons in language – by learning to talk, instead of by useless, meaningless lessons in reading.[37]

Jane Roadknight indicates that the relationship between knowledge areas within the curriculum was more conspicuous and the manner in which these related to the child's understanding was now more readily understood. Child-centred approaches were growing much stronger and the foundation of education at infant level was comprehended in relation to development at later stages of the child's education:

> Expression lessons are largely encouraged. The child expresses what it has either seen or heard in its own words, or by means of drawing or modelling; and no effort is spared to make the child self-reliant. Stories enter largely into the curriculum, preparing the way for the more formal lessons in Literature, History and Geography in the Senior Schools.[38]

Teachers recorded their syllabus of work and a daily diary that demonstrated planning and recording of work. The old-fashioned fear of school had been expelled as joy, which Jane Roadknight regarded as one of the greatest aids to the full and harmonious development of a child's powers, became a prominent element. Bold efforts to transform the classroom environment continued, the school room tone had been banished, children were not forced to imitate and repeat lessons, and teachers devoted thought and time upon the neat appearance of their schoolrooms, '. . . making them bright and pretty with suitable pictures – "few and good" is their motto – growing plants, flowers and birds, all of which have unconscious influence in moulding the aesthetic taste of the child'.[39] A loan scheme was provided by the Castle Museum and pictures were 'selected with the utmost care encouraging the child's love of the beautiful'.[40] The Castle Museum Committee lent several good works of art to some of the schools, and Jane Roadknight intended that the scheme would be extended so that more children would appreciate good art.

Nottingham Castle Museum, where, at the onset of her career, Jane Roadknight had taken her Blue Bell Hill kindergarten classes, was a squat, square building that crowned the sandstone rock, overlooking the bustling city and the extensive Trent valley beyond. In *Sons and Lovers*, D.H. Lawrence depicted the scene looking down into the industrial and residential Meadows area and along the route of the Midland railway, the railway that led towards Jane Roadknight's home in Beeston. The view was familiar to the city's teachers and children, many of whom resided in the tightly packed houses and attended the schools that Jane Roadknight had worked to transform. The busy railway track and canal extended beyond the dense black dwellings towards the glistening river and into the distance, where great 'stretches of country darkened with trees and faintly brightened with corn-land, spread towards the haze, where the hills rose blue beyond grey'.[41] Each day, when Jane Roadknight returned to her home 'where the hills rose blue beyond grey', doubtless she would have reflected upon her achievements and the way in which she had brought Froebelian pedagogy into the lives of children from the urban slums. There is a hint of pride in her words: '. . . it is gratifying to be able to report that the Infant Schools of the City as a whole rank amongst the first in the country, owing to the zeal, sympathy and intelligent cooperation of the teachers, and to the valuable lectures and demonstrations given under the auspices of the Nottingham Branch of the Froebel Society'.[42]

Jane Roadknight was far from complacent. She realised that a 'living education' should continually improve and new solutions be sought to changing problems. She established the classes for children with special needs and staffed them with selected intelligent kindergarten teachers and complemented medical inspections by offering education in personal hygiene when teachers carried out daily inspections of each child. She established home–school relationships through establishing conferences of teachers and parents. Formal reading, writing and number received careful attention in the upper divisions of the infants' schools as policy, ensuring that normal children were able to undertake standard I work between the ages of seven and eight years. Innovation was encouraged through experiments in teaching methods, especially in the use of the free timetable which helped cultivate the children's self-reliance and independence. Jane Roadknight advised teachers to undertake observations and recordings of each other's practice and stressed that it was the child's activities and needs that provided the basis of school schemes. Encouraging teachers to advance pedagogical understanding through monitoring their own practice reflects how she acknowledged individual and organic growth in both teaching and learning, thereby moving away from the strict adherence to the more mystical aspects of Froebel's gifts and occupations. By 1914 she had written about the experiments taking place in the infants' schools, with free timetables, speech training, drama, and simple eurhythmics.[43] Her philosophical idealism underpinned passionate realism that recognised the preparatory role of the school in a process of life-long learning.[44]

Just before the First World War, a report published by the Education Committee claimed the infants schools ranked among the first in the country, several of them exemplifying an intelligent adaptation of Montessori methods to English educational need. Jane Roadknight, who described Montessori's system as 'Froebelianism re-discovered in the light of modern educational Science', encouraged teachers to acquaint themselves thoroughly with its spirit without mechanical adoption of its methods in detail. During the disruption of the war years, the local authority opened evening school play centres serving over one thousand children requiring assistance and guidance in play and recreation. In 1917 the education authority was empowered to carry out a survey to qualify for a supplementary grant and as a result formulated a mission statement published as the *Educational Ideal*. Wider horizons and higher aspirations for the individual child were identified as the foundation for future stability and fulfilment. The child was seen within the context of the family, the country, the race, the needs of the nation, and the conditions of international goodwill. Teachers were expected to place children in an environment that encouraged learning through discovery based on the 'free play of their natural activities'.[45] At infant level, training commenced from 'instinctive motor reactions to perceptual objects', and from this the child progressed through stages involving manual and practical skills as well as intellectual development. 'We must also devote sedulous, though unobtrusive, attention to its emotional, moral and aesthetic activities, and to improving, stimulating and developing freedom of individual effort and initiative; the aim throughout being, as previously stated, rather to put the child into the way of learning (active attitude) than to seek to teach him (passive).'[46] The practical response was the instigation of the 'free' timetables, educational experiments, rhythmic exercises, music, an enriched curriculum, personal hygiene and courteous social habits which Jane Roadknight had painstakingly instigated and developed in the schools. Play and pleasure became important aspects within the education of the child, and through rhythmical movements, self-expression and self-discipline were developed.

Hard work and dedication to perfectionism began to take its toll, and in January 1919 the Elementary Schools' Sub-Committee reported, with regret, that 'Mrs. Roadknight, acting under Medical advice, is compelled to seek relief from full time service, and they have unanimously decided to recommend the Committee to appoint Mrs. Roadknight to give part-time service as Consulting Organiser of Infant Schools . . .'.[47] Shortly after this Jane Roadknight retired, having accomplished the daunting task of establishing and maintaining the highest quality of infant education that any authority could offer as indicated in the written reports of inspectors and in the published reports of the Education Committee.

Jane Roadknight is best described as an educational luminary whose vision and aspirations provided the foundation upon which the city of Nottingham's infants' schools flourished. She brought the ideology of freedom and play in infant education into the meanest classroom and through her dedicated teachers she anticipated the promise of the *Education Ideal*. She established and maintained, through working with and building on the work of others, the bedrock of educational understanding, so that today, although she has passed out of living memory, the impact of her work is still felt through the tradition of Froebelian practice in the city's schools.

NOTES

1. The Home and Colonial Infant School Society (1836) trained teachers for infant schools.
2. In 1870 12 per cent Standard IV or above, in the 1890s 40 per cent.
3. Minutes of the Nottingham School Board (NSB), 1870–1903, Printed Reports of School Board and Sub-Committees Book 5, p. 148.
4. *Ibid.*, p. 149.
5. *Ibid.*, p. 149.
6. *Ibid.*, p. 149.
7. Minutes of the NSB, 1870–1903, Printed Reports of School Board and Sub-Committees Book No. 7, 1885–1887, pp. 485–6.
8. F. Froebel, *The Education of Man*, trans. W.N. Hailman (New York, 1887), pp. 134–5.
9. Minutes of the NSB, 1870–1903, Printed Reports of School Board and Sub-Committees Book 7, p. 567.
10. Minutes of the NSB, 1870–1903, Printed Reports of School Board and Sub-Committees Book No. 8, p. 123, Report of the Teachers' Kinder Garten Examination, 12 May 1887.
11. *Ibid.*, p. 239.
12. F. Froebel, *Pedagogics of the Kindergarten* (New York, 1909), p. 10.
13. *Ibid.*, p. 136.
14. Minutes of the NSB, 1870–1903, Printed Reports of School Board and Sub-Committees Book No. 9, p. 135.
15. Minutes of the NSB, 1870–1903, Printed Reports of School Board and Sub-Committees Book No. 10/11, p. 175.
16. *Ibid.*
17. Minutes of the NSB, 1870–1903, Printed Reports of School Board and Sub-Committees Book No. 10/11, 1889, p. 246. 13 November 1890.
18. Minutes of the NSB, 1870–1903, Printed Reports of School Board and Sub-Committees Book No. 12, 1891, p. 308.
19. *Ibid.*
20. Minutes of the NSB, 1870–1903, Printed Reports of School Board and Sub-Committees Book Nos 10/11, p. 14.
21. Minutes of the NSB, 1870–1903, Printed Reports of School Board and Sub-Committees Book No. 14, p. 148.
22. *Ibid.*

23. The Guild of Play developed from the Settlement Movement, an international movement which aimed to alleviate the lives of children through traditional customs of song, dance and music.

24. Minutes of the NSB, 1870–1903, Printed Reports of School Board and Sub-Committees Book No. 19, 1898, p. 312.

25. Minutes of the NSB, 1870–1903, Printed Reports of School Board and Sub-Committees Book No. 22, p. 57.

26. Minutes of the NSB, 1870–1903, Printed Reports of School Board and Sub-Committees Book No. 19, p. 663.

27. D. Wardle, *Education and Society in Nineteenth-Century Nottingham* (Cambridge, 1971), p. 101.

28. First meeting was on 9 July 1903 when the School Board handed over to the LEA. The numbers were 94 Board departments with places for 28,546 children, 64 Church of England departments for 13,079 children, and 14 Roman Catholic departments with 2,473 children.

29. City of Nottingham Education Committee Minutes (CNEC) 1903–4, pp. 489–93.

30. Froebel, *Pedagogics of the Kindergarten*, p. 241.

31. Explorative movement plays were devised as the vehicle through which the child discovered the world.

32. *Ibid.*, p. 261.

33. CNEC Minutes, 1905–6, p. 499.

34. *Nottingham Evening News* (28 Oct 1905). The Froebel Society was founded in 1873.

35. CNEC Minutes, 1907–8, p. 689.

36. CNEC Minutes, 1906–7, p. 596.

37. *Ibid.*

38. *Ibid.*, p. 596.

39. *Ibid.*, p. 600.

40. CNEC Minutes, 1909–10, p. 307.

41. D.H. Lawrence, *Sons and Lovers* (Harmondsworth, 1962. First published 1913), p. 331.

42. CNEC Minutes, 1913–14, pp. 294–6.

43. *Ibid.*, p. 296.

44. CNEC Minutes, 1914–15, pp. 257–65.

45. CNEC Minutes, 1916–17, pp. 345–7.

46. *Ibid.*, p. 347.

47. CNEC Minutes 1918–19, p. 414.

INTERVIEW

The late Mrs Lindley (née Gregory), 1983.

CORRESPONDENCE

The late Professor W.G.H. Armytage.

CHAPTER ELEVEN

English Revisionist Froebelians and the Schooling of the Urban Poor

KEVIN J. BREHONY

This chapter is concerned with revisionist Froebelians in England during the period 1890 to 1914, their critique of the Froebelian orthodoxy and their interventions in the schooling of the urban poor. The organisational core of this movement was the Froebel Society, founded in 1874, and the National Froebel Union (NFU), founded in 1887. Also constitutive of the Froebel movement was a diverse mixture of institutions, journals and other publications and cultural practices. Where a movement is established, an orthodox interpretation is created by those who hold power within it. In this context, the outcomes of the attempts to revise the orthodox interpretation of Froebel may be charted through an examination of the revisions made by the NFU. This was an important component of the Froebel movement as it controlled its examinations and awarded Froebel Certificates to successful candidates. As a consequence it was an important site where Froebelian ideas and practices were codified and reproduced. By 1911 the practices desired by the revisionists had supplanted those that had been previously constituted and this may be taken as a measure of the revisionists' success.[1]

Few previous commentators have grasped fully the significance of the fact that the Froebel movement was composed overwhelmingly of women. At least one of its participants regarded it as part of the women's movement and, because it supported and enabled middle-class women to gain employment, it may be considered a part of feminist history.[2] From this it follows that the conflict between each of the Froebelian camps mainly involved women confronting other women. But at the same time, the beliefs of all the women in the Froebel movement were subject to challenge by male critics whose Darwinian notions threatened to depose the Froebelian domination of the theory if not the practice of early childhood education. Many of these, like the American psychologist and founder of the child-study movement G. Stanley Hall (1844–1924), were engaged in establishing university departments of education. Within these departments theories of pedagogy and education became rationalised and institutionalised.

The first kindergarten was opened in England in 1851 by Johannes and Bertha Ronge.[3] The Ronges were refugees from the reaction that followed the failed revolution of 1848 among the German states. As the kindergarten was itself a German import, unsurprisingly many of its early supporters were other Germans who had come for similar reasons to settle in England. What was understood as kindergarten theory and practice was also conveyed from Germany by such women as the Baroness von Marenholtz-Bülow, Madame Adèle de Portugall, Madame Michaelis, Maria Boelte, Eleonore Heerwart and Julie Salis-Schwabe.

In the absence of Froebel himself – he died in 1852 – these German women and their English supporters – like the indefatigable advocates of women's education, Emily Shirreff and her sister Maria Grey, plus a small number of male supporters such as the Manchester-based William Herford – produced an authoritative version of the kindergarten which soon crystallised into an orthodoxy.[4] This was undoubtedly assisted by the production of kindergarten manuals in which Froebel's propositions made at varying levels of abstraction were codified and simplified for the use of teachers. Of these, the most widely used were the Ronges' *A Practical Guide to the English Kindergarten*, which, by 1893, was in its eighteenth edition, and *The Paradise of Childhood* written by Edward Wiebe, a German music teacher who had emigrated to the USA.[5] At the heart of this orthodoxy were the Gifts and Occupations. These were the items that constituted Froebel's pedagogic apparatus. Although learning through play in the kindergarten was interpreted to include singing, dancing and nature study, the Gifts and Occupations were central to Froebel's system. Froebel had endowed his apparatus and his 'Mother's Book' with great symbolic significance.[6] The latter was also highly regarded for its symbolism by the orthodox or 'conservative' wing.[7]

The revisionist cause was assisted somewhat by changes in the conditions Froebelians encountered in England. The early Froebelians were confined to a ghetto of kindergartens in private schools catering mainly for the *avant garde* fractions of the middle and upper classes. But as the girls' high schools opened, further opportunities arose because these schools tended to have kindergartens attached to them. Into these kindergartens went trained Froebelian women many of whom, as girls, had been pupils at them. Among the peculiarities of the English system and which distinguished it from other national systems was the provision of infant schools for children below the age of six.[8] As state involvement in elementary schooling rapidly grew during the 1860s and 1870s, so did the number of schools. Consequently, a major objective of the Froebelians became the 'conversion' of the state schooling provided for young children to the kindergarten. The establishment of school boards after 1870 seemed to offer the potential to achieve this aim but the Froebelians identified numerous obstacles to the implementation of their strategy. These included the conditions pertaining in many of the schools: large classes and teachers untrained in kindergarten or, often, in any method.[9] When the kindergarten was implemented in the elementary schools it typically took the form of a rigid, formalised pedagogy far distant from Froebel's principles.[10]

The Elementary School Code, with its system of payment by results and its bureaucratic prescription of the curriculum, was, as many Froebelians perceived, a major obstacle to the implementation of the kindergarten. Exceptions tended to occur in infants' departments which were free from the requirements of the Code and its annual examinations. Unable to transform to their satisfaction the education provided for young children in the elementary schools, many younger Froebelians at the end of the nineteenth century attempted another strategy. This was to establish kindergartens supported by voluntary contributions and free of charge to the parents whose children attended them. But although the Froebelians associated with the free kindergartens were critical of state-regulated schooling they were sufficiently collectivist not to want a voluntary alternative to the state-run infant schools and departments. Instead, they wanted the free kindergartens to 'serve as object lessons to point the way in which the community's efforts on behalf of the young child of the slums may be directed'.[11]

This was a new departure for the Froebel movement as it involved the transformation of the kindergarten. Hitherto it had been a middle-class institution in the sense that it was patronised by that class and was also organised by it. Now, it was to be changed into one which its advocates claimed was eminently suited to the needs of the children of the urban poor.

A key moment in the development of the revisionist Froebelian child-saving ideology was the foundation, in 1881, of the Pestalozzi Froebel House in Berlin by Froebel's grand-niece, Henriette Schrader-Breymann. The practices developed there flowed, in part, from Schrader-Breymann's critical reading of Froebel and Pestalozzi and from her own sympathies for German liberal politics.[12] Thus, from the outset, this faction was at odds with literal interpretations of Froebel made by those who, the revisionist Henrietta Brown Smith claimed, exhibited 'blind and unquestioning acceptance' of the sanctity of the Gifts and Occupations and to Froebel's mystical symbolism.[13]

After living at Keilhau, the site of Froebel's 'Educational Institute', Henriette married Karl Schrader, a railway administrator and liberal politician, in 1871. They moved to Berlin in 1874, where Henriette reorganised the 'Society for Family and Popular Education'. This organisation had been set up by the Baroness von Marenholtz-Bülow to run private kindergartens which were used to subsidise the training of teachers and kindergartens for working-class children. In 1881, the Schrader-Breymanns purchased a house in Berlin for the purpose of running a training seminar. This became the Pestalozzi–Froebel House which was in many ways a precursor of the settlement houses that were established later among the poor in cities in England and the United States.[14] Within the Pestalozzi–Froebel House attempts were made to reproduce the social relations and the educative community which were thought to have existed in the kind of pre-industrial family which had been idealised by Pestalozzi and Froebel. This focus on the family but more specifically on the mother and the casting of the family in the role of community regenerator became a characteristic of all the free kindergarteners.

Often referred to as 'Spiritual Motherhood' or 'Social Maternalism', this view is sometimes seen as implying women's acceptance of male domination and their own subordination.[15] In the context of late nineteenth-century Germany, however, and also to a lesser extent that of England, spiritual motherhood was an ideology that enabled many middle-class women to 'escape the confines of the domestic sphere'.[16] It also legitimated the entry of middle-class women into certain kinds of paid employment.

Spiritual Motherhood was not the exclusive property of the Pestalozzi–Froebel House faction. It was a concept that was widely accepted within the Froebel movement and beyond. The term 'spiritual mother' was used by the Ronges.[17] Writing in 1858, some years before she helped found the Froebel Society, Emily Shirreff explained that 'what society wants from women is not labour, but refinement, elevation of mind, knowledge, making its power felt through moral influence and sound opinions. It wants civilisers of men, and educators of the young.'[18]

At the centre of this women's mission, presented by Schrader-Breymann, was a heavy emphasis on training. Men in fields such as education resisted training unless they were teaching in elementary schools, but women, in order to gain acceptance in a male-dominated world, engaged in a professionalising project. This was one of the features that distinguished those who had attended the Pestalozzi–Froebel House from other women of similar social backgrounds engaged in philanthropic voluntary work. It was thus a part of the new 'science of charity' which in England was exemplified by the Charity Organisation Society.[19] Unlike earlier forms of philanthropy, the kind advocated by Schrader-Breymann required, as did later women's settlement house founders, that women should 'go among the poor'. This was not simply in order to do good works and exercise compassion but to forge a natural rapport between rich and poor and between the educated and uneducated classes.[20]

In the words of Mary Lyschinska, one of her leading supporters in England, Schrader-Breymann's kindergarten placed the children in natural surroundings, under motherly direction, in the midst of a household, a garden and household pets. These were the props of the Pestalozzi–Froebel House faction's pedagogy which instead of fetishising Froebel's apparatus, emphasised play, nature study and the correlation of subjects around domestic occupations and nature themes.

Among the prominent Froebelians in England who adopted the revisionism of the Pestalozzi–Froebel House at a relatively early stage was Caroline Bishop (1846–1929). Like many other leading Froebelians and women discussed elsewhere in this volume, Bishop was a Unitarian. In 1881 she visited Berlin and there she saw the Pestalozzi–Froebel House. In 1883 she returned to run the Pestalozzi–Froebel House Training College while its director, Annette Hamminck-Schepel, was on holiday.[21] After her return to England, Bishop tried unsuccessfully to get the Froebel Society to adopt the pedagogy of the Pestalozzi–Froebel House. This failure, which stemmed from the hold of the Gifts and Occupations upon the Society's leaders, precipitated her resignation from the Committee of the Froebel Society and her move to Birmingham in 1883.[22] There, in 1890, Bishop moved to Edgbaston where her college, school and kindergarten had a kitchen for cooking, a room for Sloyd[23] and a garden complete with a sandheap for the younger children. An image of Bishop's domestic pedagogy is contained in her biographer's description of how what she termed the 'many-sidedness' of home life was reproduced in the many-sidedness of the community life of the kindergarten. Both the children and the adults were involved fully in the daily domestic labour associated with the kindergarten. Before the classes could begin, the rooms had to be put in order, 'the little tables and chairs must be cleared to give space for the games, gooseberries must be topped and tailed or peas shelled for the school dinner and out of these living experiences came the subject matter of the occupations poetry, story, music and games'.[24] Thus, Froebel's practice of play–work and its use as a basis for learning was still present but his apparatus was no longer central.

In 1898 a plan for an institution modelled on the Pestalozzi–Froebel House to be built in London was outlined in a lecture given by Alice Buckton, a lecturer at the Froebel Educational Institute.[25] Significantly, this lecture drew attention to the high status accorded to the role of the mother by Pestalozzi and Froebel. Buckton's lecture was given at the Sesame Club which had been formed by a 'group of friends' who wished to study and discuss how best to educate their children.[26] By 1897, it had a claimed membership of nine hundred, composed of some who used it purely as a social club and others who wished to pursue their interest in educational theories and practices. Courses on drawing were organised as were others on wood, Sloyd and nature study. In 1899, those members of the Club who were interested chiefly in these activities formed the Sesame League and they announced their intention to establish a 'House for Home Life Training' modelled on the Pestalozzi–Froebel House.

The chief significance of Sesame House lies not so much in its course of training as in its role in the free kindergarten movement. As at the Pestalozzi–Froebel House, it was intended from the outset that a free kindergarten would be opened in connection with Sesame House. In 1899 one was opened with six children in attendance.[27] By the end of its first year of operation, the kindergarten was said to contain 'forty little ones from houses in the neighbourhood, both poor and well-to-do'. In the Third Report on the work of Sesame House, it was claimed that its 'child garden' was 'the first of its kind opened in this country for the poor'.[28] This concern was concretised by an exchange between students at Sesame House and students at Caroline Bishop's Kindergarten Training College in Edgbaston. The intention was that during the exchange the Birmingham students would 'gain experience with the poor'. The kindergarten soon abandoned 'the poor' and, instead, fee-paying children were admitted so that in 1905 it contained a few children of the 'well-to-do' plus the children of a policeman, a baker and a coachman.[29] As at the Froebel Educational Institute, which had similar ambitions, lack of finance proved to be an insurmountable obstacle to the running of a free kindergarten at Sesame House.

The leading revisionist Elsie Murray, who included a survey of the free kindergartens in her history of the Froebel movement, dismissed the claims of the Sesame House kindergarten to be a true free kindergarten on the grounds that it did not 'reach the neglected little ones'.[30] She did, however, observe that the chief function of Sesame House was to act as a 'centre for the training for home life'. In contrast to the students of the Froebel Educational Institute, who were increasingly employed as lecturers and teachers, many of the Sesame House students who did not become nurses became involved in the free kindergarten movement.

What is generally recognised as the first free kindergarten in England was opened at Woolwich in 1900. The Woolwich Mission Kindergarten, as it was known, began in a room provided by a Christian Socialist vicar, the Reverend Walter Wragge.[31] It seems to have owed little to the Pestalozzi–Froebel House faction at Sesame House. Instead, it was formed and supported by a combination of the church and the settlement movement. In England the latter was started by Canon Barnett and his wife Henrietta when they founded Toynbee Hall in 1884. Their intention was to provide somewhere for philanthropic university men to visit and stay for a period in areas marked by poverty. By this means the rich and poor were to come into contact with each other, the former to perform acts of citizenship and the latter to attain citizenship through education and contact with 'cultured' men.[32] As the settlement movement grew, settlements were established specifically for women. Martha Vicinus has pointed to the differences between these settlements and those designed for men. Both exhibited a great deal of idealism tempered by a tendency towards a form of colonialism in their dealings with the poor. However, unlike the men who were in transit, the women in the settlements were there on a permanent basis as they 'were determined to turn philanthropy into a paid profession'.[33]

Many of the settlement workers and the free kindergarteners were impelled to work among the poor by religious motives. Clara Grant, the Froebelian Head of Fern Street School in the East End of London, first of all intended to be a missionary.[34] The idealist and mystical strands in Froebel's thought attracted many followers who were interested in religious questions and the specific problem of how best to teach religion. Writing about the free kindergarten movement in the US, Shapiro said that 'the benevolent men and women of the free-kindergarten crusade were simply extending sanctifying grace to the children of the urban poor through scientific philanthropy'.[35] Scientific philanthropy, he argues, was distinguishable from older forms of charity which were highly individualised. Himmelfarb has identified the beginning of a new 'scientific' attitude towards poverty in England with the founding of the Charity Organisation Society in 1869.[36] But its obsession with differentiating the deserving from the undeserving poor, the labouring poor from the residuum found little echo among the free kindergarteners. In as much as an explanation of the condition of the poor occurs in the free kindergarten literature it conforms to the prevailing moral approach. The notion that poverty was a structural condition related to casual labour, unemployment and the downturns in economic cycles endemic to capitalism was not one they were familiar with. Environmental explanations, it is true, did sometimes appear, as when Lileen Hardy wrote of the mothers of the children who attended her kindergarten that 'with the cramped house space, burdened restricted lives and big families . . . it is hardly to be expected that they will have energy, insight, time and patience to train their children well . . .'.[37] This empathy with the poor was unusual as free kindergarteners saw their pedagogic practice as particularly efficacious for the residuum. They argued that their kindergartens were 'social settlements reaching the parents through the children'.[38] From a Froebelian perspective, all mothers were deficient, to an extent, hence the need to train them. While Froebel's pedagogy, particularly as expressed in the *Mother's Songs*, drew upon the practices of 'successful' mothers, it was his view that what such mothers did unconsciously needed to be made conscious. As Her Majesty's Inspector (HMI) Thomas Rooper explained:

> It was not Froebel's idea to substitute philosophy for maternal instincts, but rather to show that in the treatment of their children by successful mothers a principle was involved which might be understood and applied by all who have to train young children, whether nurses or teachers, or even mothers . . . whose natural instincts failed to supply her with the art of managing her child.[39]

The mothers observed by the free kindergarteners were ones, according to Murray, who were 'either unfit to give any training or else are obliged to go to work and leave their children on the streets'. For Lileen Hardy, who ran St Saviour's Child-Garden in Edinburgh, the mothers of the children at her kindergarten were 'at the best of times often undisciplined children in emotion themselves'.[40] She also thought that the mothers were ignorant, physically incapable of coping and self-indulgent. They allowed their children to go to bed late, bribed them with halfpennies and, in Hardy's experience, gave to their children a higher proportion of the family income than the wealthy classes would. For a visitor to the Greet kindergarten in Birmingham, the lack of home discipline, which through contact with the mothers the kindergarten sought to ameliorate, constituted, 'one of our greatest national dangers'.[41]

In England also the free kindergarten phenomenon benefited from its possession of 'affinities' with a newly developing social and political stance towards the urban poor in England which emerged in the 1880s.[42] A major aspect of this new approach was not the ending of the deserving and undeserving distinction but a readiness to adopt collectivist strategies towards the poor. This willingness to embrace collectivism in the form of state or local state provision was a significant departure from the individualism of an earlier era. Oliver Lodge, a leading spiritualist and a professor at Birmingham University, told the Birmingham People's Kindergarten Association that too many things were left to charity and private enterprise. If he had his way, he declared, free kindergartens would be lavishly supported out of public funds.[43]

The educationalist Michael Sadler, who became President of the Froebel Society in 1904, argued that the theory of human nature found in Froebel's *Education of Man* needed 'much modification before we can apply it to the backward races of Africa or to the degenerates of our great cities'. However lacking in 'progressive' sentiments this approach might appear, it was one which, in many respects, was shared by the Socialist, one-time Froebelian and founder of the nursery school Margaret McMillan and by many of the free kindergarteners with whom she had much in common as well as the Froebelians' great rival, Maria Montessori.[44]

Despite the problems associated with such an ambiguous term, 'collectivism' is arguably a much more illuminating label for this new mode of state regulation than either Socialism of the Fabian variety or even New Liberalism which were both subsumed by it.[45] For Froebelian revisionists like Elsie Murray, the free kindergartens were a means of bringing 'true education' to bear on 'social questions'. This was to be done by providing the children who attended them with 'the conditions that are the right of every child, . . . including decency, cleanliness, fresh air, sunlight, gentle guidance, and sympathy born of understanding'.[46]

Notably, Murray's list of essential conditions for the care of young children makes no mention of school knowledge. This was far from uncommon among the revisionists. Lucy Latter, a teacher at the 'Invicta' Board School at Blackheath, was only one of many who argued for the abolition of all exercises in reading, writing and counting for the under fives.[47] The absence of any reference to curriculum in Murray's list implied that the state elementary school system, because of its insistence on the primacy of school knowledge, did not provide the desired 'true education' for the children of the urban poor. Rather fortuitously, these sentiments corresponded to ones held by Robert Morant, Permanent Secretary to the Board of Education, who, prior to taking up that appointment, was a member of the Council of the Froebel Society.[48] Writing to Margaret McMillan he expressed the view that 'what subjects are taught and how they are taught do not matter anything like so much nowadays as attention (a) to the physical condition of the scholars and of the teacher and (b) to the physiological aspect of the school'.[49]

A second pressure that was to impel the revisionist cause was the critique of what was seen as Froebel's metaphysics by some members of the newly emerging academy. In contrast, members of the academy claimed, on the basis of psychological insights, to have produced a more scientific pedagogy. A key figure in this, alongside the American pragmatist philosopher and educationalist John Dewey (1859–1952), was G. Stanley Hall who was critical of Froebel's theory of play.[50] His use of an evolutionary or Darwinian perspective to criticise the Froebelian orthodoxy generally was echoed in England by Graham Wallas, a prominent Fabian and an active member of the London School Board.[51]

While the free kindergarteners wrote about their practice or had it written about by others, the main work of revising Froebel in England was conducted by women located at some distance from the free kindergartens in the colleges.[52] Excluding Margaret McMillan, who in many respects was a Froebelian revisionist who spanned the divide between practice and theory but who drew upon discourses other than those in the Froebelian tradition, there were four main figures among the revisionists. At the turn of the century all were fairly recent arrivals on the Froebelian national stage. They represented a new generation of Froebelian leaders who were based mainly in the training colleges. Froebelians who clung to the symbolism of the gifts and occupations tended to belong to a former generation whose institutional base was in the private kindergartens. There they were locked in a position of isolation which was reinforced by the rejection of their pedagogy by the majority of elementary school teachers. Furthermore, their social class location cut them off from the world of mass elementary schooling designed specifically for the working classes. Many elementary school heads would not employ middle-class women teachers and the experiences of some of the few who, like the

Fabian Society pamphleteer Katherine St John Conway, attempted to teach what a character in D.H. Lawrence's *The Rainbow* called 'dirty, board-school brats' show that the experience was a far from happy one.[53] Her health broke down while struggling to teach a class of seventy infants in the working class district of St Philips in Bristol.

The first of the four revisionists to be considered here is Grace Owen (1873–1965). She was trained in Froebelian methods at the Blackheath Kindergarten Training College. Owen obtained a BSc from the prestigious Teachers' College, Columbia University at New York and while she was there her account of a mission kindergarten in New York was published in 1900 in the English Froebelian journal *Child Life*. She also published several other descriptions of similar kindergartens in the United States.[54] She went on in 1923 to become an Honorary Secretary of the Nursery School Association of Great Britain of which she was a founder member and a lecturer at Manchester University where she taught Susan Isaacs. She was also the Principal of the Mather Training College for Nursery and Junior School Teachers 1917–24 and the Principal of the City of Manchester and Mather Training College 1924–6.

Grace Owen was not the only revisionist Froebelian to draw her inspiration from developments in the USA. The most prominent advocate in England of Dewey's revision of Froebel was Maria Elizabeth Findlay (1855–1912). She was a sister of J.J. Findlay who was the principal promoter of Dewey's educational ideas in England and who also taught Susan Isaacs when Professor of Education at Manchester University.[55] Maria Findlay's career was typical of the new professional women who came to prominence in the Froebel movement at the turn of the century. She was educated privately and at a Moravian school in Germany before commencing a career as a teacher in girls' high schools. After gaining an external BA degree from the University of London, she became head of the Stockton-on-Tees High School for Girls. She held this post for a number of years until she left to spend a term studying psychology at Edinburgh. Following this period of study, Findlay spent three years as head of the City High School in Montreal. This period of teaching was followed by three years in the United States studying under G. Stanley Hall and at the schools of Colonel Parker and John Dewey.

Findlay returned to England in 1898 and she became an instructor at Southlands Training College and a Lecturer and Organiser of Method at the Froebel Educational Institute. In 1901, she became a member of the Council of the Froebel Society and, subsequently, of the Governing Body of the NFU. In addition to her writing and teaching, Maria Findlay attempted to express revisionist Froebelianism in practice at the Mayland Mill School which was situated in Joseph Fels's land resettlement scheme. Joseph Fels (1854–1914) was an American who subsidised a number of progressive causes including some of Margaret McMillan's initiatives to ameliorate the health of children of the labouring poor.[56] Fels was a 'single taxer', a follower of Henry George, who accumulated a large fortune through the manufacture of Naptha Soap. The Mayland Mill School he financed is described in *School and Life*.[57] For a year, from 1908 to 1909, the school was under the reluctant control of the local authority as Morant, the Permanent Secretary to the Board of Education, had virtually forced it to open.[58]

She also contributed an article entitled 'The Training Of Teachers In The United States Of America' to one of the Board of Education's *Special Reports* series.[59] In this article, Maria Findlay presented the case made also by other revisionists for the proposition that the 'reform of school methods based on principles of mental development could be effected only by teachers who understood those principles'.[60] She included in her article an account of the work of Colonel Parker and John Dewey. She described, for example, how, at Cook County Normal School, Colonel Parker made 'life' the basis of the curriculum. In her judgement, Parker's philosophy of education was 'most akin to that of Froebel' but instead of the Gifts and Occupations the children at Cook County studied 'Anthropology and the lives of primitive races yet living, natural science and myth, industries and games, civic government and popular song . . .'.[61]

At the age of thirty-three Elsie Riach Murray became a student at Maria Grey Training College. After a period lecturing on Froebelian principles and methods at Stockwell Training College she was appointed head of the kindergarten at Maria Grey Training College. Under her direction, Maria Grey became the main centre for the diffusion of a revisionist Froebelianism connected to the work of Dewey. Her book *Froebel As A Pioneer In Modern Psychology* presented a reading of Froebel that held his psychology to have been a precursor of that of McDougall, Stout and Sully.[62] The knowledge produced by these male psychologists constituted a distinct threat to the foundations of Froebelian ideas whether they were revisionist or orthodox. But in spite of her efforts to assimilate the idealist Froebel to contemporary 'scientific', Darwinian thinking in education her efforts ended largely in failure. The problem was, as an anonymous reviewer in the *Times Educational Supplement* observed, 'the stones are from the Froebelian quarry, but the plan of the resulting edifice is Miss Murray's own'.[63]

Murray also expounded the revisionist view of the symbolism that surrounded the Gifts and Occupations and criticised the orthodoxy as defended by Susan Blow.[64] A former pupil of the Hegelian, German-American Maria Kraus-Boelte, Blow was the leader of the conservative faction within the International Kindergarten Union. She was a tenacious defender of Froebel's symbolism and of a literal adherence to Froebel's practices, and while the orthodox position had its adherents in England it was Blow who best articulated it.[65] Her involvement indicates that the struggle for hegemony within the Froebel movement was not simply a matter for the Froebelians in England but was one of international proportions.

Writing in 1920, the Froebelian Alice Woods, formerly head of Maria Grey Training College, registered the impact of Dewey. Following him, she wrote, the modern Froebelian 'leads the older child along the lines of primitive man, and no longer limits him to the rigid apparatus of the older Froebelians, but provides him with sticks and stones, sand and clay, wood and bricks as the Froebelians always did, adding pins, hammer, nails and string'.[66] Like the other revisionists, Murray quoted Dewey approvingly. But it was Maria Findlay who made most use of Dewey's critical appropriation of Froebel. Her description of Dewey's Laboratory School was cast unmistakably in Deweyean terms. At the school, she wrote, 'The children are there employed at various industries with a view, not only to form habits of industry and helpfulness, but also to bring them into right relations to society, and to promote rational intellectual development. Knowledge is sought for an answer to the problems which arise in connection with manual work.'[67] Having absorbed the Deweyean critique of Froebel, Maria Findlay began to assail the 'conservative' Froebelians who clung to the idealist and mystical legitimation of their practices. The first of her attacks on the old school of Froebelians occurred in 1900 in an article entitled 'Miss Blow on Froebel's Philosophy of Education'. She criticised Susan Blow again at the Conference of the Froebel Society in 1901 where she presented a paper entitled, 'Kindergarten Games'.[68] Later, in 1909, Maria Findlay wrote a series of articles for *Child Life* criticising Susan Blow's book *Educational Issues In The Kindergarten*.[69] The value of kindergarten games, argued Elsie Murray, lay chiefly in the opportunities which they provided for social training and not, as Blow argued, in their symbolism. Murray was clear as to the practices she wanted to see discarded. At the Froebel Society's conference in 1903 she went on to the offensive in a paper graphically entitled 'That symmetrical paper folding and symmetrical work with the gifts are a waste of time for both students and children',[70] and in the same year another revisionist, Henrietta Brown Smith, attacked the kindergarten occupations in *Child Life*.[71]

Henrietta Brown Smith's career exemplifies the extent to which the revisionists in the Froebel movement managed to gain an institutional foothold in the expanding field of schooling. It also exemplifies the processes by means of which the revisionist reading of Froebel, (the challenge of Montessori notwithstanding), came to dominate the field of early childhood education for the best part of the twentieth century. A student at Maria Grey, she taught for some years and then returned to college. In 1901 she obtained a Higher Certificate of the NFU with first class distinctions in the Theory of Education and Class Teaching.[72] She subsequently became Mistress of Method at the British and Foreign School Society's college at Saffron Walden, which opened in 1884. Women who wished to become infant teachers were introduced to kindergarten methods there. After that Brown Smith lectured at Goldsmiths' College and in 1921 she was appointed an HMI for infant and nursery schools and later for training colleges.

On the surface, the Deweyean critique of Froebel was concerned mainly with the apparatus and the idealist baggage that accompanied it, but at a deeper level it rejected the exclusively child-centred and individualist approach of the conservative Froebelians. Dewey had abolished, in his own thought at least, any contradiction between the needs of the individual and the needs of society. In *The Child And The Curriculum,* for example, Dewey counselled: 'Abandon the notion of subject-matter as something fixed and ready-made in itself, outside the child's experience; cease thinking of the child's experience as also something hard and fast; see it as something fluent, embryonic, vital; and we realize that the child and the curriculum are simply two limits which define a single process.'[73]

In similar vein, Maria Findlay argued that in formulating the general aims of education there was merit in both the child-centred and society-centred positions but what was important was the question of 'the relative emphasis' to be laid on them. With regard to the curriculum, recapitulation theory held, for her, the key to bridging the two approaches.[74] From the point of view of the child, she suggested that its 'natural, spontaneous' interests arose in the order that they emerged in the 'race'. The first interest to emerge was 'activity'. This interest could only be satisfied by engaging in industries which met 'the three primary goads driving the savage, of the primitive forest and of our London slums alike',[75] which were food, clothing and shelter. The 'savages' of the London slums were referred to mainly as the 'residuum'.[76] Members of this category were described by the economist Alfred Marshall as having 'a poor physique and a weak character' and moreover were 'limp in body and mind'.[77] Their condition had moral causes and was closely associated with drunkenness and other vicious habits. Findlay's conflation of images of the 'residuum' with ones of 'race' were quite common in late nineteenth-century discourse on poverty but they were a far cry from the symbolism of the sphere and the cube of Froebel's Gifts and his bucolic songs and plays. The most suitable curriculum activities for these needs were not, she argued, those of manual training and laundry work but 'cooking, weaving and constructing'. These activities not only aroused the thinking powers of children who wished to discover easier ways of doing things but they also had 'ethical value' in that they forged close bonds 'between the child and his fellows'. But the stress on socialised labour in Findlay's account did not imply curriculum construction for its own sake. Like Dewey, she held that the school had a wider purpose than that of merely providing children with the appropriate conditions for growth. Schooling, in her view, needed to 'counteract the arrestive tendencies of the monotonous toil' to which people are condemned. Adopting an evolutionary perspective, Findlay looked back to a 'golden age', a time that predated the division of labour and asked rhetorically, 'Must not the savage woman have been necessarily placed on a higher level than the mass of our people who toil in factories and workshops at one small piece of work endlessly repeated?'[78] Thus was the Romantic critique of industrial capitalism harnessed to a pedagogic practice intended to discipline the residuum.

The achievements of the women discussed here were little short of remarkable. At the personal level they broke through the constraints and barriers that constituted the domestic ideology which confined many of their sisters to home and hearth. Their pursuit of academic knowledge and qualifications in a period when women were routinely denied them was single-minded and courageous. In the slums, they endured great personal hardship in the course of their attempts to ameliorate the condition of the poor and they displayed great resourcefulness in raising the necessary funds to sustain their work.

Collectively they not only revised Froebel but put in place the main out-lines of a pedagogic practice which was based on the study of the develop-ment of young children and made their perceived needs the point of departure of an educational process. The work in the 1920s of Susan Isaacs at the Malting House was almost in a direct line of descent from the revisionist Froebelians.[79] Whitbread, the historian of the nursery and infant school, states of the free kindergartens that 'they were undoubtedly healthy and happy places for the few three-to-six-year-old slum children lucky enough to attend them'.[80] Leaving aside the methodological problems involved in actually demonstrating this assertion, it is one, almost certainly, which few could dissent from. The plight of the children of the urban poor at the beginning of the twentieth century was undeniably grave as the Interdepart-mental Committee on Physical Deterioration and the annual Reports of the Medical Officer of the Board of Education revealed. While it might be argued at the very least that the Froebelian pedagogy was probably a more positive experience than, as Sir John Gorst put it, being 'beaten with canes' in the public elementary school, Foucault and his followers argue that there is no difference, that both approaches are forms of power.[81] Arguably, pessimism of this kind disables any political and social action aimed at the amelioration of the poor and the oppressed.

Nevertheless many of these women exhibited an attitude to the poor which bordered on a form of class cultural aggression. And in so far as their notions became embodied in the expanded welfare state of the twentieth century, a critical appraisal of their contribution cannot evade their role in the construction of a disciplinary regime. Of course, the attitudes they exhibited towards the poor were of their time and their class culture. Moreover, solutions to problems are, to an extent, always formulated with one eye on the means to address them. Educators can do little to alter the structural causes of poverty which is why, even on those rare occasions when they recognise them, they choose to do what they are capable of which is to attempt to educate. Arguably, poverty has not been eliminated, but those changes that have occurred in its manifestations have not been the result of schooling alone. What the free kindergartens did was to illustrate, along with many others, the necessity for state action in order to ameliorate the lot of the slum child. They also managed to install at the heart of early years' education the notion that its concern was for the whole child and not just for its cognitive capabilities.

The subsequent history of the free kindergartens was less illustrious than that recorded here. Altogether, twelve free kindergartens were opened in England and Scotland between 1900 and 1910. Following the 1918 Education Act the free kindergartens together with Margaret McMillan's school at Deptford became Britain's first nursery schools supported by funds from the Local Education Authorities. Since then the growth of nursery schools has been constrained by successive governments that chose not to heed the message of the nineteenth-century Froebelians which is still relevant today: that an education based on play and the needs of childhood is the right of every young child.

NOTES

1. E.R. Murray, *A Story of Infant Schools and Kindergartens* (1912).
2. A. Buckton, 'Sesame Child Garden and House for Home Training', *Child Life* 1, 1 (1899), pp. 32–6.
3. P. Woodham-Smith, 'History of the Froebel Movement in England' in E. Lawrence, ed., *Friedrich Froebel And English Education* (1952), p. 36.
4. W.H. Herford, *The Student's Froebel* (1905).
5. M.S. Shapiro, *Child's Garden: The Kindergarten Movement from Froebel to Dewey* (Pennsylvania State University Park, 1983).
6. F. Froebel, *Mother's Songs, Games and Stories* (1900).
7. M. Wroe, 'The Reconciliation of Opposites', *Child Life* IX, 36 (1907), pp. 191–4.
8. P. McCann and F.A. Young, *Samuel Wilderspin And The Infant School Movement* (1982).
9. International Health Exhibition, *The Health Exhibition Literature* (1884).
10. Murray, *A Story of Infant Schools and Kindergartens.*
11. *Ibid.*
12. A.T. Allen, 'Spiritual Motherhood: German Feminists and the Kindergarten Movement 1848–1911', *History of Education Quarterly* 22, 3 (1982), pp. 319–39.
13. H. Brown Smith, *Education By Life* (1925).
14. A.T. Allen, ' "Let us live with our children": Kindergarten Movements in Germany and the United States, 1840–1914', *History of Education Quarterly* 28, 1 (1988), pp. 23–48.
15. J. Lewis, *Women in England 1870–1950* (Brighton, 1984).
16. C. Steedman, *Childhood, Culture and Class in Britain: Margaret McMillan 1860–1931* (1990).
17. J. Ronge and B. Ronge, *A Practical Guide to the English Kindergarten* (1865).

18. E. Shirreff, *Intellectual Education and its Influence on the Character and Happiness of Women* (1858).

19. G. Himmelfarb, *Poverty and Compassion* (New York, 1992).

20. *Ibid.*; Allen, Spiritual Motherhood.

21. E. Last, *Memoir of Caroline Garrison Bishop* (1936).

22. Murray, *A Story of Infant Schools and Kindergartens.*

23. Sloyd, or Slojd, was a system of manual training originating in Sweden which aimed to develop exercise of judgement and manual dexterity by progressive exercises. It became popular in England in the late nineteenth century.

24. Last, *Memoir.*

25. Buckton, 'Sesame Child Garden and House for Home Training'.

26. Anon., 'Sesame Club Notes', *Child Life* 1, 1 (1899), pp. 53–5.

27. Anon., 'Free Kindergartens in Great Britain', *Child Life* VII, 26 (1905), p. 95.

28. Anon., 'Sesame Club. The Third Year's Record of Sesame House', *Child Life* V, 17 (1903), pp. 43–4.

29. 'Free Kindergartens in Great Britain', p. 95.

30. Murray, *A Story of Infant Schools and Kindergartens.*

31. J. Attfield, *With Light of Knowledge* (1981).

32. Himmelfarb, *Poverty and Compassion.*

33. M. Vicinus, *Independent Women* (1985).

34. C.E. Grant, *Farthing Bundles* (1929).

35. Shapiro, *Child's Garden.*

36. Himmelfarb, *Poverty and Compassion.*

37. L. Hardy, *The Diary of a Free Kindergartner* (1917).

38. Murray, *A Story of Infant Schools and Kindergartens.*

39. T.G. Rooper, *School and Home Life* (1896).

40. Hardy, *The Diary of a Free Kindergartner.*

41. Report of the Birmingham People's Kindergarten Association, 1905–1906, p. 5.

42. G. Stedman Jones, *Outcast London* (Harmondsworth, 1984).

43. Murray, *A Story of Infant Schools and Kindergartens.*

44. M. McMillan, 'Froebel Yesterday and Tomorrow', *Child Life* XI, 48 (1909), pp. 117–18; M. Montessori, *Pedagogical Anthropology* (1913).

45. S. Hall and B. Schwarz, 'State and Society, 1880–1930' in M. Langan and B. Schwarz, eds., *Crises in the British State 1880–1930* (1985), pp. 7–32.

46. Murray, *A Story of Infant Schools and Kindergartens.*

47. L.R. Latter, 'How far is it possible to adapt the kindergarten system to public elementary schools as now existing?', *Child Life* V, 19 (1903), pp. 137–43.

48. Froebel Society Council Minutes, 20 February 1899.

49. B.M. Allen, *Sir Robert Morant* (1934); A. Mansbridge, *Margaret McMillan* (1932).

50. K.J. Brehony, 'An "Undeniable" and "Disastrous" Influence? John Dewey and English Education (1895–1939)', *Oxford Review of Education* 23, 4 (1997), pp. 427–45.

51. G. Wallas, 'A Criticism of Froebelian Pedagogy' in M. Wallas, ed., *Men and Ideas: Essays By Graham Wallas* (1940), pp. 133–50.

52. Hardy, *The Diary of a Free Kindergartner.*

53. K.S.J. Conway, *The Cry of the Children* (Manchester, 1894); L. Thompson, *The Enthusiasts* (1971); D.H. Lawrence, *The Rainbow* (Harmondsworth, 1978).

54. G. Owen, 'An English Student's Impressions of American Kindergartens', *Child Life* II, 6 (1900), pp. 97–102.

55. Brehony, 'An "Undeniable" and "Disastrous" Influence?'.

56. Steedman, *Childhood, Culture and Class in Britain.*

57. Various writers, *School and Life* (1914), pp. 121–86.

58. Public Records Office ED 21/5272.

59. M.E. Findlay, 'The Training of Teachers in the United States of America' (eds. Board of Education), *Special Reports on Educational Subjects* (1902), pp. 421–60.

60. *Ibid.*

61. *Ibid.*

62. E.R. Murray, *Froebel As A Pioneer In Modern Psychology* (1914).

63. *Times Educational Supplement* (6 October 1914).

64. S.E. Blow, *Symbolic Education* (1915).

65. S.E. Blow, 'The Kindergarten' in International Kindergarten Union. Committee of Nineteen, eds., *The Kindergarten: Reports Of The Committee Of Nineteen On The Theory And Practice Of The Kindergarten* (Boston, New York [etc.], 1913), pp. 1–230; Blow, *Symbolic Education.*

66. A. Woods, *Educational Experiments in England* (1920).

67. Findlay, 'The Training of Teachers in the United States of America'.

68. *Journal of Education* Vol. XXIII (February 1901), p. 53.

69. M.E. Findlay, 'Educational Issues in the Kindergarten', *Child Life* XI, 45 (1909), pp. 19–22; 46, pp. 54–6; 47, pp. 77–80.

70. E.R. Murray, 'That symmetrical paper folding and symmetrical work with gifts are a waste of time for both students and children', *Child Life* V, 17 (1903), pp. 14–18.

71. H. Brown Smith, 'Hindrances in the Training of Kindergarten Students', *Child Life* V, 20 (1903), pp. 195–7.

72. *Child Life* IV, 14 (1902), p. 119.

73. J. Dewey, *The Child and the Curriculum and The School and Society* (Chicago, 1956).

74. See S.J. Gould, *Ontogeny and Phylogeny* (Cambridge, Mass., 1977).

75. M.E. Findlay, 'Anthropology and the New Education' in *School and Life* (1914), pp. 31–49.

76. Himmelfarb, *Poverty and Compassion.*

77. Quoted in Stedman Jones, *Outcast London.*

78. Findlay, 'Anthropology and the New Education'.

79. D.E.M. Gardner, *Susan Isaacs* (1969).

80. N. Whitbread, *The Evolution of the Nursery-Infant School* (1972).

81. J. Gorst, 'Presidential Address. Section L – Educational Science 1901. London' (eds. British Association for the Advancement of Science), *Report of the British Association for the Advancement of Science* (1901), pp. 858–68.

PART FIVE

Women Theorists in
the Early Twentieth Century

CHAPTER TWELVE

The Montessori Phenomenon: Gender and Internationalism in Early Twentieth-Century Innovation

PETER CUNNINGHAM

We need to consider seriously the 'Montessori Phenomenon' if we are to understand educational innovation and change. We need to explore, as I have tried to do in a variety of other contexts, the interplay of economic, social and cultural conditions that underlie developments in educational practice.[1] Individual theorists and practitioners make their impact, as we see throughout the studies in this book, by means that are themselves culturally specific, working within or outside an established system of schooling, conveying ideas and exerting influence in a whole variety of ways.

Understanding the process of educational change entails a cautious approach to much of the literature on Maria Montessori which has been hagiographic.[2] It is indeed part of the 'phenomenon' I wish to investigate, that she inspired such adulation. In the work of Rita Kramer,[3] on the other hand, we have had a meticulous and detailed narrative of Maria Montessori's life, offering a wealth of detail on her activity and movements; Kramer also engages sensitively with the personality, confronting the uncomfortable contradictions in her subject's behaviour. What this chapter seeks to do is to tease out the significance for the process of educational innovation of aspects of Maria Montessori's personality, work and teaching.

A contemporary comparison of Montessori and Froebel hinted at character, epoch and even race as contributory factors.[4] In the later twentieth century we might want to consider gender, too; it is a question of some significance for the general theme of this book, what part Maria Montessori's gender played in the impact of her innovations in Britain. When surveying the development over the longer term of British early years teaching, a simple and striking contrast appears between the official endorsement on the one hand of ideas emanating from the German Friedrich Froebel, and on the other hand the marginalising of methods devised by an Italian woman. Too many

other factors come into play in the process of transmission and implementation of educational ideas and practices for the contrast to survive scrutiny in
these stark terms. Extensive consideration needs to be given to the different
historical location of the two innovators and the cultural conditions prevailing at their time, as well as the contrasting circumstances in which their ideas
were conveyed across national and cultural boundaries.

What can the case of Maria Montessori tell us about the proposal and
reception of progressive ideas in different cultures and why they are differen-
tially received? The question arises as to how she achieved such an enormous
impact, but further, in Britain (and in the USA too) how she soon became
marginalised by the educational establishment. An attempt at exploring these
issues below falls into four parts. First, what part did her personality and her
career play in all this? Secondly, what was the significance of her scientific
authority and her evident practical skills? Thirdly, in the projection and
reception of her ideas on a world stage, what was the significance of her
natural charisma and gender? Finally, in the economic and cultural climate
of the time, what aspects of patronage, promotion and the market may have
been significant?

The present account is located largely in the years around 1910–14 when
Maria Montessori's ideas took Britain by storm and when her name became
a catchword of educational innovation. It was the culmination of an educational ferment which had steadily gained momentum over the previous decades, accompanying the growth of universal elementary schooling from the
Education Act of 1870, coincidentally the year of her birth.

Born in Ancona, to a well-educated and liberal-minded mother and a
father, a government accountant who shared his wife's liberal political views,
the family moved to Rome when Maria was five. She turned out to be intelligent, mathematically inclined and determinedly studious, and at the age
of thirteen persisted, with her mother's support and against her father's
wishes, in seeking a place at technical school. This almost outrageous step
for a middle-class girl was rewarded by high grades and progression to a
technical institute. Here she set her mind at first on becoming an engineer,
but subsequently switched to the goal of medicine, unprecedented for a
woman in Italy. There was general disapproval, but her mother supported
her in this ambition. She enrolled at the University of Rome to study physics,
mathematics and natural sciences, and at the age of twenty-two entered
on a course of medicine. Obstacles were overcome, and influence wielded,
though the story is unclear and subsequent accounts suggest that some form
of papal intervention was secured to enable the realisation of her goal.
Fellow students expressed their hostility towards her, but she apparently
remained unperturbed and won their acceptance, graduating in medicine
in 1896.

For the next two years Maria Montessori studied anthropology and worked at the university's Psychiatric Clinic, which included the care of mentally handicapped children. Publicly, in print, she began to explore the links between delinquency and the lack of adequate care for retarded and disturbed children. Her article 'Social Miseries and New Scientific Discoveries' in a political review of 1898 was widely quoted and reprinted in the educational press under the title of 'Educational Awakening'. Her subsequent invitation to address this theme for the nation's teachers at a pedagogical conference in Turin led to further acclaim. Whilst praising philanthropic effort, she stressed the necessity of applying modern scientific knowledge if the real needs of backward and deficient children were to be met. 'Our efforts', she said, 'will have to go into gaining an understanding of those children who have the most difficulty adapting to society and helping them before they get into trouble.'[5]

In the course of her work with the mentally retarded, she had studied closely the work of Seguin, and developed the principle that was to inform her work with normal children: that education of the senses must precede that of the intellect. She evidently had a powerful presence on the podium and spoke too on feminist platforms, evoking ecstatic applause from her audiences. In 1899 she was appointed Director of a new medical–pedagogical institute, an 'orthofrenic' training school for teachers of deficient children. She spent long hours teaching, observing, experimenting with different methods, making sketches and models for teaching materials, and she regarded the two years of practice she enjoyed here as her 'true degree in pedagogy'.[6] She adapted apparatus developed earlier by Itard and Seguin, modifying it on the basis of the children's reactions, and it was this material and the manner of its presentation which later became the Montessori method. By the age of thirty her work had been reported in hundreds of newspaper articles in Italy, France, Germany and England.

At this point, however (Kramer suggests that it may have been for personal reasons), she relinquished her prestigious directorship and the practice of medicine, and returned to the University of Rome as a student of educational philosophy, anthropology, and experimental psychology. In pursuit of her anthropological and pedagogical studies, she visited elementary schools and observed children at close quarters in classrooms. From 1904 to 1908 she lectured, by all accounts with liveliness, immediacy and relevance, in the School of Pedagogy at the university.

During this period a new social housing project was opened in one of the poorest parts of Rome by a group of wealthy bankers and the directors approached Maria Montessori for assistance in setting up a children's centre. Consequently, on the feast of the Epiphany, 6 January 1907, the first Casa dei Bambini was opened under her direction. The Casa gave her an opportunity to continue her observations, to experiment further and to develop her method. In 1909, with the encouragement of a patroness, she wrote, in the space of a month, the immensely influential description of her work at the Casa later translated as *The Montessori Method*. The method was characterised by free choice for the child as a self-activated learner in a prepared environment of programmed materials, 'constant education of the senses by various games and carefully thought-out apparatus . . . the simple forms of manual exercise and manual labour, training of limbs and bodies, marching, singing, modelling, drawing, patient observation of animals and plants'.[7] Social education was also an essential part of the work of the Casa dei Bambini, children helping to prepare and serve meals and to tidy and clean the learning environment. The role of the teacher was to observe the children and to intervene only when necessary.

Inferences about her personality can begin to be drawn from this account of her early career. Maria Montessori was evidently highly intelligent, well-organised and determined, with an inclination to apply her intellectual analysis to psychological and social problems, and to manage solutions. Her vision was both scientific and humanitarian. A more detailed exploration of some of these traits in the context of the cultural, economic and social circumstances of her age is necessary to explain the impact which she had, the 'Montessori phenomenon'.

Dr Montessori's medical and scientific qualifications undoubtedly lent her innovatory ideas both an authority and a very specific appeal to a particular audience in Britain. At the Casa dei Bambini, she had developed a scientific method of education consisting of observation, experimentation and analysis. The title of her book, as originally published in Italian in 1909, *Il Metodo della Pedagogia Scientifica applicato all'educazione infantile nelle Casa dei Bambini*, would have an immediate appeal to British educationists many of whom were already in pursuit of a 'scientific pedagogy'. There had been a marked revival of interest in the contribution to a 'science of education' of the early German psychologist Herbart. The influential commentator Edmond Holmes saw Maria Montessori as 'adapting the principle to which Froebel devoted his life and to which she is devoting hers, to conditions which 100 years of scientific progress have profoundly modified'.[8]

In Britain, as elsewhere in Europe and in North America, the child study movement was by 1910 well established and perhaps at the peak of its influence. Though supported by many women, its most prominent protagonists had been men who boasted qualifications in science, medicine and education that still eluded most women. In the 1880s, James Sully, Professor of Psychology and Philosophy at the University of London, began to write on child development as a science, and Francis Galton established his 'Anthropometric Laboratory' for the assessment of individual children.

Compulsory schooling began conveniently to provide cohorts of children for large-scale studies. In 1894 the Child Study Association was founded and two years later the Childhood Society, the latter arising from the British Medical Association with rather more of a medical emphasis to its work. In 1907 the two organisations combined and launched the journal *Child-Study*.[9]

In the pages of *Child-Study* responses to Dr Montessori's scientific approach can be traced. A reference in February 1913 to discussion meetings on the Montessori Method recorded attendance as being keen and overflowing, comparing them to first nights at sensational plays.[10] This number of the journal carried three articles on Montessori, one by Mme Pujol-Segalas, who is described as 'a practical worker', one by Robert R. Rusk, MA, BA, PhD, 'a scientific critic', and the third by Frank Smith, BA, BSc, 'a scientific experimenter'. Even the 'practical worker', a former pupil of Maria Montessori and co-founder of an experimental girls' college, laid great emphasis on the scientific basis of her work. Comparing Montessori with Froebel, despite her admiration for both and her recognition of what they had in common, she identified Froebel as essentially a philosopher, whereas 'Doctor Montessori proceeds as a scientist, formulating the law, according to the results of carefully conducted and many times repeated experiments'.[11]

It was the slow process of experiment and analysis, implying more precision, that would produce a 'more complete synthetical apprehension' of any subject. 'At the present day, when life has a tendency to become dangerously artificial, it is necessary that the educationalist should make an effort to attain, through the study of the child, to a truer and more practical knowledge of the human needs and possibilities.'[12]

Robert Rusk addressed himself to the pedagogical and psychological principles and practice of Dr Montessori. In pedagogical terms, Maria Montessori's achievement had been the persuasive results of a series of trials, applying techniques used for teaching 'deficients' to the teaching of 'children at a stage of development corresponding to deficients, that is ... infants'.[13] The hypothetical relationship between normal infants and people with learning difficulties appears dubious now, but a scientific experimental approach is clearly endorsed by Rusk, who was keen to assert psychology as 'a positive, not a regulatory science'. Pestalozzi, he considered, sought to psychologise education, but lacking in his day any psychology of the school child, he ended up by mechanising instruction.[14]

Frank Smith's approach was to replicate some of Dr Montessori's experiments with children of 'fairly poor' parents in an urban elementary school. Using the colour discrimination apparatus, he set out to test the claim of the didactic nature of the material and the influence of age upon performance. His conclusions amounted to a considerable criticism of the particular task and profound doubts about the usefulness or relevance to a child's education of a highly artificial and mechanistic exercise. Nevertheless he concluded with a wish to see experiments continuing on a much wider scale, acknowledging the 'admirable tone' of the dottoressa's book, paying tribute to her patient investigations and to her pursuit of a scientific pedagogy: 'For we are all groping towards the truth, and the road thereto is long and difficult.'[15]

A further attraction of the Montessori system, deriving from its scientific basis, was the demand it made for properly trained personnel. Indeed Maria Montessori demanded 'directresses' rather than teachers, implying a very different relationship between adult and child and reinforcing the idea of scientific basis and profound principle, which need to be fully understood. This coincided with contemporary concerns in Britain to raise the 'culture' of elementary school teachers generally, and to improve the quality of their education and training. Thus the emphasis on proper training and a long apprenticeship for young teachers was welcomed.[16] 'The directress is a psychologist rather than a teacher – she observes and experiments, never a correction, hardly ever a word of command. No need for prizes and punishments. Any teaching given is simple, short, objective and nearly always individual. Collective lessons at this stage in children's lives are few and far between.'[17]

Dr Montessori's scientific turn of mind was not just analytical, but practical too. In the early days at the Casa dei Bambini she paid every attention to details of organisation and provision including prescription of the children's diet and even recipes for their meals. Her practical skills were recognized by contemporaries, in matters of institutional organisation and in the development and design of specialised apparatus by which her methods are perhaps most commonly remembered. The didactic apparatus was certainly ingenious, and derived from scientific observation. There was a superficial parallel to be drawn with Froebel's 'Gifts' and 'Occupations'. More substantial were her debts to Seguin's apparatus for sense training, but she had considerably adapted and developed it through her own observations of children at work. For some progressives, such apparatus was very attractive. Norman MacMunn, for example, author of the influential book *The Child's Path to Freedom*, himself much preoccupied with designing and making curriculum materials for particular learning objectives, delivered a lecture on 'Montessorism in the Secondary School'.[18] But for others her apparatus became the stumbling block, seen as too limiting in itself, or too dogmatically employed in her method.

Jerome Bruner described Maria Montessori as a 'strange blend of the mystic and the pragmatist'.[19] Whilst her scientific skills and practical abilities attracted the attention of avant-garde educationists, it was her personal charisma which facilitated the dissemination of her ideas and methods on the world stage. This charisma may be associated with the more idealistic aspects

Fig 12.1 *Books by and about Maria Montessori and her teaching methods were often extensively illustrated with photographs and almost invariably included a frontispiece portrait of Maria herself. This frontispiece to* The Montessori Method *(1912) conveys her role of scientist, technician and observer of children.*

of her innovations, or what Bruner labelled the 'mystic', and to understand the 'Montessori phenomenon' we need also to consider that aspect in the context of its time. With other educational reformers, Rousseau, Froebel and Steiner, for example, there was an element of idealism bordering on the 'mystical' or the 'spiritual' that attracted many followers. Distinctive in the case of Maria Montessori is the international stage on which she played in the early twentieth century, and the personal attraction conveyed in part in her gender and her nationality.

Increasing ease of foreign travel and communications allowed child study and psychology to flourish as an international pursuit at the turn of the century. In 1909, for example, Sigmund Freud from Vienna lectured for the first time in the USA. Maria Montessori had travelled to London and Paris in pursuit of her researches in the late 1890s.

In 1899 she undertook a national lecture tour in Italy in support of a new campaign for retarded children. Her appearances caused a great stir on account of her gender, and her physical elegance as well as her powerful oratory featured in press reports. Her lectures also took a feminist turn, and she addressed an international women's conference in London which attracted a great deal of public attention, including a formal audience with Queen Victoria. Despite growing status as a national figure, she 'retreated' for some years to further work in pedagogy and experimentation, as we have seen, but in the years after the opening of the Casa dei Bambini, a marked characteristic of Dr Montessori's educational ideas was the rapidity with which they spread on an international, indeed a global, scale. Rousseau's ideas had in printed form spread quite rapidly around the Western world, and the practices of Pestalozzi and Froebel had been disseminated internationally through their writings and through the medium of visitors to Burgdorf and Yverdon. In those cases the momentum took a decade or two to develop, but in the case of Montessori it was a matter of years.

As for the Montessori phenomenon, the rapid spread of 'this remarkable movement' was recorded in June 1912 in the *Times Educational Supplement*.[20] One year previously the method had been established by law in all the public schools of Switzerland, Montessori schools had been established in Paris, New York and Boston by June 1912, and others were about to open in India, China, Mexico, Korea, Honolulu and the Argentine Republic. A good rail network made European travel increasingly easy, and the Casa dei Bambini in Rome and other Montessori establishments were much visited by educationists from Britain. As the *Times Educational Supplement* described it, the 'pilgrimage to Rome' had become the educationists' 'Grand Tour'. A Montessori Society for the United Kingdom was established and it accredited a resident representative in Rome.

A significant gender distinction appears in the way *The Times* reported this phenomenon: 'English ladies' were being 'sent to Rome to learn the system on the spot', whilst 'Englishmen are learning Italian so as to be able to speak directly with the Dottoressa'. Lily Hutchinson, an infants' school teacher, applied to the London County Council Education Committee for travel expenses to attend a Montessori course in Rome.[21] This request did not pass without provoking some debate, one member arguing that trips abroad for teachers were becoming far too frequent and not worth the money spent on them, whilst a clergyman, Rev. W.J. Sommerville, objected that the Montessori system was 'the greatest bit of rubbish ever invented and he could only regard it as sickly sentimentality run mad'.[22] But the proposal was agreed to. Some of Maria Montessori's visitors subsequently exerted considerable influence back in their own countries, an outstanding example being Helen Parkhurst, who ten years later developed her 'Laboratory Plan' at Dalton, Massachusetts.

International dissemination may have begun with visits to the Casa dei Bambini, but following the translation of her book into many languages, Maria Montessori herself journeyed about the world. From 1915 to 1918 she lived in Barcelona; she travelled to give courses in Europe, the USA and India, and her students opened schools in Russia. Between 1919 and 1938 a six-month training course was run in London every alternate year over which she personally presided. In 1934 she fled Mussolini's Italy for the Netherlands and in 1939 moved on to live in India and Ceylon, returning to the Netherlands where she spent her final years.

Verbal accounts, as well as photographs, testify to the personal magnetism which Maria Montessori exercised. Kramer has described her ability to win round a hostile audience at the British Psychological Society in 1919 through 'her presence, a combination of charm and conviction, that attracted those who heard her speak in a way that her writings alone could never have done'.[23] Her status as the first female doctor in Italy was bound to hold some fascination. Her gender can be seen to evoke both positive and negative responses. Edward Parnell Culverwell, the Irish professor, was adulatory:

> A new light has appeared in the educational world. The remarkable advance made by Dr Maria Montessori, of Rome, in the theory and practice of the home and school education of children up to seven years of age, will ultimately place her name with those of Pestalozzi and Froebel as one of the greatest in the history of educational progress . . .[24]

Culverwell admired Dr Montessori for identifying that 'the dominating fact in education' is the need for the teacher to rely on the spontaneous tendencies of the pupil. He was impressed by the

> relentless logic with which she applies what she considers fundamental. . . . It is a strange distinction for a woman, that in dealing with children she should exhibit a degree of logical consistency far beyond that to which any educationist of the sterner sex has attained. No one had ever dreamed of limiting the intervention of the teacher to the same extent.[25]

In a similar vein, Percy Nunn, Director of the London Institute of Education, admired her 'masculine logic'.[26] But a negative sexism may certainly be inferred in the writings of her American arch-critic, William Heard Kilpatrick,[27] who consistently referred to her as 'Madam Montessori' when all the rest of the world knew her as a qualified doctor.

Her powerful influence over some followers, however, was more particularly associated with her Roman Catholicism. The Catalan government, attracted by her radical educational ideas, had appealed to Dr Montessori for assistance in school reform, as a consequence of which she settled there for a number of years, but the adulation which she received from Catalan teachers appears to have had some basis in their common faith. Following an emotional Christmas midnight mass in Barcelona, she reportedly defended her distinction from the romantic literary idealism of Rousseau by asserting her own interpretation of herself as a 'rigorous scientific investigator': 'I seek to discover the man in the child, to see in him the true human spirit, the design of the Creator: the scientific and religious truth.'[28] Her sense of mysticism coloured her perception of science and deepened as her life progressed:

> We give the name scientist to the type of man [*sic*] who has felt experiment to be a means guiding him to search out the deep truth of life, to lift a veil from its fascinating secrets, and who, in this pursuit, has felt arising in him a love for the mysteries of nature, so passionate as to annihilate the thought of himself.[29]

In teaching, she wrote, it would be inadequate to rely mechanically on bare experiment, to limit the preparation of teachers to technique alone: 'We must, instead, make of them worshippers and interpreters of the spirit of nature.'[30]

Adelia Pyle, daughter of an American millionaire related to the Rockefeller family, one of several young American women who became devoted followers of Maria Montessori, eventually converted to Catholicism. Edward Mortimer Standing, who first met her in 1921, became a lifelong collaborator and went on to write her first official biography. He believed that she was 'sent into the world to shed new light on the unfathomed depths of the child's soul' and that she herself had 'felt the duty of going forth as an apostle on behalf of all the children in the world, born and as yet unborn . . .'.[31] Her charisma, which worked so well in some contexts, eventually served her ill, and critics made the harsh observation that 'she had followers and sycophants but no real colleagues'.[32] Rita Kramer has clearly exposed the central paradox that in a movement dedicated to liberty, freedom of action and even of expression was stifled. Freedom for the individual child was advocated in her method (though the clear limits to that freedom offered a target for some of her critics), but was in stark contrast to her style of dissemination. Though she lamented a lack of true collaborators to continue her research, she was unable to accommodate disagreement with her own ideas. Maria Montessori had no time for those who saw her innovation as one contribution to a constantly evolving research of teaching and learning. A highly publicised schism within the English Montessori Society occurred in the winter of 1920–21 when a large majority of the membership took exception to the autocratic conception of Dr Montessori's Rules of Authorisation, and at her reluctance to delegate the function of training teachers in her method.[33]

The dogmatism and inflexibility of her method may also have been associated with the patenting and marketing of her apparatus, and there is a significant gender dimension to this. By contrast with the female acolytes in her entourage, those who promoted her work in the academic, professional and commercial world were predominantly male.

> Two things chiefly mark the recent movement of change in English education. The first is a stronger sense of the responsibility of the State for the upbringing of its future citizens. The other is an equally strong sense of the need for individuality in training and for recognizing varieties of parental conviction.[34]

In the West in 1910 her methods promised both a solution to wider social problems of racial degeneration, which appealed to predominantly (though not exclusively) male educationists, and a better education for middle-class children, which appealed particularly to middle-class mothers who represented a potential market. Both of these dimensions coloured the 'Montessori phenomenon'.

It was one of Maria Montessori's American visitors, Prof. Henry W. Holmes of the Education Division, Harvard, who suggested an English translation of her *Pedagogia Scientifica*, to which he contributed an introduction when it appeared under the Heinemann imprint in 1912. Its title in translation, *The Montessori Method*, implies both a 'patenting' and a commodification of the pedagogical system. The Irish professor Edward Culverwell, a mathematician and physical scientist before he turned educationist, was another academic who actively supported and propagated her work, through his public lectures and through his book.

The initial promoter par excellence of Montessori's work in Britain was the educationist Edmond Holmes; he was able to do so from a position of considerable influence. Coming from a former Chief Inspector of Elementary Schools, the forthright criticism of most state elementary education which he published in 1911 following his retirement, and his advocacy of a more child-centred approach to curriculum and teaching method, were powerful and influential.[35] In the same year he visited Rome on behalf of the Board of Education. His published report coincided with the appearance of the first English language edition of *The Montessori Method* and was sold out in a few days.[36] The *Times Educational Supplement* reported that interest in the Montessori system was 'increasing daily'.[37] A Montessori Society was inaugurated in England, and by June 1912 a Committee had been formed which included such prominent educationists as Edmond Holmes himself, Michael Sadler, Albert Mansbridge and Lord Lytton. Female members were Lady St Cyres, Lady Isabel Margerson, Mrs George Montagu. Mr Bertram Hawker, another committee member, had been en route to Australia to deal with his properties there when he had been introduced to the Casa dei Bambini by the British ambassador in Rome.

Overwhelmed by what he saw, he immediately returned to his home in East
Runton, Norfolk, where he set up an experimental school for 12 children
aged 3–5 chosen from the local elementary school, with approval of Norfolk
LEA, and directed by the first Montessori-trained teacher in Britain, Miss
Lydbetter.

In November the Montessori Society and the Child Study Society held a
joint conference in London to discuss the Montessori movement, and throughout Britain both Prof. Culverwell and Bertram Hawker gave public lectures
which attracted large audiences. The discussion and debate which followed
was not wholly uncritical of all aspects of Dr Montessori's work and principles,
and some prominent progressive educationists were sharp in their public
criticism. At a conference which attracted as many as 250 delegates held at
East Runton in 1914, these disagreements surfaced and resulted in the formation of a more broadly based 'New Ideals in Education' group, abandoning
any exclusive association with her.

Many of her British critics, like William Boyd, Lecturer in Education at the
University of Glasgow, were enthusiasts for the fundamental principles of
individuality, freedom and early education through the senses. But some
decried the limitations to freedom for children in her method and found
her apparatus too restrictive. Others regarded her scientific claims and method
as inadequate, and some accused her of a lack of originality. Margaret
McMillan shared Maria Montessori's convictions about the physiological
basis of education, and had herself found inspiration in the work of Seguin,
especially with his St. Simonian ideas about the social application of gospel
principles in improving the lot of the poor through educational provision.
McMillan's hostility in print towards Montessori, however, is attributed by
Steedman to a personal jealousy over credit given for the discovery of Seguin's
ideas.[38]

Charlotte Mason, who had developed her own principles of home education from the 1880s, considered the Montessori system too restrictive, insuffi-
ciently encouraging of vigorous and energetic play and over-concerned with
intellectual development, such as the early development of writing and reading.[39] Others made similar claims. A.S. Neill, from a more extreme libertarian
angle, found the Montessori method highly intellectual and lacking in emo-
tionalism, too scientific, too orderly and too didactic. It was a system in which
adults remained in control of the environment, and children were to work
with her apparatus but not to play with it.[40] Whilst Susan Isaacs accommo-
dated aspects of Maria Montessori's approach, her influential experimental
work owed more to alternative emphases from Freud on personality development and from Dewey on social learning and a 'real life' context.[41]

J.A. Green, Professor of Education at Sheffield and editor of the *Journal
of Experimental Pedagogy*, thought her scientific work shallow, describing *The*

Montessori Method as 'the Swiss Family Robinson of educational literature . . .', a 'collection of pretty stories' rather than an account of scientific procedures.[42] Boyd was another who identified many contradictions and flaws in her argument and her practice and found her system and apparatus eclectic and heterogeneous. He accused her, too, of an unscientific temper of mind. It reveals, he thought, 'the glowing faith of a devotee or the sentiment of a romancer rather than the critical attitude of a scientist', but above all he lamented the lack of a coherent and unified scheme of thought.[43]

It was this absence of philosophy which ultimately dissatisfied the British Froebelians and led them to make unfavourable comparisons between Maria Montessori and Friedrich Froebel. Elsie Murray, Vice-Principal of Maria Grey Training College and long-serving council member of the Froebel Society, visited Rome to study Dr Montessori's system at first hand, and found herself admiring the social experiment of the Casa dei Bambini. However, she opposed the narrow preoccupation with sense-training and its apparent neglect of the more 'open-ended' creative work facilitated by the Froebel Gifts. She felt the focus on the individual was at the neglect of groupwork, and she regretted too the early introduction of writing, and consequently of reading, by Dr. Montessori.[44] This opposition from the Froebelians was long-lasting: Nathan Isaacs was scathing about 'the incompatibility of her gospel of freedom and spontaneity with her intensely directive doctrine of actual training' and the 'quite untenable pretensions of a would-be "scientific" pedagogy which . . . is just another old-fashioned claim to have found the real elixir of pedagogic life, the one true pedagogy'.[45] More recently Joachim Liebschner, in an ostensibly cool and objective historical study, is disparaging in the tone of his suggestions that the main function of the Casa dei Bambini was to pre-empt vandalism in the tenement, and that the Montessori training courses in the 1920s 'provided teachers with an easy solution to the problem of how to occupy children'.[46]

Culverwell, an early supporter and energetic promoter of Montessorism, who was attracted not only by Dr Montessori's scientific principles but also by what he saw as the democratic ideal of liberty for individual pupils, nevertheless feared the consequences of uncritical application of any kind of 'system', and was critical of the marketing of the method as a 'total package'.

If, as I argue, the subsequent fate of the Montessori phenomenon in Britain has as much to do with commercial as with academic and professional interests, then the role of certain entrepreneurs needs to be understood. Holmes's 1912 pamphlet for the Board of Education reported that twenty-six separate items of apparatus were on sale from: 'Societa Umanitaria, Casa di Lavoro, Milan (costing £11.12s plus carriage in UK), with the hope that manufacture of apparatus will soon commence in UK (reducing the price to £7 or 8)'. The *Montessori Method*, published the same year, announced that her patent rights in the didactic apparatus for the US and Canada were controlled by House of Childhood, Inc., New York. The tenor of commercialism thus pervaded dissemination of Montessori's ideas and methods from an early juncture.

Following the rift amongst the 'New Ideals' group at East Runton in 1914, the old Montessori Society committee was disbanded and a new group formed, whose 'official organiser' was C.A. Bang, a long-standing manager of William Heinemann, Montessori's British publisher. Bang organised official Montessori teacher training courses and represented himself in correspondence as Maria Montessori's official spokesman, whilst Heinemann advertised their wares as 'the only authorised books on the Montessori method'. Meanwhile, the educational suppliers Philip and Tacey had acquired exclusive rights to the manufacture and marketing of the apparatus in Britain and, though less stridently than their American counterparts, warned that the Didactic Material must be used complete, and applied intelligently, according to the principles of the Montessori method. William Boyd objected to the rather sordid commercialism and the slight on teachers' intelligence implied in this dogmatic marketing.[47]

Samuel McClure, American publisher and journalist, had been responsible for 'breaking' the Montessori story in the USA. Talented publicist that he was, he assumed the role of agent and impresario, organising Maria Montessori's tours and public appearances in North America on a thoroughly commercial basis. *McClure's Magazine* epitomised an important new genre of the cheaper serious journal for a new middle-class readership, pitched between the older elite reviews and the more popular sensational periodicals. From 1911 there was extensive coverage in *McClure's* of Montessori's work, which triggered attention to her from other American periodicals, where 68 references over the years 1910–1914 have been traced.[48] Some of these included the teachers' press, but most were more general periodicals sometimes of an intellectual or techical character, such as *Bookman* (New York), *Literary Digest* (New York), or the *Popular Science Monthly* (Garrison, New York) and *Technical World Magazine* (Chicago).

The articles on Maria Montessori from *McClure's* reappeared in Britain in *The World's Work: An Illustrated Magazine of National Efficiency and Social Progress*.[49] This relatively new journal, founded in 1902, was edited by Henry Norman MP and also published by Heinemann. *The Times* found it worthy of comment:

> An especially strong and varied number of the *World's Work* marks the conclusion of the first ten years of its existence with excellent articles on the Montessori system, sea-going trains, dancing, lighthouses, India, excavation work in Palestine and other 'live' subjects. It is a typical example of a magazine which is emphatically doing good work in the world and for the Empire.[50]

Maria Montessori herself, in her preface to the English language version of *The Montessori Method,* paid tribute to 'the Harvard professors who have made my work known in America and to McClure's Magazine, no less than to the Editor of the *World's Work'.*[51] A significant category of this periodical literature in the USA was practical journals like *Good Housekeeping Magazine* (New York), *Woman's Home Companion* (New York) and *Home Progress* (Cambridge, Mass.). The initial success of Maria Montessori in America and in Britain has a good deal to do with a new model of motherhood. In the closing decades of the nineteenth century, an extension to all classes of a previously very limited conception of 'the home' entailed women gaining a central role in this complex and most important venue of social life.[52] Publications on household management from the 1860s served individual families, but increasingly by 1900 was highlighting the family as a breeding and training ground of the new imperial race. Jose Harris has pointed to a greater emotional investment in children as one result of a declining birth rate, and the ability of middle-class mothers to excel at and to enjoy motherhood, probably to a greater extent than at any previous time in human history. One manifestation of this was the popular 'child-study' movement which greatly enhanced the self-confidence and self-awareness of mothers who kept detailed diaries of their children's development, and aroused popular scientific interest in relations between mother and child. Child-rearing had now become a matter of intellectual curiosity as well as of maternal duty.

The role of the mother had been a significant one in the writings of both Pestalozzi and Froebel. Maria Montessori herself was a mother, but as she was unmarried, her son had been brought up elsewhere and the relationship remained shrouded in secrecy until later in her life. Some commentators have seen her deprivation in this regard as a key to her work at the Casa dei Bambini. Jane Roland Martin has investigated the domesticity of the Casa dei Bambini, and argues that most contemporary commentators overlooked that aspect.[53] An obvious exception in this regard is the account by Dorothy Canfield Fisher, who in 1913 published *A Montessori Mother,* evidently a popular book as it went through six impressions by 1920. Fisher focuses most movingly on the social aspects of the children's education, and it is here that the photographic medium is used to such evocative effect. Photographs had featured too in accounts of Maria Montessori in *McClure's* and *The World's Work,* and Montessori's lectures also made use of visual representation through the medium of film. These media offered a vividness and immediacy that had been unavailable to earlier generations in the international promulgation of an educational practice. The illustrations of children in Fisher's book have a romantic appeal, both in their representation of children and also, one suspects, for the intended audience, in the setting of Italian architecture and gardens. Mothers, to whom Fisher's book would clearly appeal, were able to purchase kits of Montessori apparatus for home use from the American suppliers, despite the supposed strictures on their use, which have been described above. Hence the Montessori method became potentially a commodity for a mass market.

The educational ferment in Britain in the years 1910–14 has been referred to above. It was a receptive environment for international ideas and practices. In Britain the *Times Educational Supplement* provides a useful source through which to trace the reception of Dr Montessori's ideas. Knowledge in Britain of Montessori's work coincided not insignificantly with the launch of this new supplement to 'The Thunderer', as *The Times* was affectionately known, the newspaper of the Establishment and the newspaper of record. It was launched on a wave of interest in and optimism about education in 1910 at the beginning of a new king's reign. It claimed in its first leading article:

> Educationally, England is one of the most interesting countries in the world. This is only just being realized by administrators and students not only in other countries but in our own. . . . Competent observers all over the world realize that during the last few years an extraordinary change has come over the spirit of educational administration in England . . . We have spread our educational investments. We have tried to be true to different sides of the truth. . . . The result is that, for those who have eyes to see, England is an educational laboratory.[54]

Into this educational laboratory stepped Maria Montessori. She had scientific credentials and a scientific approach when science was being looked to for solutions to educational questions. She had charisma, the fascination of her gender when women were coming to play a more prominent and public role in education, and the exoticism of her Roman origins, when Rome was still a cultural cynosure in various respects. And she acquired powerful promoters, especially in the commercial field when childhood and education were becoming commodified and marketed with the assistance of media such as photography and film.

But passionate debate raged in the laboratory, and despite gaining some influential patrons Maria Montessori's methods ultimately failed to gain official sanction, remaining on the fringe of educational practice. Notwithstanding, her ideas, her practices, and her very presence had contributed powerfully to the development of 'progressive' education.

NOTES

1. Peter Cunningham, *Curriculum Change in the Primary School since 1945* (London, 1988); Peter Cunningham and Philip Gardner, *Elementary School Teachers: Texts and Testimonies 1918–1939* (London, 2000); 'The impact of wartime evacuation upon teacher attitude and practice' (1998–2001), research project directed by Peter Cunningham and Philip Gardner, ESRC Award no. R000237211.

2. Anna Maccheroni, *True Romance: Dr Maria Montessori As I Knew Her* (Edinburgh, 1947); E.M. Standing, *Maria Montessori: Her Life and Work* (1958).

3. Rita Kramer, *Maria Montessori: A Biography* (Chicago, 1976). See also: Sol Cohen, 'The Montessori Movement in England, 1911–1952', *History of Education* 3, 1 (1971), pp. 51–67.

4. M. Pujol-Segalas, 'Maria Montessori's Method of Self-Education', *Child-Study* VI, 1 (Feb. 1913), p. 3.

5. Kramer, *Maria Montessori*, p. 75.

6. *Ibid.*, p. 89.

7. *Times Educational Supplement (TES)*, 4 June 1912, pp. 69–70.

8. *TES*, 5 Nov. 1912, p. 127.

9. Prior to this the Child Study Association had published *The Paidologist* 1894–1907.

10. 'Editorial Notes', *Child-Study* VI, 1 (Feb. 1913), p. 1.

11. Pujol-Segalas, 'Maria Montessori's Method', p. 3.

12. *Ibid.*

13. R. Rusk, 'The Montessori Method: Its Principles and Practices', *Child-Study* VI, 1 (Feb. 1913), p. 6.

14. *Ibid.*, p. 7.

15. F. Smith, 'The Montessori Method and Colour Discrimination', *Child-Study* VI, 1 (Feb. 1913), pp. 8–14.

16. *TES*, 5 Nov. 1912, p. 127.

17. *TES*, 4 June 1912, pp. 69–70.

18. Norman MacMunn, 'Montessorism in Secondary Schools', *Report of the Montessori Conference at East Runton 1914* (1914), pp. 78–90.

19. Jerome Bruner, *Toward a Theory of Instruction* (Cambridge, Mass., 1966), p. 34.

20. *TES*, 4 June 1912, pp. 69–70.

21. Lily Hutchinson was later to translate *The Advanced Montessori Method* (London, 1917) published by William Heinemann.

22. *The Times*, 12 Dec. 1912, p. 13.

23. Kramer, *Maria Montessori*, p. 264.

24. E.P. Culverwell, *The Montessori Principles and Practice* (1913), p. 1.

25. *Ibid.*, p. 22.

26. Cited in Kramer, *Maria Montessori*, p. 264.

27. W.H. Kilpatrick, *The Montessori System Examined* (Boston, 1914) (London, 1915).

28. Cited in Kramer, *Maria Montessori*, p. 251.

29. Maria Montessori, *The Montessori Method* (912), p. 8.

30. *Ibid.*, p. 10.

31. Standing, *Maria Montessori*, pp. 8, 42.

32. Kramer, *Maria Montessori*, pp. 262, 276.

33. *Ibid.*, pp. 243, 272–6.

34. *TES*, 6 Sept. 1910, p. 1.

35. Edmond Holmes, *What Is and What Might Be* (1911).

36. Board of Education, *The Montessori System of Education* (Educational Pamphlets, no. 24) (London, 1912); Dorothy Canfield Fisher's popular book *A Montessori Mother* was published in London in 1913, with an introduction by Edmond Holmes, 'Author of *What Is and What Might Be*'.

37. *TES*, 4 June 1912, pp. 69–70.

38. Carolyn Steedman, *Childhood, Culture and Class in Britain: Margaret McMillan, 1860–1913* (London, 1990), pp. 195, 227.

39. *The Times*, 3 Dec. 1912, p. 4.

40. John Shotton, *No Master High or Low* (Bristol, 1993), pp. 71–3.

41. See chapter 5 in Adrian Wooldridge, *Measuring the Mind: Education and Psychology in England c. 1860–1990.* (1994).

42. W. Boyd, *From Locke to Montessori: A Critical Account of the Montessori Point of View* (1914), p. 208.

43. *Ibid.*, p. 190.

44. E.R. Murray, *Infants' Schools and Kindergartens* (London, n.d. [1912]), ch. 12.

45. Nathan Isaacs, 'Critical Notice', *Journal of Child Psychology and Psychiatry*, 7 (1966), pp. 155–8.

46. Joachim Liebschner, *Foundations of Progressive Education: The History of the National Froebel Society* (Cambridge, 1991), pp. 77–8.

47. Boyd, *From Locke to Montessori*, p. 14.

48. H.W. Wilson Company's *Reader's Guide to Periodical Literature*. Significantly, the following volume of the *Readers' Guide to Periodicals* (1915–1918) reflects a diminished coverage, only eleven different articles in four years, the titles of which tend to be more questioning or critical: 'Is Montessori the educational Columbus?' in *Sunset* (June 1915), followed by 'Montessori Cult's Eclipse' (October). The title 'Derivation of the Montessori didactic apparatus' in *Elementary School Journal* (December 1917) reflects one theme of the general critique, the alleged lack of originality in her work.

49. Josephine Tozier, 'The Montessori Schools in Rome', *The World's Work* 19 (Feb. 1912), pp. 251–65; 'The Montessori Apparatus', *The World's Work* 19 (March 1912), pp. 384–98.

50. 'Review of Reviews and Magazines', *The Times*, 2 Dec. 1912, p. 10.

51. Montessori, *The Montessori Method*, p. viii.

52. Jose Harris, *Private Lives, Public Spirit: Britain 1870–1914* (1993), pp. 79–84.

53. Jane Roland Martin, 'Romanticism Domesticated: Maria Montessori and the Casa dei Bambini', in Jane Roland Martin, *Changing the Educational Landscape: Philosophy, Women and Curriculum* (1994).

54. *TES*, 6 Sept. 1910, p. 1.

CHAPTER THIRTEEN

Susan Isaacs: Pioneering Work in Understanding Children's Lives

MARY JANE DRUMMOND

In this chapter I shall consider, first, Susan Isaacs' legacy to her students and successors in terms of what she has to tell us about children. Drawing largely on her own accounts of her work at the experimental school in Cambridge, the Malting House, where she was the principal teacher between 1924 and 1927, I will illustrate the richness of her understanding of children's lives and their astonishing capacity for learning in both intellectual and social domains. Secondly, I shall illustrate the application of this rich, principled understanding to educational concerns, to everyday practices in early childhood and in primary schools. Susan Isaacs' thinking is complemented by her interpretation of the work of other people, whose insights she integrated into her own 'practical vision'. These include Piaget and Montessori, both of whom she criticised but did not reject, and, more importantly, Freud, Dewey, Froebel and Klein. Thirdly, I shall speculate about the central themes in the life of this remarkable woman, who has left us such generous gifts. I shall draw on Susan Isaacs' own extensive publications, and on the work of her only English biographer, Dorothy Gardner, who was also Susan Isaacs' student, colleague and friend. A brief account of the Malting House School is also given by Van der Eyken.[1] It is not the least remarkable aspect of Susan Isaacs' unique contribution to educational progress that it remains so under-documented by other educationalists in this country.

Susan Isaacs' brief summary of the aim of education, in *The Children We Teach*,[2] is used by Dorothy Gardner to describe the woman herself: it will serve here as an appropriate opening to this appreciation of the life and work of this great educator:[3]

> The aim of modern education is to create people who are not only self-disciplined and free in spirit, gifted in work and in enjoyment, worthy and desirable as persons, but also responsible and generous in social life, able to give and take freely from others, willing to serve social ends and to lose themselves in social purposes greater than themselves.

My starting point is an examination of the great gifts that Susan Isaacs left her students and successors in the shape of her meticulous observations and her searching reflections on them. Her two most substantial publications,[4] for which she was awarded a doctorate from the University of Manchester in 1933, are crammed with detailed anecdotal records of the children at the Malting House school. The sheer bulk of the material is as amazing as the vividness of the reader's encounters with these 'full-blooded', living, learning children.[5] These records were collected by Susan Isaacs and her colleagues themselves. In the final year of the school, according to Van der Eyken,[6] Geoffrey Pyke, the founder and paymaster of the school, was persuaded to provide shorthand typists, who would record all the children's activities and their interactions, 'practically complete', in Susan Isaacs' words, in the form of 'strictly verbatim and objective records'. It seems, however, that the stenographers' observations were not used in either the 1930 or 1933 publications, and although Susan Isaacs mentions the possibility of making the 1927–8 records available as a whole, Van der Eyken comments that the greater part of her writing about the school remains unpublished. Certainly, the projected third book based on the Malting House material, *Individual Histories*, was never written.

More important than the abundance of the published material, however, are the conditions in which it was collected. Susan Isaacs' own definition is that the records were amassed 'under relatively free conditions'; two main aspects of this relative freedom characterise the life of the school. First, there was 'an all-round lessening of the degree of inhibition of children's impulses' compared to other schools or family groups.[7] Some practical considerations, particularly for the children's safety, did set a number of limits on their behaviour. But by today's standards there were very few, and by today's sensitivities, the limits were set in the most unlikely places. For example, in the garden at the Malting House were several outbuildings, one of which had a most enticing and accessible sloping roof. The rule was not, no climbing, but a much more daring and child-friendly one: only one child on the roof at a time (implicitly an invitation to climb!). By contrast, there was virtually no constraint on the children's verbal expression, their intellectual impulses, their expressions of infantile sexuality, their anal and urethral interests, their feelings, including anger and aggression, their views on everything that happened around them, and their questions. The result was, as Susan Isaacs claims, and as generations of readers have excitedly discovered for themselves, 'a greater dramatic vividness of their social and imaginative and intellectual life as a whole'.[8]

Secondly, the physical environment, the materials provided, and the ways in which the educators responded to the children's impulses, led the children to be much more generally active – curious, creative, exploratory, inventive

Fig 13.1　*This picture of Susan Isaacs and some of her pupils in the garden of the Malting House School illustrates the extreme informality of the 'relatively free conditions' and the close attention that Susan Isaacs gave to what the children had to say. The original caption, reprinted below, reveals some persisting anxiety about this apparently anarchic approach to schooling:*

　　'*A discussion with Susan Isaacs outside the tent pitched in the gardens of the Malting House. Some children have taken their shoes off, others have kept them on. There were few rules.' W. Van der Eyken and B. Turner, Adventures in Education (1969).*

– than they would have been in any more orthodox school or classroom. The children passed their days moving freely between a large hall, plentifully equipped, with a gallery and a piano, four small rooms, one used largely as a science laboratory, and a large garden with animals, including, at different times, mice, rabbits, guinea-pigs, two cats and a dog, hen and chickens, snakes and salamanders, silkworms, a wormery and a freshwater aquarium. There were two lawns, abundant fruit trees, real bricks for building, space for bonfires, a seesaw with hooks so that weights could be fitted underneath, and more, much more. Indoors, the provision was no less stimulating: small movable pulleys which could be screwed in where desired; a full-sized lathe, and wood-working equipment; the laboratory contained tripods, gauzes, flasks and test tubes; there were also modelling materials, textiles, paint and writing materials; cupboards full of Montessori equipment; microscopes and dissecting instruments. In a memorable phrase, Susan Isaacs captures the distinguishing features of the observations she and her colleagues made, hour by hour, and day by day: 'there was more for us to see; and we could see it more plainly'.[9]

For example, having recorded the children's interest in melting (a piece of modelling wax had fallen on the hot-water pipes and melted), and their experiments with other materials in the bonfire in the garden, Susan Isaacs arranged for Bunsen burners to be fitted in the classroom so that the children could see the results of their enquiries more clearly. Many observations of their ensuing activity were recorded, such as these (the children's ages at the time of the observation are given in brackets, in years and months):

29.1.26.   Frank (6.3) and Christopher (5.4) used the Bunsen for some time, altering the flame constantly with the air supply. Priscilla (6.5) joined them, and they held glass rods in the flame, watching them when they 'went soft', and discovering accidentally that they could join two pieces together by fusion when soft.

1.2.26.   Frank, Dan and Priscilla again experimented with glass and the Bunsen. They found they could divide a long rod by pulling it into two when soft in one place.

Phineas (2.11) was crying bitterly at being left by his mother, but he laughed with delight when he saw the flame of the Bunsen, and said, 'I can see it burning. Oh, it's out now'.

4.11.26.   Phineas (3.9) and Lena (3.10) spent ten minutes or so experimenting with the steam coming out of the mouth of the kettle. They put their hands into it cautiously, saying, 'It's hot near the spout'.

15.11.26.   The elder children were boiling some water in a flask, and Dan (5.6) removed the wire gauze from the tripod, so that a fierce flame came directly on to the flask. Soon the flask broke and the water splashed out. Mrs. I. said, 'I wonder how that happened?' Jane (10.5) said, 'Perhaps it was because we had taken the gauze away'. Dan added, 'Yes, we had put too much heat on too quickly, and if the gauze had been there, or if we'd turned the gas tap on very slowly, probably it wouldn't have cracked'. And added, 'We found that out'.

16.11.26.   Jane (10.5) put a bulb of mercury into a flask of water which she was heating, and watched the mercury rise. She presently said, 'Let's boil it longer this time, and then it will come right up' – not having yet discovered that boiling water maintains a constant temperature. She agreed with Mrs. I. to go on boiling and watch, and marked the highest point reached by means of a piece of stamp-paper.[10]

The importance of records such as these is not in the challenge they offer to present-day educators, whose concerns about health and safety are all too easily aroused, but in the use that Susan Isaacs makes of them, and many,

many others like them. The observations do not remain inert on the page, to alarm or horrify; they are put to work, as Susan Isaacs pieces together an analytical account of the development of children's intellectual and emotional powers. In the 1930 volume, the analysis is organised around the three broad categories of *Discovery, Reasoning* and *Thought,* and in its 1933 successor, the material is divided into two parts: *Social Relations* and *The Deeper Sources of Love and Hate.* Subdivisions of the first part include 'Hostility and Aggression' and 'Friendliness and Cooperation', and of the second 'Sexuality' and 'Guilt and Shame'.

The range of children's powers documented in these two volumes is still extraordinary, even after generations of educators, psychologists and other researchers have added to our sum of knowledge about young children. In Susan Isaacs' account, the children's living interests are evergreen, comprehensive and cosmopolitan, their appetite for understanding virtually insatiable. No avenues are closed off from their enquiries. And Susan Isaacs is just as ready to describe the children's experiments with pulleys, their imaginative play, and their 'looking inside' freshly dissected animals, as she is to note their anal and urethral interests, and instances of both tenderness and cruelty in their treatment of living animals. Priscilla, for example (aged 6.5), is described as offering to marry the first boy who pulls a worm in half; and Harold, not quite five, is observed peering through the frosted glass to see Mrs I. on the lavatory, shouting with glee: 'I can see her! I can see her combinations!'[11] Susan Isaacs' position on this inclusiveness is stoutly defended. Her argument was always that adults – educators and parents – must strive to see children as they really are, not as adults would like them to be. 'I was not prepared to select . . . only such behaviour as pleased me, or as fitted into the general convention as to what little children . . . should feel and talk about', she writes in the introduction to *Social Development in Young Children,* and continues: 'I was just as ready to record and to study the less attractive aspects of their behaviour as the more pleasing, whatever my aims and preferences as their educator might be.'[12] To see children as Susan Isaacs saw them is to see them whole, with all their strengths and weaknesses intact.

Susan Isaacs was not, of course, a naive or inexperienced observer when she opened the Malting House School. She had had one year of training as an infant teacher and then taken a first in philosophy at the University of Manchester. She had lectured in a teacher training college and worked for a Master's degree on a research project in the department of psychology at the University of Cambridge. The most significant of her professional strengths, however, was, I believe, her knowledge and understanding of psychoanalysis, and of how the insights of this new discipline could be applied to the care and education of young children. She had started her first analysis in 1920 (or 1921, Gardner is unclear); she went on to have a second with Otto Rank, and to qualify as a psychoanalyst herself, beginning to take patients in 1923.

All of these experiences can be seen at work in Susan Isaacs' original intention to write one book based on her Malting House material, not two. She was convinced that her data threw light on both intellectual and social/ emotional aspects of development. Regretfully, she abandoned this plan and divided the material, while continuing to insist that 'in fact, the children lived a whole and complete life'.[13] We see this life in its wholeness in another of her major works, *The Children We Teach*. In this account of children's learning and development between the ages of 7 and 11, Susan Isaacs continues to emphasise the inextricable interconnectedness of affect and cognition, of emotional and intellectual growth: 'The thirst for understanding . . . springs from the child's deepest emotional needs – a veritable passion.'[14] She urges her readers never to overlook the child's strong, spontaneous, constant impulse towards understanding, which can be seen in every interaction, every form of activity, every verbal and non-verbal expression, the only key to the meaning of the child's life as a whole.

It seems appropriate to conclude this section about children and children's learning with Susan Isaacs' own spirited claim for the vital importance – to educators of every kind – of focused, first-hand observations of children: 'The actual interests and the everyday experiences of our children offer us the only direct way into their hearts and minds.'[15] Susan Isaacs' observations of actual, everyday children offer all her readers just such a way; our understanding of children, their hearts and minds, their cruelty and tenderness, their lavatory humour and their rigorous logic, has been immeasurably and permanently enriched by the texts based on her Malting House and psychoanalytic experiences. But there is more.

Here I shall turn to another aspect of Susan Isaacs' legacy to present-day educators: the application of her unparalleled knowledge of children, the educational implications of her work for children right through the preschool and primary years. The written record is frustratingly incomplete: there is little documentation of her seminars and lectures during her years at the Department of Child Development at the University of London Institute of Education, or of her many years as a part-time lecturer in psychology for various bodies (including the University of London, the London County Council, and Morley College). However, Gardner's biography quotes letters and tributes from many contemporary academics and educationalists, all of whom testify to the enormous influence Susan Isaacs exercised on people's lives and on their work with children in many different spheres. We may safely assume then, that the generations of teachers and other professionals who worked with and studied under Susan Isaacs were as familiar with the application of her insights as with the evidence on which she drew in her books, essays and articles.

The clearest expression of Susan Isaacs' views on schooling, as it was and as it might be, can be found in her short book *The Children We Teach*

(1932) and, admittedly at second hand, in the fascinating *Memorandum for the Plowden Committee*, written by Nathan Isaacs, her second husband, and submitted to the Plowden Committee in 1965 on behalf of the Froebel Foundation.[16] Nathan Isaacs' memorandum is a remarkably fresh – and regrettably still relevant – plea for the 'root-and-branch rethinking – and eventual reconstruction – of our whole scheme of primary education'.[17] His section headings can act as a summary of his argument. He presents 'A Radical Thesis for the Long Term', submitting in its defence 'The Fresh Psychological Evidence' for what is 'Wrong with Current Education'. He concludes with 'The Moral for both Education and Teaching'. His wife's influence is apparent on every page, and her work is frequently cited; another source of insight and argument is Nathan's own experience as observer and educator at the Malting House (where he worked full-time from 1926), when he was amassing material for his work on *Children's 'Why' Questions* (printed as an appendix to *Intellectual Growth in Young Children*).

The final chapter of Susan Isaacs' own earlier text, *The Children We Teach*, reads like a rehearsal for Nathan Isaacs' memorandum. She begins by reminding her readers of the key characteristics of the Malting House School: 'the environment . . . fostered the children's own doing and thinking. The physical setting and the educational technique were designed to call out the *children's* activity, rather than the teacher's.' From this simple beginning, Isaacs builds up three broad practical principles, 'which if fully understood, would profoundly affect the whole organisation of life in the Primary school, as well as all the details of the curriculum and of methods of teaching'.[18] These principles are given in summary below.

- 'It is *the children's activity* that is the key to their full development.' It is the child's own doing, thinking and talking that are the chief means to education: the teacher's part is to call out the children's activity and to meet their spontaneous interests, which offer all the opportunities needed for their education.
- 'The children's activity is most fruitful when it is most concrete and practical.' Even at ten and eleven children need experiences with real things 'that can be seen and handled and made and measured'.
- The child in the primary school needs 'the chance to put his experience into words, to describe, to discuss and to argue'. The free use of spoken language, as they talk about what they are doing, with their fellows and with their teachers, is one of 'the most valuable means of intellectual and social growth'.[19]

How disappointed Susan Isaacs would have been to think that more than 30 years after she had offered this admirably simple set of principles by which to construct effective primary education, her husband would have felt it necessary to go over the very same ground again in his memorandum to the Plowden Committee. And even more disappointed that after *another* 30 years of educational reform and debate, her basic 'broad practical principles' are as far as ever from being generally implemented through the primary years.

Of equal importance for today's educators are Isaacs' ground-breaking insights into the forms and functions of children's imaginative play, and their significance in children's learning. In a paper given in 1943 to a meeting of the British Psycho-Analytical Society, Susan Isaacs acknowledges the influences of Freud and Melanie Klein on her thinking, but the synthesis she offers is distinctly her own. The paper, 'The Nature and Function of Phantasy',[20] is written from a theoretical perspective, but any one of the significant points she makes in this text could have been illustrated with examples of the individual children described in the pages of *Social Development in Young Children*. She bases her argument on a description of the very young child's emotional life; she demonstrates that love and hate, gain and loss, desire and deprivation, power and powerlessness are the child's earliest companions: 'meanings, like feelings, are far older than speech'.[21] The young child's tumultous feelings and impulses are experienced in phantasies and expressed in play. At the same time, all young children are learning to live in and understand the external world, as well as their internal mental worlds; this learning too is embodied in play. Their experimental and imaginative play is thus, Susan Isaacs concludes, at one and the same time, an attempt to adapt to reality, and an active means of expressing phantasy. In a passage suggesting interesting parallels with key constructs in Froebel's educational thought, she describes children's imaginative play as the bridge between their inner and outer worlds, by which they pass from reflection on the symbolic values and meanings of things and people, to active enquiry into their real construction and real ways of working. Putting it another way, Susan Isaacs argues that make-believe play is significant not only for the child's creative intentions (as the child functions as artist, novelist, poet), but also for the child's growing sense of reality, scientific attitudes and the growth of reason (as the child acts on the world as physicist, biologist, engineer, sociologist). Both the 1930 and the 1933 volumes are stiff with evidence that substantiates this claim; 'the children's own doing and thinking' was the core of the Malting House curriculum and their play was an essential and indivisible part of it.

In *Intellectual Growth in Young Children* Susan Isaacs describes another aspect of play, its temporal dimension. She argues that the child's ability to evoke the *past* in imaginative play is closely connected with a corresponding power to evoke the *future* through 'as if' hypotheses.[22] In this passage, Susan Isaacs once again constructs play as an act of bridging contiguous worlds. Taken together, Susan Isaacs' arguments, in these and other texts, seem to be both anticipating and deconstructing Piaget's succinct position that 'Play is a form of thought' (in *Play, Dreams and Imitation in Childhood*,[23] of which the original French title, it should be noted, is *La Formation du Symbole*). The kinds of thinking developed and exercised in play are, in Susan Isaacs' view, crucially important ones for all children's development as rational, expressive, compassionate human beings. The implications of this view for the children's educators are abundantly clear: there is simply no case to be made for the exclusion of play from the lived curriculum of children in their primary years.

There is considerable evidence that Susan Isaacs was only too well aware of the ways in which contemporary primary education fell short of the principles and practices she advocated. To give just one example, Dorothy Gardner quotes from a stirring letter, written in 1936, containing some 'forthright criticisms' that have a good deal of relevance for educators today:

> Specifically, we teach reading and writing and the formal arts far too early, substituting sterile attempts to compose with the pen for living communication by word of mouth. The time that is spent in formal work on the three Rs would be far better employed in allowing the children to pursue the activities they so much seek connected with the business of living – washing, cooking, cleaning, searching out facts about the way the home is kept going and the life of the town maintained . . . Today the school deliberately deadens [children's] interest in these things and idolatrises the formal tools of learning . . . There is an extraordinary disproportion between the time and trouble put into teaching children to read and write at far too early an age and our concern with the real use of these things to serve personal and social life.[24]

In all this, however, it is striking how Susan Isaacs never attempts to do teachers' thinking for them. She does not proffer a pedagogic programme, nor specify methods, aims, objectives, targets or outcomes. She describes the environment she created for children's learning ('generous' is one of her epithets for it), and demonstrates its educational effects. She describes the inner life of the children she knows best, and demonstrates its educational significance. She continually emphasises the 'strength and spontaneity of [children's] wish to know and understand'.[25] Gardner concludes that no one who studied with Susan Isaacs would ever forget that 'children cannot be emotionally satisfied unless they can also learn, nor really learn unless their emotional needs are met'.[26] But for Susan Isaacs, teachers and other educators are learners too, who must do their own thinking and feeling. Rather than hector her readers and her students with admonitions about best practice, Susan Isaacs sends them back to the children, to the evidence from which she forged her own magnificent understanding. Gardner quotes from an examiner's report on a psychology course in a teachers' training college, in which Susan Isaacs writes:

> I do wish we could give up teaching these dreary old theories of play. It seems to me pathetic that students spend so much time on discussing Schiller, Groos, etc. instead of . . . going direct to children at play and seeing for themselves what play does for children's development.[27]

It is arguable, however, whether simply 'going direct to children at play' would enable Susan Isaacs' students, or early childhood educators today, to see what she saw, without the benefit of her commentary and analysis. It is in this aspect of her work that her experiences of psychoanalysis, as both client and analyst, seem to me to bear the richest fruit. In a revealing paper given in 1938, though not published until the year of her death, Susan Isaacs argues that psychoanalytic research is profoundly important in the study of children because of its essential concern with '*the meaning of the child's experiences to himself*' (Susan Isaacs' italics).[28] The discipline of psychoanalysis is the foundation that underpins Susan Isaacs' conviction that all of children's behaviour has meaning and significance. The corollary of this assumption is that chief among the educator's responsibilities is the necessity of trying to understand children's behaviour, in all its forms, giving respectful attention to the significance and strength of their constant and spontaneous search for meaning. Her own commitment to this work of attentive enquiry was fuelled by her interest in 'everything that little children do and feel'[29] and her compelling awareness of 'the desperate need of children to be *understood*'.[30] Not, we note, their desperate need to be obedient or compliant pupils, or their need to be inducted into the disciplines of formal schooling.

Finally, I shall offer some personal reflections on what I believe I detect beneath the bland surface of the biographer's admiration, and the eloquent, dispassionate argument of Susan Isaacs' own writings. (In a fascinating oxymoron, she refers in passing to 'genuine lovers and dispassionate students of children', a description in which I assume she includes herself.[31]) Dorothy Gardner's biography is introduced by a tribute from Susan Isaacs' contemporary, the psychoanalyst D.W. Winnicott. His terms of praise evoke a magnificent character '... this sturdy soul ... a truly great person ... a struggling, striving, radiant human being'.[32] But I have become convinced that there is a more sombre side to this astonishing woman, whose influence, according to Gardner, pervaded a whole profession.

One shred of evidence can be found in the dedication of *Social Development in Young Children* to her own (third) analyst, Joan Riviere, a close colleague of Melanie Klein. Riviere, says Susan Isaacs, 'taught me to understand my own childhood'. It is worth considering some of the key events in that childhood. Born in Bolton in 1885, the ninth child of William and Miriam Fairhurst (of whom seven then survived), Susan Isaacs' first experience of loss came very early, when Harry, the brother nearest her in age, contracted pneumonia and died when she was seven months old. She was still at the breast and her mother weaned her very suddenly. She was only four when her mother fell ill; she died two years later, after a long illness. Dorothy Gardner's account of these years includes a harrowing anecdote, which she presumably had from Susan Isaacs herself:

Mrs Fairhurst's illness increased, unsatisfactory housekeepers came and went. It was clear that more help was needed and so a nurse was employed who also helped with household affairs. William Fairhurst gradually came to feel great affection for this nurse and married her not long after the death of his wife. Susan's last meeting with her mother was inexpressibly painful because a comment made by the six-year-old little girl revealed the growing affection between her father and the nurse. Her mother was too ill to bear it and demanded that Susan should ask God to forgive her for telling such a lie, which the child felt powerless to do when what she had said was in fact true. Then someone came into the room and took her away. She never saw her mother again. The memory of her mother's white face and anguished eyes remained with Susan all her life.[33]

It is quite clear, even from the cautious Gardner, that Susan Isaacs' life with her new stepmother was not a happy one, though there is little detail to go on (Gardner does not even give the stepmother's name). These early events are certainly enough to help us see why Susan Isaacs would later teach her students ('She often said in her lectures', comments Gardner) that by the end of the first year of life, a child could experience the whole range of human emotions, including loss and grief. And in a lecture for which we have Gardner's own student notes, Susan Isaacs said: 'for real happiness, we must be able to admit sorrow and guilt'. At the very least, these scraps of evidence, taken together, give some insight into the force with which she emphasises 'the desperate need of children themselves to be *understood*'.[34]

Another important source of evidence of Susan Isaacs' perspective on children and childhood is to be found in the 1948 book *Troubles of Children and Parents*, a reissue of the letters she wrote between 1929 and 1938 in *The Nursery World*, using the pen name of Ursula Wise to respond to the real questions of anxious and enquiring parents. Her correspondents were concerned about every conceivable topic related to the upbringing of young children (for example, spoiling, masturbation, nail-biting, night terrors, whether parents should take a holiday). 'Ursula Wise's' replies are candid, forthright and principled; they may not always have been what the parents had wanted to hear. One example is particularly relevant here. A long letter about corporal punishment concludes: 'Do, please put me right about this, "to smack or not to smack" etc.'

Susan Isaacs replies:

First of all, let me say that I wish I could understand how it is possible for anyone seriously to claim that smacking a child hurts her more than it hurts the child. I confess that I feel that to be a complete humbug. I have such vivid memories of being smacked when I was a child myself, and when I compare those feelings with my own as a grown woman when I have smacked children, it seems to me the sheerest nonsense to suggest that it hurts me now more to smack a child than it hurt me to be smacked when I was a child.[35]

This passage, and many others like it, do much to demonstrate that Susan Isaacs, the grown woman, was still and always intensely aware of the inner life of children, and that she accepted and tried to understand their emotional lives as a whole. This awareness was, I have already suggested, both reinforced and exercised by her practice as a psychoanalyst. Gardner claims that this aspect of her work meant more to her than any other, and it was certainly her determination to pursue her own practice, and to work as a training analyst, that was her chief reason for never accepting a full-time post in the Department of Child Development, in spite of the prodigious workload involved in the part-time appointment.

Her absolute commitment to understanding children was matched by her conviction that she could put this understanding to good use on their behalf. In her last illness, Gardner records her as saying: 'It seems such a waste to have to go, when I could be helping people . . .'[36]

In a sense, this phrase 'helping people' can be read as a pitifully abbreviated summary of her life's work, not just in the years at the London Institute, but throughout her life. She worked astonishingly hard, according to the colleagues and ex-students who contributed to Gardner's chapter of eulogies, and Joan Riviere wrote of her, after her death: 'We are missing her very sadly in our work, as indeed I have long foreseen.'[37] This tribute, however heartfelt, does little to convey the quite extraordinary demand that psychoanalytic work made on Susan Isaacs and her colleagues, some of its earliest practitioners. The pages of *Childhood and After*, a collection of essays on clinical and psychoanalytical subjects, document any number of hair-raising case-studies. For example, she describes Jack, four years old, who exhibits a 'compulsion to undress' which she tries to frustrate. Then she changes her mind.

> I therefore decided that it was wiser now to be quite neutral in this matter, and confine my comments to interpreting his compulsion to undress, and all the details of his actions. When I did not again say he must not, he at once took all his clothes off. He climbed up on the table, and defecated there. The expression on his face was friendly and his tone of voice gentle, as he now said to me 'Now wipe it up'. I did this; and when the table was clean again, Jack took a black crayon and wrote letters and drew on the table – *the first time* he had written or drawn with any of the crayons during the analysis, so far. He evidently felt that if he were allowed to make a gift of his faeces to me, and I was willing to clear them away, he could feel greater trust in himself and in me. This, together with my interpretations of his anal wishes and anxieties, was felt as a proof that the contents of his body were not so disgusting and dangerous to me, or to himself, as he had feared they would be.[38]

Where did Susan Isaacs find the strength to endure such encounters? (And there are others quite as alarming.) From her rock-like inner assurance that the child's 'desperate need to be understood' had to be met, and if that meant meeting hatred and defiance along the way, so be it. 'All children', she writes, 'at one time or another are rebellious and defiant . . . Not all our human wisdom and good will can avoid the conflict which arises inherently in the child's early and imaginative life.'[39]

At the age of fifteen, Susan Isaacs declared herself an agnostic (apparently under the influence of her brother Enoch). Her father promptly brought her home from school where she stayed, doing nothing but household work, for some considerable time. Gardner's chronology is vague and incomplete for this part of Susan Isaacs' life, but she does add the chilling detail that Mr Fairhurst, her father, did not speak to her for two of those years. With these early experiences in mind, a reading of some of Susan Isaacs' mature work becomes almost unbearably poignant. For example:

> In analytic work, when the earliest love for mother or father, which has been buried under the layers of hatred and defiance, is brought to life, the pain and suffering of the patient in realising the depth and extent of this love and of the complex interplay of his love and hate, may be extreme.[40]

We can, of course, only speculate as to whether Susan Isaacs is here writing of herself, as well as others.

Less speculative though is my enduring impression that for Susan Isaacs, the knowledge of how to help people, to use her own expression, was never as important as the act of giving that help. She writes most beautifully of the supremely human act of giving: 'The gift is not only a sign that the giver loves, it is also a sign that the recipient is believed to be loving, not hating and hateful.' And, even more sweetly and succinctly: 'Both giving and gift are love itself.'[41]

These terms, giving and gift, are, in my reading, the strongest and the grandest themes to emerge from Susan Isaacs' work. She wrote early in her professional life of children's need for a generous environment, generous in warmth of feeling and opportunities for spontaneous activity. And this is her great achievement. Her life was a giving, her company, her teaching, her psychoanalytic practice, the generous environment. Perhaps her most important gift was her grasp of what she calls the most profound problem of the mental life: the relation between understanding and purpose, between the activity of knowing and those of wishing and feeling.[42] It is a problem that she convincingly and gloriously solved in her life's work. In the late paper already cited, she writes, in the context of children's lives, that learning depends upon interest and that interest is derived from desire, curiosity and fear.[43] Her own learning, her own desire, curiosity and fear, were all given away, in the service of children, with the overarching purpose of making a life, not just an education, that was fit for them.

NOTES

1. W. Van der Eyken and B. Turner, *Adventures in Education* (1969).

2. S. Isaacs, *The Children We Teach* (1932).

3. D. Gardner, *Susan Isaacs* (1969), p. 171.

4. S. Isaacs, *Intellectual Growth in Young Children* (1930) and *Social Development in Young Children* (1933).

5. 'full-blooded' is an epithet used by Nathan Isaacs, who writes of young children's learning as 'their own full-blooded active building up of knowledge' in M. Hardeman, ed., *Children's Ways of Knowing: Nathan Isaacs on Education, Psychology and Piaget* (New York, 1974), p. 169.

6. Van der Eyken, *Adventures in Education.*

7. Isaacs, *Intellectual Growth*, p. 12.

8. *Ibid.*

9. *Ibid.*

10. *Ibid.*, pp. 129, 134.

11. Isaacs, *Social Development*, p. 140.

12. *Ibid.*, p. 19.

13. Isaacs, *Intellectual Growth*, p. ix.

14. Isaacs, *Children We Teach*, p. 113.

15. *Ibid.*, p. 117.

16. The director of the Froebel Foundation was, at that time, Evelyn Lawrence, who had taught at the Malting House, and who married Nathan Isaacs shortly after Susan's death. According to Gardner, Susan Isaacs herself expressed a wish that Nathan, ten years her junior, should take such a step.

17. Hardeman, *Children's Ways of Knowing*, p. 160.

18. Isaacs, *Children We Teach*, p. 169.

19. *Ibid.*, pp. 169–71.

20. M. Klein *et al.*, *Developments in Psycho Analysis* (1952), pp. 67–121.

21. *Ibid.*, p. 89.

22. Isaacs, *Intellectual Growth*, p. 104.

23. J. Piaget, *Play, Dreams and Imitation in Childhood* (1951), p. 167.

24. Gardner, *Susan Isaacs*, p. 166.

25. Isaacs, *Children We Teach*, p. 113.

26. Gardner, *Susan Isaacs*, p. 149.

27. *Ibid.*, p. 155.

28. S. Isaacs, *Childhood and After: Some Essays and Critical Studies* (1948), p. 84.

29. Isaacs, *Social Development*, p. 113.

30. *Ibid.*, p. 13.

31. *Ibid.*

32. Gardner, *Susan Isaacs*, p. 6.

33. Gardner, *Susan Isaacs*, p. 21.

34. Isaacs, *Social Development*, p. 113.

35. S. Isaacs, *Troubles of Children and Parents* (1948), p. 37.

36. Gardner, *Susan Isaacs*, p. 138.

37. Gardner, *Susan Isaacs*, p. 144.

38. Isaacs, *Childhood and After*, p. 167.

39. *Ibid.*, pp. 23, 35.

40. *Ibid.*, p. 28.

41. *Ibid.*, p. 39.

42. Isaacs, *Children We Teach*, p. 70.

43. Klein, *Developments*, p. 108.

Select Bibliography

The footnotes to each contributor's chapter refer readers to primary sources, particular archives and specialist works. The following titles are listed because we consider them useful routes into the field of gendered studies of educational history. Most of these books use gender as a category of analysis. Some of them, however, have been included as lively studies of the ideologies of a particular period within which women educationists were operating. This is by no means a comprehensive bibliography of the field. We have chosen these books and articles because they illuminate aspects of the issues integral to our project.

Place of publication is London unless otherwise stated.

The emergence of liberal educational ideology, particularly the Unitarian contribution

KNUD HAAKONSON (ed.), *Enlightenment and Religion: Rational Dissent and Political Opposition* (Cambridge, 1996).

RAYMOND V. HOLT, *The Unitarian Contribution to Social Progress in England* (1938).

ISAAC KRAMNICK, *Republicanism & Bourgeois Radicalism: Political Ideology in Late Eighteenth-Century England and America* (Ithaca & London, 1990).

DORINDA OUTRAM, *The Enlightenment* (Cambridge, 1995).

NEIL MCKENDRICK, JOHN BREWER and J.H. PLUM, 'New Worlds of Childhood' in *The Birth of a Consumer Society: The Commercialisation of Eighteenth Century England* (1982).

ROBERT E. SCHOFIELD, *The Lunar Society of Birmingham* (Oxford, 1963).

ROLAND STROMBERG, *Religious Liberalism in Eighteenth-Century England* (1954).

RUTH WATTS, *Gender, Power and the Unitarians in England 1760–1860* (1998).

Eighteenth-century and early nineteenth-century women and educational ideas

MELISSA A. BUTLER, 'Early Liberal Roots of Feminism: John Locke and the Attack on Patriarchy', *American Political Science Review* 72, 1 (1978), pp. 135–50.

KAREN GREEN, *The Woman of Reason: Feminism, Humanism and Political Thought* (Cambridge, 1995).

JO MANTON, *Mary Carpenter and the Children of the Streets* (1976).

S.H. MYERS, *The Bluestocking Circle* (Oxford, 1990).

SAMUEL F. PICKERING JNR, *John Locke and Children's Books in Eighteenth Century England* (Tennessee, 1981).

ALAN RICHARDSON, *Literature, Education and Romanticism: Reading as Social Practice, 1780–1832* (Cambridge, 1994).

CATHERINE MACAULEY, *Letters on Education* (1790).

MITZI MYERS, 'Impeccable Governesses, Rational Dames, and Moral Mothers: Mary Wollstonecraft and the Female Tradition in Georgian Children's Books', *Children's Literature* 14 (1986), pp. 31–59.

RUTH A. SYMES, 'Catherine Cappe of York (1822)' in *The Uses of Autobiography* ed. Julia Swindells (1995).

CLAIRE TOMALIN, *The Life and Death of Mary Wollstonecraft* (1974).

MARY WOLLSTONECRAFT, *Vindication of the Rights of Woman* (Harmondsworth, 1986).

Evangelical ideology in the late eighteenth and early nineteenth centuries

IAN BRADLEY, *The Call to Seriousness: The Evangelical Impact on the Victorians* (New York, 1976).

WILLIAM OWEN CHADWICK, *Victorian Miniature* (1960).

LEONORE DAVIDOFF and CATHERINE HALL, *Family Fortunes: Men and Women of the English Middle Class 1780–1850* (1987).

BOYD HILTON, *The Age of Atonement: The Influence of Evangelicalism on Social and Economic Thought 1785–1865* (Oxford, 1988).

MARY G. JONES, *The Charity School Movement: A Study of Eighteenth-Century Puritanism in Action* (Cambridge, 1938).

MITZI MYERS, 'Hannah More's Tracts for the Times: Social Fiction and Female Ideology' in *Fettered or Free? British Women Novelists, 1670–1815* ed. Mary Anne Schofield and Cecilia Macheski (Ohio, 1986), pp. 264–84.

F.K. PROCHASKA, *Women and Philanthropy in 19th Century England* (Oxford, 1980).

Nineteenth-century feminism

KATHRYN GLEADLE, *The Early Feminists: Radical Unitarians and the Emergence of the Women's Rights Movement, 1831–51* (Basingstoke, 1995).

PAM HIRSCH, *Barbara Leigh Smith Bodichon: Feminist, Artist and Rebel* (1998).

JUDITH JOHNSTON, *Anna Jameson: Victorian, Feminist, Woman of Letters* (Aldershot, 1997).

PHILIPPA LEVINE, *Victorian Feminism 1850–1900* (1987).

CLARISSA CAMPBELL ORR (ed.), *Wollstonecraft's Daughters: Womanhood in England and France 1789–1920* (Manchester, 1996).

JANE RENDALL, *The Origins of Modern Feminism: Women in Britain, France and the United States, 1780–1860* (Basingstoke & London, 1985).

JANE RENDALL (ed.), *Equal or Different: Women's Politics 1800–1914* (Oxford, 1987).

ROBERT B. SHOEMAKER, *Gender in English Society 1650–1850: The Emergence of Separate Spheres?* (1998).

BARBARA TAYLOR, *Eve and the New Jerusalem: Socialism and Feminism in the Nineteenth Century* (1983).

MARTHA VICINUS (ed.), *A Widening Sphere: Changing Roles of Victorian Women* (Indiana, 1977).

Women and school teaching

DINA COPELMAN, *London's Women Schoolteachers: Gender, Class and Feminism 1870–1930* (1996).

FELICITY HUNT (ed.), *Lessons for Life: The Schooling of Girls and Women 1850–1950* (Oxford, 1987).

FELICITY HUNT, *Gender and Policy in English Education: Schooling for Girls 1902–1944* (1991).

P.W. GARDNER, *The Lost Elementary Schools of Victorian England* (1984).

LEE HOLCOMBE, chapters 2 and 3 in *Victorian Ladies at Work: Middle-Class Working Women in England and Wales 1850–1914* (Newton Abbot, 1973).

JOHN P. MARMION, 'The Beginnings of the Catholic Poor Schools in England', *Recusant History* 17, 1 (1984), pp. 67–83.

JANE MILLER, *School for Women* (1996).

GEOFFREY PARTINGTON, *Women Teachers in the Twentieth Century in England and Wales* (Windsor, 1976).

SUSAN SKEDD, 'Women Teachers and the Expansion of Girls' Schooling in England, c. 1760–1820' in *Gender in the Eighteenth Century* (eds.) Hannah Barker and Elaine Chalus (Harlow, 1997).

GILLIAN SUTHERLAND, *Elementary Education in the Nineteenth Century*, History Association pamphlet no. 76 (1971).

FRANCES WIDDOWSON, *Going Up into the Next Class: Women and Elementary Teacher Training 1840–1914* (1980).

Schools for middle-class girls

GILLIAN AVERY, *The Best Type of Girl: A History of Girls' Independent Schools* (1991).

CAROL DYHOUSE, *Girls Growing up in Later Victorian and Edwardian England* (1980).

SHEILA FLETCHER, *Feminists and Bureaucrats: A Study in the Development of Girls' Education in the Nineteenth Century* (Cambridge, 1980).

NONITA GLENDAY and MARY PRICE, *Reluctant Revolutionaries: A Century of Headmistresses 1874–1974* (1974).

JANET HOWARTH, 'Public Schools, Safety-nets and Educational Ladders: The Classification of Girls' Secondary Schools, 1880–1914', *Oxford Review of Education* 11, 1 (1985).

JOSEPHINE KAMM, *Indicative Past: A Hundred Years of The Girls' Public Day School Trust* (Oxford, 1971).

JOYCE SENDERS PEDERSON, 'Some Victorian Headmistresses: A Conservative Tradition of Social Reform', *Victorian Studies*, 24 (1981), pp. 463–88.

Women and higher education

VERA BRITTAIN, *The Women at Oxford: A Fragment of History* (1960).

JOAN N. BURSTYN, *Victorian Education and the Ideal of Womanhood* (New Jersey, 1984).

SARA DELAMONT and LORNA DUFFIN (eds.), *The Nineteenth-Century Woman: Her Cultural and Physical World* (1978).

CAROL DYHOUSE, *No Distinction of Sex? Women in British Universities 1870–1939* (1995).

SUSAN J. LEONARDI, *Dangerous by Degrees: Women at Oxford and the Somerville College Novelists* (New Brunswick and London, 1989).

JUNE PURVIS, *A History of Women's Education in England* (Buckingham, 1991).

GILLIAN SUTHERLAND, 'The Movement for the Higher Education of Women: Its Social and Intellectual Context in England c. 1840–80' in

Politics and Social Change in Modern Britain P.J. Walter (ed.) (Brighton, 1987).

GILLIAN SUTHERLAND, 'Emily Davies, the Sidgwicks and the Education of Women in Cambridge' in *Cambridge Minds* ed. Richard Mason (Cambridge, 1994).

GILLIAN SUTHERLAND, ' "The Plainest Principle of Justice": and the Higher Education of Women' in F.M.L. Thompson (ed.), *The University of London and the World of Learning 1836–1986* (1990).

RITA MCWILLIAMS TULLBERG, *Women at Cambridge* (Cambridge, 1998).

Sexual and social politics of education

BARRY H. BERGEN, 'Only a Schoolmaster: Gender, Class and the Effort to Professionalise Elementary Teaching in England 1870–1910' in Jenny Ozga (ed.), *Schoolwork: Approaches to the Labour Process of Teaching* (Milton Keynes, 1988), pp. 39–60.

PATRICIA HOLLIS, *Ladies Elect: Women in English Local Government 1865–1914* (Oxford, 1987): see ch. 2 'The London School Board 1870–1904' and ch. 3 on 'English Provincial School Boards' (1870–1903).

JANE MARTIN, *Women and the Politics of Schooling in Victorian and Edwardian England* (1999).

JANE ROLAND MARTIN, *Changing the Educational Landscape: Philosophy, Women and Curriculum* (1994).

ALISON ORAM, *Women Teachers and Feminist Politics 1900–1939* (Manchester, 1996).

JUNE PURVIS, *Hard Lessons: The Lives and Education of Working-Class Women in Nineteenth-Century England* (Oxford, 1989).

LILIAN LEWIS SHIMAN, *Women and Leadership in Nineteenth-Century England* (Basingstoke, 1992).

CAROLYN STEEDMAN, CATHY URWIN and VALERIE WALKERDINE (eds.), *Language, Gender and Childhood* (1985).

GABY WEINER, *Feminisms in Education* (Buckingham, 1994).

EILEEN JANES YEO, 'Social Motherhood and the Sexual Communion of Labour in British Social Science, 1850–1950', *Women's History Review* 1, 1 (1992) 63–87.

The kindergarten and child study movements

ANN TAYLOR ALLEN, 'Spiritual Motherhood: German Feminists and the Kindergarten Movement 1848–1911' in *History of Education Quarterly* 22, 3 (1982), pp. 319–39.

ROSEMARY ASHTON, *Little Germany: German Refugees in Victorian Britain* (Oxford, 1989).

D.E.M. GARDNER, *Susan Isaacs: The First Biography* (1969).

RITA KRAMER, *Maria Montessori: A Biography* (Chicago, 1976).

EVELYN LAWRENCE (ed.), *Friedrich Froebel and English Education* (1952).

JOACHIM LIEBSCHNER, *Foundations of Progressive Education: The History of the National Froebel Society* (Cambridge, 1991).

JOACHIM LIEBSCHNER, *A Child's Work: Freedom and Guidance in Froebel's Educational Theory and Practice* (Cambridge, 1992).

ELSIE MURRAY, *A Story of Infant Schools and Kindergartens* (1912).

CAROLYN STEEDMAN, ' "The Mother Made Conscious": The Historical Development of Primary School Pedagogy', *History Workshop Journal* 20 (1985), pp. 149–63.

CAROLYN STEEDMAN, *Childhood, Culture and Class in Britain: Margaret McMillan 1860–1931* (1990).

Index

Page numbers in *italics* denote illustrations.

241